T0201256

Transformational
Security
Awareness

Transformational Security Awareness

What Neuroscientists, Storytellers, and Marketers Can Teach Us About Driving Secure Behaviors

Perry Carpenter

WILEY

Transformational Security Awareness: What Neuroscientists, Storytellers, and Marketers Can Teach Us About Driving Secure Behaviors

Published by
John Wiley & Sons, Inc.
10475 Crosspoint Boulevard
Indianapolis, IN 46256
www.wiley.com

ISBN: 978-1-119-56634-2
ISBN: 978-1-119-56637-3 (ebk.)
ISBN: 978-1-119-56635-9 (ebk.)

Manufactured in the United States of America

V10009638_042619

For general information on our other products and services please contact our Customer Care Department within the United States at (877) 762-2974, outside the United States at (317) 572-3993 or fax (317) 572-4002.

Wiley publishes in a variety of print and electronic formats and by print-on-demand. Some material included with standard print versions of this book may not be included in e-books or in print-on-demand. If this book refers to media such as a CD or DVD that is not included in the version you purchased, you may download this material at http://booksupport.wiley.com. For more information about Wiley products, visit www.wiley.com.

Library of Congress Control Number: 2019933733

For Siobhan, Sage, and Lily: the best reasons imaginable to help build a more secure planet. Oh - and thanks for putting-up with all the puns . . .

About the Author

Perry Carpenter, C|CISO, MSIA currently serves as Chief Evangelist and Strategy Officer for KnowBe4, the world's most popular security awareness and simulated phishing platform.

Perry has been a recognized thought leader on security awareness and the human factors of security for well-over a decade. His broad background makes him uniquely positioned to understand nuances of awareness strategy that can be elusive. Perry's security awareness-related experiences spans multiple pivotal roles: from being a general employee receiving awareness training; to being an awareness program manager running complex global programs; to being the primary market analyst advising security leaders about awareness trends, success practices, and vendor platforms; to now helping lead the efforts of the world's largest and most successful security awareness and simulated phishing platform. Perry draws from this experience, along with cutting-edge research in the fields of marketing, communication, behavior science, and organizational culture management to inform his perspectives and advice for creating awareness programs that are transformational.

Before joining KnowBe4, Perry led security awareness, security culture management, and anti-phishing behavior management research at Gartner Research (NYSE:IT), in addition to covering areas of IAM strategy, CISO Program Management mentoring, and Technology Service Provider success strategies. With a long career as a security professional and researcher, Carpenter has broad experience in North America and Europe, providing security consulting and advisory services for many of the world's best-known brands.

Perry holds a Master of Science in Information Assurance (MSIA) from Norwich University in Vermont and is a Certified Chief Information Security Officer (C|CISO).

You can connect with Perry on LinkedIn at: https://linkedin.com/in/perrycarpenter.

About the Technical Editor

Matt Stamper, CISA, CISM, CIPP/US, ITIL, brings a broad, multi-disciplinary understanding of cybersecurity best practices. His diverse domain knowledge spans IT service management (ITSM), cybersecurity, cloud services, control design and assessment (Sarbanes-Oxley, HIPAA-HITECH), privacy (GDPR, CCPA), enterprise risk management (ERM), and IT risk management (ITRM).

Matt excels at conveying complex cybersecurity and IT concepts to boards of directors, executive management, as well as professional service providers. His executive and board-level experience with managed services, cybersecurity, data centers, networks services, and ITSM provide a unique perspective on the fast-changing world of enterprise IT, IoT, and cloud services.

Stamper was a Research Director within the Security and Risk Management Practice at Gartner (NYSE:IT). During his time at Gartner, Stamper met with CISOs and CIOs across the globe to address cybersecurity program development, security incident response, and other security topics. Matt was the co-author on the Magic Quadrant for IT Risk Management Solutions and wrote research on incident response and covered breach and attack simulation technologies. Matt is also the co-author of the CISO Desk Reference Guide (Volumes 1 & 2).

You can connect with Matt on LinkedIn at: https://www.linkedin.com/in/stamper/

Credits

Associate Publisher
Jim Minatel

Editorial Manager
Pete Gaughan

Production Manager
Kathleen Wisor

Project Editor
Tom Dinse

Production Editor
Athiyappan Lalith Kumar

Technical Editor
Matt Stamper

Copy Editor
Kim Wimpsett

Proofreader
Evelyn Wellborn

Indexer
Johnna VanHoose Dinse

Cover Designer
Wiley

Cover Image
© wildpixel/iStockphoto

Acknowledgments

Wow! Writing a book is such a big process; draining at times, and life-giving at others. During the writing of this book I had times of intense focus and productivity when it felt like words and information were gleefully flying from my fingertips to my keyboard and onto my screen, sitting there virtually smiling back at me. And there were other times when, frankly, I felt like finding a box of toothpicks and stabbing the entire contents of the box, toothpick by toothpick, into my eyes just to make it end.

Ok . . . that's a bit of an exaggeration. But you wanna' know what's not an exaggeration? Sure you do. So, I say this in all seriousness: Though my name adorns the wonderfully designed cover of this book, it is only able to do so because of a list of countless other names. The names of people who have provided me with so much help and encouragement throughout my life and career.

I'll start with the most important group in my life: my family. To my amazing wife, Siobhan: Thank you for always believing in me; for dealing with my craziness; and for helping me become a better version of myself, every day. You have the biggest heart of anyone I know. I'm so lucky to call you my bride and my friend. To my kids, Sage and Lily: I love you more than words can express. You make me prouder than you'll ever know.

Thanks to my mom and dad for always encouraging me to be multidisciplinary in my thinking and skills development. That multidisciplinary thinking is at the core of this book.

There are so many great people who've helped me throughout my career; many of whom I've never thanked. First and foremost are George Brooks and David Newton, two managers who took chances hiring a young, relatively inexperienced guy who dropped out of law school because he wanted to plunge into the wonderful world of software development. If not for your faith in me, the chances you took, and the responsibilities that you gave me nearly 20 years ago, this book would certainly not exist.

By far the two people who shaped the way that I've approached my security career more than anyone else are Greg Schaffer and Whitney Bell. I have no idea how you both put up with me, but you did. I think of your patience, guidance, trust, and mentorship often. And I hope that, in some little way each day, I'm able to reflect your values back into the world.

During my time at Gartner, I had the privilege to make great friends, have wonderful managers, and work with some of the brightest folks on the planet. To Ray Wagner, Andrew Walls, Ash Ahuja, Michele Caminos, Joanna Huisman, Tom Scholtz, Jeffrey Wheatman, Paul Proctor, Neil Wynne, Neil MacDonald, Ant Allan, Gregg Kreizman, Earl Perkins, Terry Hicks, and countless more, thank you for your friendship, guidance, and mentorship.

For those who helped lead awareness efforts with me at my previous employers. Thank you! Roy Eggensperger for being my partner in crime way back in the 2006-ish timeframe and wanting to help move our awareness program forward in new, interesting, and crazy ways. And to Amber Styles-Emberson, Vladimir Skoric, and Kym Patterson, thank you for your tireless efforts in creating and running an innovative large-scale program under enormous internal pressure and external scrutiny.

I have so many great coworkers at KnowBe4 that I work with every day and who encouraged me to tackle this project. First and foremost, I need to thank Roger Grimes. Thank you for believing that I can not only have a book proposal accepted, but also believing that I can deliver on my mission for the book.

To Stu Sjouwerman for giving me the go-ahead to effectively split my attention for six months and for reading and providing encouraging feedback on my earliest drafts. You are an amazing CEO, leader, mentor, and friend.

Thanks to Kevin Mitnick for your friendship and encouragement. I learn something interesting and fun (and often, scary) every time we get together.

And, thank you to Kathy Wattman, Kendra Irimie, Mary Owen, Laurie Haynes, Roger Grimes, Erich Kron, Amanda Tarantino, Rob Henley, Greg Kras, and Alin Irimie. I could not ask for a better or more supportive group of folks to work with daily. Each of you are amazing and inspiring in so many ways.

Thanks to Jim Shields, Rob McCollum, Richard Leverton and all the amazing people at Twist & Shout for being the creative force and production expertise behind *The Inside Man*. This video series was a dream realized for me and was probably the most fun project I've worked on in my career.

Believe it or not, even though I work for a vendor serving the security awareness market, I've received a ton of encouragement and support from other vendors in this space as I let them know about this book. Special thanks to Lance Spitzner (SANS Security Awareness), Lisa Plaggemier (InfoSec Institute), Tom Pendergast (MediaPro), and Masha Sedova (Elevate Security). Your faith in my handling of the material and encouragement throughout this project mean more to me than you can possibly know.

Thanks to Beth Beerman and Kathy Michael of the International Association of Security Awareness Professionals (IASAP) for your support and for sending some of your members my way to be interviewed. Having the voices of practitioners as part of this book helps ensure that the concepts are connected to how they can be implemented in the real world.

A HUGE thank you to BJ Fogg and Stephanie Weldy for reviewing the sections on the Fogg Behavior Model and for working through several iterations of text and graphics to ensure that I've captured the essence of the model faithfully and that it is applied accurately. Your support and input shine through and will make the behavior-related aspects of this book have the gravitas they deserve.

This book wouldn't have been possible without the constant help and encouragement provided by the folks at Wiley Publishing. Jim Minatel, Tom Dinse: you both made this process as painless as possible. In everything from first-timer, newbie questions to schedule issues, to strange requests about wording, graphics, and more, you were constantly encouraging and supporting. Thank you! Thank you also, to Athiyappan Lalith Kumar for being a thorough and thoughtful editor. Additionally, there is an amazing team of professionals who believe that the printed word is still incredibly powerful. These people do all the heavy lifting to ensure that a project like this is successful. Thank you! It was fantastic working with you all!

And, finally, thanks to my technical editor and reviewer, Matt Stamper. I'm so glad you were able to lend your CISO and executive strategy lens to this work. I appreciate all the thoughtful comments, suggested edits, points to ponder, and encouragement that you lent along the way. This project was a great excuse to work together and to get to know you better.

-Perry Carpenter

Contents at a Glance

Contents

Foreword

Perry Carpenter is a highly respected cybersecurity guru who I've gotten to know over the last two years. He has 15+ years of experience in the field both as a practitioner and as an analyst. He's sharp, is incredibly analytical, has a knack for psychology, and is a prolific writer. I first met Perry when he started working at KnowBe4, but I'd heard of him when he was an analyst at Gartner through KnowBe4's CEO Stu Sjouwerman. Perry and I always play off of one another on webinars that we put on together for KnowBe4. We have a natural chemistry that is sometimes hard to find. A big reason for that natural chemistry is one of the first things that drew me to him—our mutual love of magic. We both have such a fascination with it that we took turns showing each other magic tricks one day.

Social engineering threats have been around since before I was born. Con artists continue to get better. That's a big reason why I look at security awareness as an absolute necessity—because humans can be easily influenced to reveal confidential information or to perform actions through manipulation and deception. Regardless of what the software does, humans can be tricked to do whatever another human wants. There's no software in the world that can protect a system against a pretext. People must realize that technology alone won't protect them. That's why it's crucial to implement entertaining, relevant, and informative security training to make it matter to employees personally (appeal to self-interest), which helps change behavior.

Perry has put together a comprehensive book about security awareness programs that every security professional should read. It covers a variety of topics related to security awareness including the psychology of the behaviors behind getting someone to perform a certain act or care about a certain topic, the use of marketing and communications tactics to enhance security awareness training, leveraging social pressures to change culture, and more. He's also added a compilation of voices from the cybersecurity industry who provide their advice about how to put on your best security awareness training.

Not only does Perry address the "how" behind putting together a comprehensive and effective security awareness training program, he addresses the ever important "why." Why should people care about it? Why would it appeal to him/her personally? He even breaks it down to simplify why you should have a security awareness training program in the first place. Knowing the ultimate purpose and goal of your security awareness program is important because it correlates directly to the impact of your program.

One thing that I particularly enjoyed about his book was that he talked in detail about the importance of repetition when it comes to effectively getting a message across, and then he proceeds to summarize and repeat the most important points at the end of each chapter in the book. Perry also uses a line throughout the book that I'm a big fan of: "Just because I'm *aware* doesn't mean I *care*." Keep that in mind as you develop your security awareness program. Plan for it and work with human nature rather than against it to make your program more effective and to go beyond mere awareness. When we connect with people on an emotional level, the chance of them actually caring increases dramatically. Your ultimate goal should be to change end-user behavior and to shape the organization's overall security culture.

We can't argue that the world is in desperate need of better equipped security awareness leaders. And the human element is the most important one when it comes to your cybersecurity program. Beyond technology, beyond software, people are truly your last line of defense. At the end of the day, it all comes down to people. Perry has a way of masterfully exploring how people think and why they act the way they do. This is a fascinating read and, once again, something I'd recommend to everyone in the cybersecurity field.

—Kevin Mitnick

Introduction

I have a confession to make. This may sound strange, but pondering human thought and behavior is one of my favorite things to do. I think it's always been that way for me. I've wanted to know what makes people tick. Because of that, I've gone down a few interesting roads of study, from music, to religious studies, to magic and misdirection, to social engineering, to training as a street hypnotist and theatrical mind-reader, to taking classes in pickpocketing, to learning the ins and outs of public speaking and influence tactics, to graphic design, and more.

In all of this, I think I've actually been trying to understand why I do the things that I do and think the things that I think. You see, I've always felt a bit different. And that difference was confirmed to me late in life when I was diagnosed with Asperger's syndrome (a neurological difference also known as autism spectrum disorder, or ASD). In many aspects of life, this neurodiversity has served me well. I see the world in a different way. And that off-centered view of things has helped me find solutions or phrase answers in ways that can sometimes elude others. And, often, I'm sure that my way of approaching things has resonated not because it is better or more insightful; rather, it can resonate because it is quirky enough to cut through someone's pre-established filters.

In other areas of life, the social areas, I often felt (and sometime still feel) like an alien or a social anthropologist seeking to better understand the strange and wonderful inhabitants of this world. That *seeking to understand* is something that I still do every day. So, pondering human thought (psychology), our behavior (behavior science), and group dynamics (culture) is ceaselessly interesting and fun. The best part of it (professionally) is that I've had the opportunity in my career to make this quest part of the mandate for my daily job.

The Security Awareness Connection

The various roles throughout my professional life have offered me a unique vantage point when it comes to security awareness programs and to the security awareness market. I've seen security awareness from virtually every conceivable angle.

- I've been the recipient of security awareness training at former employers.
- I've designed and implemented security awareness programs at multiple Fortune 500 companies.
- I've served as the Gartner analyst covering the security awareness market, authoring the Magic Quadrant for the space, advising vendors, and helping security awareness program managers design their programs.
- And now, I help shape the awareness market and seek to serve security awareness leaders around the world by working within the security awareness vendor community.

Over the 15 or so years that I've been directly involved in building my own programs, advising security leaders and vendors, or helping shape the future of KnowBe4, I've learned a thing or two about what makes a security awareness program viable and scalable for long-term success. I've seen what does and doesn't work. And I've helped to build real, functional, security awareness programs that have shaped the behavior of employees as well as molding the way that organizations perceive and value security within their broader culture. Isn't that our goal? I'm pretty sure you agree. After all, if that's not what you are hoping to achieve, you probably wouldn't be reading this.

I'm resisting the urge to summarize the entire book for you right now. But, as I do that, there are a few things that I can't help but allow to leak forward and spill onto this page. Specifically, I want to let you in on the main thesis of this book. It's this: the concept of "security awareness" can suffer from a fatal flaw, what I call the *knowledge-intention-behavior gap*. Just because your people are *aware* of something doesn't mean that they will *care*. And, even if they *care* and *intend* to do the right thing, a whole host of situations and contexts can interfere with the follow-through (the desired *behavior*). So, there is a gap between *knowledge* and *intention*. And there is a gap between *intention* and *behavior*.

A *transformational* security awareness program proactively accounts for the *knowledge-intention-behavior gap*. It does so by working with, rather than against, human nature. And it does so by setting an intentional, eyes-open, focus on the idiosyncrasies of human nature, human behavior, human thought and reasoning, social dynamics, the power of emotion, and more. A transformational security awareness program will allow these realities to define the program strategy rather than just tossing out the next security video or dragging everyone through the doldrum of the next annual PowerPoint fest.

Thinking Forward

I was very intentional about the cover image for this book. Take another look at it now. When we think about the concept of transformation, it's easy to think about a caterpillar's transformation into butterfly. But all too often, we think about the butterfly emerging from the cocoon. That's great—but it's the *end* of the story. Notice, however, in the cover photo, you see the caterpillar casting the *shadow* of a butterfly. It's about the future potential of what exists in the now.

This book is about helping you see the potential of what is possible and then helping you plan practical ways to move toward that transformational outcome. So, in the same way that you can look at a caterpillar and imagine the future butterfly, I want to you imagine. Imagine yourself, your program, your people, and your organization a year from now: *transformed*.

Let the Fun Begin

Let's make this a conversation. I'd love to know your thoughts as you progress through the book. Keep me up-to-date on any transformational stories you have. Or, let me know if I can help with anything.

Lastly, if you enjoy this book and think it's helpful, recommend it to others, write a review, and buy copies to give to all your friends, family, and co-workers this holiday season. OK, that last part was somewhat in jest. But I do sincerely hope to hear from you.

You can connect with me on LinkedIn (`/in/perrycarpenter`), on Twitter (`@perrycarpenter`), or on the Web (`https://TheSecurityAwarenessGuy.com`).

Perry Carpenter
March 2019

The Case for Transformation

1 You Know Why. . .

If you think technology can solve your security problems, then you don't understand the problems and you don't understand the technology.
                                    Bruce Schneier, *Secrets & Lies*

Ok. So, if you are reading this book, you likely already know why you need it. The world is in desperate need of better equipped security awareness leaders. The headlines and statistics make it clear that security technologies—no matter how good they become—will never be 100 percent effective. Cybercriminals will find gaps and points of ineffectiveness in the technologies and exploit them. It's the age-old arms race.

In that age-old arms race, regardless of if we are talking about computer security or physical security, cunning criminals have realized that they can effectively and reliably bypass an enemy's defensive systems by exploiting vulnerable humans. The main tactic here falls under the simple heading of *social engineering*: the process of getting someone to believe something, reveal something, or do something that works to further an attacker's goals.

Security professionals are in a quandary. Many of them feel that they could build secure systems if only those pesky end users wouldn't ruin everything. Security teams develop robust policies that clearly define appropriate behavior, but the users don't follow the policies; in fact, they go around the policies.

But there is hope. Our job as security leaders is to deal with these issues head on, and that's where this book comes in. Welcome to the world of *Transformational Security Awareness: What Neuroscientists, Storytellers, and Marketers Can Teach Us About Driving Secure Behaviors.* Over the next couple hundred pages, we'll peer into many fascinating (and sometimes frustrating) aspects of human nature. And we'll discover methods and tactics that we can use to shape the hearts, minds, and actions of our end users.

First, let's set the stage. In this chapter, we'll build the case for why a focused approach to security awareness training is critical for our security programs. This is foundational. You can use the information presented here to justify your investment of time and resources working on end-user training. And it provides enough ammo to shut down any naysayers who might argue that security awareness is a waste of time.

Humans Are the Last Line of Defense

Here's the truth: humans are the most important part of your cybersecurity program. Ignore them at your own peril.

It doesn't matter how much money we spend on technology, planning around human factors must be a critical part of the planning and implementation process. Why? Because humans are involved at every stage of the game.

- Humans determine the need for new technologies.
- Humans determine the need for new processes.
- Humans select the technologies to purchase and implement.
- Humans define process standards to be followed.
- Humans review and tweak the settings of the business technologies purchased.
- Humans review and tweak the settings of the security technologies purchased.
- Humans design and code the applications you develop in-house.
- Humans review the agreements that you have with third-party organizations.
- Humans decide how to respond to suspicious incidents within your organization.
- Humans decide how to respond to someone trying to tailgate into your building.
- Humans make both conscious and unconscious decisions as to how they will react to the systems and information that they interact with each day.
- Humans are your employees, contractors, shareholders, and customers.

Everything and everyone in your organization is impacted by the decisions and behavior of other humans.

There are other dimensions as well. Human behavior can range from negative to neutral to positive. Negative human behavior can be either unintentional (negligent) or intentional (malicious). Similarly, human behavior that is neutral, positive, helpful, or good is either intentional or unconscious. Figure 1.1 illustrates this point and can help you see how human behavior can fall into one of four quadrants, or zones. In Part 3 of this book, I'll propose some strategies for how to work with the types of behaviors associated with each zone in Part 3 of this book.

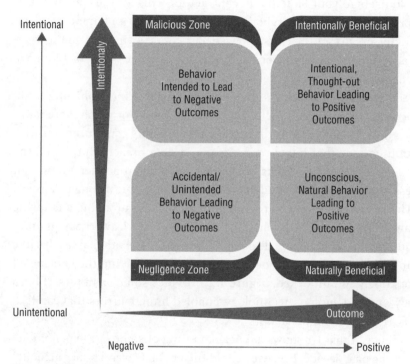

Figure 1.1: Continuum of behavior from unintentional to intentional with malicious/harmful to beneficial outcomes.

As you think about the continuum of human behavior, slow down for a moment and consider the number of human touchpoints in every part of your organization. I'm sure you can quickly see that we do ourselves a disservice by simply hoping that technology-based systems will ever provide an adequate level of protection. When all other processes, controls, and technologies fail, humans are your last line of defense. What are you doing to equip them to be effective?

Data Breaches Tell the Story

Conduct even a cursory amount of research into the history of data breaches and you'll see the danger posed by human errors. Your users—all your users—contribute to the security posture of your organization. This ranges from the decisions and behaviors of your executive team and board of directors to your general end users to your IT staff and contractors. This isn't just an end-user population problem. It's an everybody problem because it's a human problem. As Walt Kelly, creator of the classic newspaper comic strip *Pogo*, put it when creating a poster for the first-ever Earth Day observance in 1970, "We have met the enemy and he is us."[1]

From the issues that we all think about such as clicking a phishing link, falling for more sophisticated social engineering scams, or much more mundane issues such as not securely disposing of documents containing sensitive information, we see that human error leads to data breach. But, here's the problem: as security technologists, we tend to put a disproportionate amount of our messaging and focus around data breaches that occur through technical means. The result can easily be that organizations end up doing a fantastic job helping employees suss out phishing emails but still leave them ignorant and unequipped to make secure decisions across a host of other areas. It's like closing and locking the front door of your house but leaving the garage and back doors open and unlocked. Figure 1.2 provides some examples of both technology-enabled and non-technology-enabled human errors that can lead to security incidents and breaches.

For reference, Table 1.1 shows a quick sampling of some of the major data breaches of the past decade. Because I could fill a book (several books actually) with a listing of data breaches, I'm limiting the list to one significant breach each year.

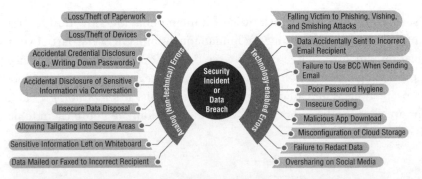

Figure 1.2: Examples of both analog and technology-enabled human errors that lead to security incidents and breaches.

Table 1.1: Example data breaches and their human factor causes

Year	Organization	Impact	Human Factor Cause
2008	Bank of New York Mellon[2,3]	Multiple issues contributed to a data breach impacting up to 12.5 million BNY Mellon customers. The first issue was that sensitive data on the tape was not encrypted. Then the tape went missing. The incident was caused by the loss of a backup tape that was handed off to a third party for storage with nine other tapes. When the tapes arrived at the off-site storage building, one was missing; the other nine were accounted for.	Loss of unencrypted backup tape
2009	Heartland Payment Systems[4,5]	Heartland Payment Systems was breached by hackers using a common SQL injection vulnerability. The result was the loss of 130 million credit and debit card numbers and more than $140 million in breach-related expenses.	Poor coding (SQL injection)
2010	CitiGroup[6,7]	Approximately 600,000 CitiGroup customers received year-end tax statements with their Social Security numbers printed on the outside of the mailing envelope delivered by the U.S. Postal Service.	Formatting error oversight
2011	RSA Security[8,9,10]	Attackers were able to breach RSA Security's network by sending two different phishing emails over a two-day period. The two emails were sent to two small groups of employees; you wouldn't consider these users particularly high-profile or high-value targets. The email subject line read "2011 Recruitment Plan." Seeds for RSA SecureID two-factor authentication token were exfiltrated. In addition to dealing with the public outcry and loss of face in the security community, RSA Security spent approximately $66 Million reissuing physical tokens to SecureID customers.	Spear-phishing attack with malware payload

(continued)

Table 1.1: Example data breaches and their human factor causes *(continued)*

Year	Organization	Impact	Human Factor Cause
2012	Yahoo![11]	Attackers embarrassed Yahoo! and shocked the security community by posting the usernames and passwords of 450,000 users associated with the Yahoo! Contributor Network. The attackers used a common SQL injection vulnerability. Adding insult to injury, the passwords that the attackers accessed were in plaintext.	Poor coding (SQL injection vulnerability) and user passwords stored in plaintext
2013	Target[12]	Credentials from one of Target's HVAC contractors were stolen via a phishing attack that downloaded and launched malware. These credentials were used to gain access into Target's networks and move laterally across systems. The effects resulted in the loss of data from approximately 40 million credit and debit cards as well as personal information associated with 70 million Target shoppers.	Phishing attack with malware payload
2014	eBay[13,14]	Credentials from a number of (up to 100) eBay employees were compromised to gain network access. The attackers were able to exfiltrate data from 145 million customers.	Phishing attack leading to credential theft
2015	Anthem[15]	The records of approximately 78.8 million current and former customers were exposed as the result of a successful phishing attack potentially carried out by a foreign government. An investigation found that the phishing email was opened by a single employee at an Anthem subsidiary in February 2014, nearly a year before the breach was discovered and reported.	Phishing attack with malware attachment

Year	Organization	Impact	Human Factor Cause
2016	Democratic National Committee (DNC)[16]	It's hard to overestimate the impact that the DNC hack had. As the result of a credential harvesting attack, hackers were able to access the email account of John Podesta, campaign manager for Hillary Clinton. The emails were leaked and were the source of a number of embarrassing media stories that may have influenced the results of the 2016 U.S. Presidential Election.	Phishing attack leading to credential theft
2017	Equifax[17,18]	The Equifax breach of 2017 exposed the personal information (including Social Security numbers) of approximately 145 million people. In addition to the data breach, Equifax's incident response and public reporting was extremely unorganized and caused great confusion to consumers wanting to know if their data was exposed.	Hack enabled by internal miscommunication and failure to apply patches in a timely manner
2018	Exactis[19]	Exactis is a large data broker located in Florida. Security researchers found a fully exposed database containing personal information of nearly every U.S. citizen and millions of businesses. It contained data such as phone numbers, email addresses, personal habits, and information on the children (including age and gender) for each of the named individuals.	Unintended disclosure/misconfiguration of cloud storage

So, what do these incidents point to? Simple: human behavior matters. There are extremely negative ramifications associated with falling victim to social engineering attacks, as well as with everyday mistakes, oversights, and lapses of judgment. We have a duty to instill good security hygiene into our user populations.

RESOURCES ON DATA BREACHES AND SECURITY INCIDENTS

There's no getting around it: publicly reported data breaches and security incidents are a big deal. They provide real-world answers to the question, "What's the worst that can happen?" Data breaches also help organizations see concrete examples of the types of behaviors or oversights that can lead to negative impacts.

Your organization might also find value in using breach-tracking databases to validate your own incident response practices. Do so by creating threat models to see where the security controls broke down resulting in the breach.

Here are links to a few annual and ongoing studies that you should take time to review:

- Identity Theft Resource Center (ongoing data breach list and analysis): `https://www.idtheftcenter.org/data-breaches/`
- IBM Cost of Data Breach Study: `https://www.ibm.com/security/data-breach`
- Privacy Rights Clearinghouse (ongoing data breach list and research tools): `https://www.privacyrights.org/data-breaches`
- Symantec Internet Security Threat Report: `https://www.symantec.com/security-center/threat-report`
- Trend Micro (various reports and studies): `https://www.trendmicro.com/vinfo/us/security/research-and-analysis/threat-reports`
- Verizon Data Breach Investigations Report: `http://www.verizonenterprise.com/verizon-insights-lab/dbir/`

NOTE When reviewing each of these reports, it is important to understand that the numbers reported in each will likely differ. One of the main reasons is because the company that is analyzing and reporting on the data may define a key reporting term/category differently than another.

For instance, one may have a category for "social engineering" attacks, and another may lump social engineering in with a category like "hacking" or may have a category for "malware" but not account for how the malware got on the system in the first place (social engineering, human error, process error, and so on).

Auditors and Regulators Recognize the Need for Security Awareness Training

What is the goal of an audit or of a specific regulation? Both are really focused around the same thing—establishing and measuring against a specific standard (or set of standards) devised to provide a baseline amount of protection or risk management for an organization. As they establish these baselines, they generally do so by looking at "failure" trends; in other words, analyzing "what went wrong" in the situations that created an awareness for the need for audit or regulatory oversight. And, in analyzing such scenarios, auditors and regulators seek to catalog the discrete factors contributing to the failure. They then postulate the inverse, looking to identify and codify best practices, the controls if you will, that would help an organization avoid that failure in the future.

Given the connection between the human element and data breaches, it's easy to see why auditors and regulators are making security awareness training a key element in their audit and regulatory requirements. To serve as examples, here is a list of ten regulations and standards across a variety of industries that specify the need for security awareness training:

- Bank Protection Act
  - Outlined in 12 CFR § 568.3.
  - Requires that covered entities provide initial and periodic training of officers and employees in their responsibilities under the security program.
- Canada's Personal Information Protection and Electronic Document Act (PIPEDA)
  - Outlined in Principle 4.1.4.
  - Organizations must implement "policies and practices" to protect personal information.

- Federal Information Security Management Act (FISMA)
  - Outlined in §3544.(b).(4).(A),(B).
  - To ensure effectiveness of information security controls over resources supporting Federal operations and assets, such organizations must establish, "security awareness training to inform personnel, including contractors and other users of information systems that support the operations and assets of the agency, of information security risks associated with their activities; and their responsibilities in complying with agency policies and procedures designed to reduce these risks."
- Federal Financial Institutions Examination Council (FFIEC)
  - Outlined in the Information Security Booklet II.C.7(e).
  - For covered entities, this specifies management's responsibility to provide training that supports security awareness and strengthen compliance with security and acceptable use policies. Example areas called out for focus include use of endpoint devices, login requirements, password guidelines, phishing and other social-engineering tactics, loss of data through email or removable media, and unintentional posting of confidential or proprietary information on social media.
- General Data Protection Regulation (GDPR)
  - Outlined in Article 39.1.(b).
  - For covered entities (any organization that processes or retains the personal data of EU residents), the GDPR specifies that a data protection officer must, "monitor compliance with this Regulation, with other Union or Member State data protection provisions and with the policies of the controller or processor in relation to the protection of personal data, including the assignment of responsibilities, awareness-raising and training of staff involved in processing operations, and the related audits."
  - Additionally, see Article 70.1 (v).
  - Promotes common training programmes and facilitates personnel exchanges between the supervisory authorities and, where appropriate, with the supervisory authorities of third countries or with international organisations.

- Gramm-Leach Bliley Act (GLBA)
  - Outlined in the Safeguards Rule §314.(4) and in the Financial Privacy Rule §6801.(b).(1)-(3).
  - Ensures proper security-related employee training and management. Provide appropriate safeguards for the protection of customer information against unintended disclosure or misuse.
- Health Insurance Portability and Accountability Act (HIPAA)
  - Outlined in the Privacy Rule §164.530.(b).(1) and the Security Rule §164.308(a)(5)(i).
  - Requires that covered entities "train all members of its workforce on the policies and procedures with respect to protected health information" and that they "implement, a security awareness and training program for all members of its workforce (including management)."
- Massachusetts Data Security Law (Standards for the protection of personal information of residents of the Commonwealth)
  - Outlined in 201 CMR 17.03.
  - Mandates training to maintain a comprehensive information security program. The training should focus on reasonably fore-seeable internal and external risks to the security, confidentiality, and/or integrity of any electronic, paper, or other records containing personal information. Training must be "ongoing" and must be given for not only permanent employees but also temporary and contract employees.
- North American Electric Reliability Corporation Critical Infrastructure Protection Standard NERC CIP
  - Outlined in §CIP-004-3(B)(R1).
  - Responsible entities "shall establish, document, implement, and maintain a security awareness program to ensure personnel having authorized cyber or authorized unescorted physical access to Critical Cyber Assets receive ongoing reinforcement in sound security practices. The program shall include security awareness reinforcement on at least a quarterly basis." Example communication mechanisms include emails, memos, computer-based training (CBT), posters, articles, presentations, meetings, and so on. They also highlight the need to show management support and reinforcement.

- Payment Card Industry Data Security Standard (PCI DSS)
  - Outlined in requirement 12.6.
  - Covered organizations must "implement a formal security aware-ness program to make all personnel aware of the importance of cardholder data security," and ensure that employees receive training, "upon hire and at least annually."

LOOKING FOR LINKS TO COMPLIANCE REQUIREMENTS FOR SECURITY AWARENESS TRAINING?

Many vendors serving the security awareness and training market main-tain web pages dedicated to cataloging regulations and standards related to security awareness training. Here are a few:

- **InfoSec Institute:** https://resources.infosecinstitute.com/cat-egory/enterprise/securityawareness/compliance-mandates/
- **KnowBe4:** https://www.knowbe4.com/resources/security-aware-ness-compliance-requirements/
- **TeachPrivacy:** https://teachprivacy.com/privacy-training-and-data-security-training-requirements/

Traditional Security Awareness Program Methods Fall Short of Their Goals

For decades in the computer industry and for millennia throughout the history of humanity, those seeking to promote "secure behaviors" have fallen into a trap. They believe that exposing people to the right information will naturally result in those people adopting the appropriate behavior and mind-set.

Those of us who are parents can already see the logic flaw. Just because we tell our kids what we expect, even when we tell them why, doesn't mean that they will do what we are hoping. You can tell them that you want their room cleaned by 5 p.m. And you can show them a picture of a clean room, remind them what a clean room looks like, and even give them a lecture about the virtues associated with having a clean room. But their desire to keep playing video games, with LEGOs, or with their iPhone can easily override your hopes.

Our adult selves aren't any different. Want proof? I think we'd all admit that we, on occasion, disregard what a speed limit sign says. Speed limit signs exist for a reason, safety, specifically the safety of the driver and others on (and around) the roads. And speed limits are a legal control, not just a suggestion. But, how many of us take speed limit signs as suggestions? We read the sign, look at our surrounding conditions (rain, pedestrians, presence/absence of police, our schedule constraints or lack thereof), and make a context-driven risk assessment about how fast we can drive. *Our users treat our security controls in much the same way that we treat speed limits: as suggestions or as impediments to progress.*

For several years now, I've included the following two phrases in most of my presentations or interactions with security awareness leaders:

- "Just because I'm aware doesn't mean that I care."
- "If you try to work against human nature, you will fail."

Take a moment to review Table 1.2, and think about each of those statements and the related implications:

Table 1.2: The reality of human nature and security awareness programs

Statement	Implication
"Just because I'm aware doesn't mean that I care."	Awareness doesn't lead to caring. And, if I don't care about something, I'm unlikely to go out of my way to engage with it or perform related tasks.
"If you try to work against human nature, you will fail."	Humans are wired in specific ways. We don't like to do things that are difficult, awkward, or require change.

So, just giving people good security information won't cut it. In the next chapter, I'll remind you of these statements and implications, but I'll open the doorway to hope by adding a "Resolution" column that will help frame how we work within the reality of human nature. That's really the purpose of this book: to help you overcome the sticking points of insecure human behavior by working with human nature rather than against it. After all, do you care more about what your employees *know* or what they *do*?

NOTE

That's really the purpose of this book: to help you overcome the sticking points of insecure human behavior by working with human nature rather than against it. After all, do you care more about what your employees *know* or what they *do*?

Key Takeaways

We've reached our first "Key Takeaways" section. I'm including this section in each chapter as a way of helping distill the "So what?" For you, I'm assuming you already knew the answer to that before you picked up this book. However, let me boil down my main thoughts into a few bullets.

- *Humans are your last line of defense.* Regardless of how good our security technology is or becomes, there will be a percentage of attacks that slip through the technology or bypass the technology entirely. Humans will be your last line of defense in cases where these are not machine-to-machine interactions. Not training employees is therefore unwise and negligent.
- *Data breaches are a commentary on the importance of end-user training.* In many ways, the history of data breaches and publicly disclosed cybersecurity incidents is a study in how human decisions and behavior are critical in an organizations' security program.
- *Auditors and regulators advocate for training.* The large body of audit, regulatory requirements, and recommended best-practice standards all point to employee training as a critical element in an organization's cybersecurity program.
- *It's time to step up our game.* Unfortunately, even when organizations implement a security awareness training program, they fail to do so as effectively as possible for a variety of reasons, but, primarily because they haven't successfully bridged the gap between *awareness* and *caring* or the gap between *knowing* and *doing*. As an industry, we can do better, and we certainly have a lot to gain by doing so.

So, where do we go from here? In the next chapter, I'm going to provide a high-level view of what a more effective and impactful approach entails. Subsequent chapters will break this down even further, examining the different components, subcomponents, and considerations. After that, we will be in a great position to walk through how to put all the pieces together to build the effective and sustainable program your organization needs and your employees deserve.

References

1. https://en.wikipedia.org/wiki/Pogo_(comic_strip)#%22We_have_met_the_enemy_and_he_is_us.%22
2. https://www.bankinfosecurity.com/bank-new-york-mellon-investigated-for-lost-data-tape-a-862
3. https://www.reuters.com/article/us-bankofnymellon-breach/bank-of-ny-mellon-data-breach-now-affects-12-5-mln-idUSN2834717120080828
4. https://www.computerworld.com/article/2527185/security0/sql-injection-attacks-led-to-heartland--hannaford-breaches.html
5. https://www.privacyrights.org/data-breaches?title=heartland
6. https://www.aol.com/2010/03/02/citibank-may-have-printed-your-social-security-number-on-the-out/
7. https://money.cnn.com/galleries/2010/news/1006/gallery.biggest_bank_blunders/2.html
8. https://www.theregister.co.uk/2011/04/04/rsa_hack_howdunnit/
9. https://nakedsecurity.sophos.com/2011/04/04/rsa-release-details-on-security-breach/
10. https://www.washingtonpost.com/blogs/post-tech/post/cyber-attack-on-rsa-cost-emc-66-million/2011/07/26/gIQA1ceKbI_blog.html?utm_term=.546b71045e1d
11. https://www.csoonline.com/article/2131970/identity-theft-prevention/yahoo-security-breach-shocks-experts.html
12. https://krebsonsecurity.com/2014/05/the-target-breach-by-the-numbers/
13. https://www.pcworld.com/article/2360762/what-ebay-taught-us-about-malware-your-own-data-can-be-used-to-dupe-you.html
14. https://www.bankinfosecurity.com/ebay-a-6858
15. http://fortune.com/2017/01/09/anthem-cyber-attack-foreign-government/
16. https://www.washingtonpost.com/news/politics/wp/2018/07/13/time-line-how-russian-agents-allegedly-hacked-the-dnc-and-clintons-campaign/?noredirect=on&utm_term=.e95de15651be

17. https://www.theverge.com/2017/10/3/16410806/equifax-ceo-blame-breach-patch-congress-testimony

18. https://krebsonsecurity.com/2017/09/breach-at-equifax-may-impact-143m-americans/

19. https://www.wired.com/story/exactis-database-leak-340-million-records/

2 Choosing a Transformational Approach

The methods that will most effectively minimize the ability of intruders to compromise information security are comprehensive user training and education. Enacting policies and procedures simply won't suffice. Even with oversight the policies and procedures may not be effective: my access to Motorola, Nokia, ATT, Sun depended upon the willingness of people to bypass policies and procedures that were in place for years before I compromised them successfully.

Kevin Mitnick, Congressional Testimony, March 2, 2000

Let's start with a simple question: why are you implementing a security awareness training program? That question may seem overly basic, but having helped thousands of security leaders with their programs, I can tell you from experience that most people haven't stopped to analyze what they are really trying to accomplish. Instead, they know that they should "do some security awareness," but they don't really know what that means, and they don't know where to start. Add to that the fact that most people tasked with running a security awareness program have several other job duties on their plate, and you can see why it's so easy to end up with programs that are ineffective. They end up creating something that may help serve a bare-bones compliance purpose, but then the stack of competing priorities mount so high that the awareness program manager is forced to move on and deal with the other tasks on their plates. In the back of their mind, they know that they *should* do more, and they have every intention to do more *someday*, but the daily firefights always push *someday* further and further into the future.

So, before going any further, I'll ask again: Why are you implementing a security awareness training program? As you think about that question, consider your hopes for the program and your vision of what a great outcome would look like. This chapter will walk you through the premise of what a transformational security awareness program entails and how to begin that journey.

Your "Why" Determines Your "What"

Knowing your "why" may be the best indicator of your likelihood of having an impactful program. That's because having a clear idea of why you are building your program will naturally point to the types of things you'll need to focus on. Said another way, once you have a clear vision of your program's purpose, you can start planning the best way to achieve that purpose: *why* you are doing it will inform *what* you should do.

I've found that there are four main reasons (the "whys") that drive organizations to implement a security awareness training program.

- ■ **Compliance:** We do it because the regulations or auditors require it.
- ■ **Information dissemination:** We do it to "get the word out" about policies, expectations, news, concerns, best practices, and so on.
- ■ **Behavior shaping:** We do it to actively influence and manage the security-related actions of employees.
- ■ **Culture shaping:** We do it to help mold the organization's collective core values, beliefs, attitudes, and actions as they relate to security.

Figure 2.1 illustrates the four whys.

Figure 2.1: The four main reasons why organizations create security awareness training programs.

We'll explore the implications for each "why" in just a bit. But, for now, be gut-level honest with yourself about your program's driving purpose as it exists today. Also, be gut-level honest about what your current organizational culture will tolerate. Thinking through your answers to questions like the following will help. How much awareness training is enough? What formats for training will your organization support? How often can you train? What are your challenges and limitations? And, how will you know if your program is achieving its goals?

Down the Rabbit Hole

When I was discussing the proposed content of this project to Jim Minatel at Wiley Publishing, he immediately said, "Oh, you are going for a true liberal-arts view of security awareness." Yes! Jim got it. And I'm hoping that you will "get it" as well because for far too long the security industry has approached awareness in an extremely one-dimensional way.[1]

The frenetic pace and competing priorities that security professionals face daily is the biggest contributor to one-dimensional thinking and shallow approaches to security training. As you have undoubtedly seen, the negative effects of this are far-reaching. People aren't equipped to make good security decisions. That leads to security failures. And then leaders question the validity of security awareness programs and their ability to provide a positive value. They question not only the ROI associated with the time that employees spent on the training but the value of doing training in the first place.

This leads some within the security industry to advocate the following line of thought: because security incidents still happen in organizations that previously provided security awareness training directly related to a cause leading to an incident, security awareness is of little-to-no value, and only technology will help an organization prevent security issues.[2,3]

Heck, even respected security experts like Bruce Schneier have made similar comments. In a 2013 blog post, Bruce wrote, "I personally believe that training users in security is generally a waste of time and that the money can be spent better elsewhere. Moreover, I believe that our industry's focus on training serves to obscure greater failings in security design."[4] While I have a lot of respect for Bruce, I think that his perspective here doesn't align with reality. I also think that it doesn't align with his broader thinking in the areas of security and technology. As an example, Bruce has a very well-known quote. . .the one that I used as an intro to Chapter 1: "If you think technology can solve your security problems, then you don't understand the problems and you don't understand the technology."[5]

So, what does it mean when even our industry's best and most respected thinkers have such contradictory opinions about the value and ability of security awareness training to reduce an organization's security risk? I personally think it signals frustration with the status quo and a hope for something better. We know that current security technologies have inherent failures, allowing for users to make unintentional or intentional decisions that lead to security incidents. At the same time, despite receiving training, users still make these unintentional or intentional decisions.

As an industry, we will always have to solve (and evolve) for both sides of the equation (technology and humanity). Not implementing standard and reasonable technology-based tools proven to improve an organization's security posture would be negligent. Similarly, not acknowledging that technology will never be 100 percent effective at preventing cybercriminals from creating well-crafted attacks targeting humans, such as emails or other messages that reach your end users, is also negligent. Neither approach is mutually exclusive of the other. And whenever we create stronger security protocols intended to help our organizations, there will be a group of employees who will intentionally or unintentionally find ways to bypass those controls. The human element must be a factor in the deployment of technology, and it should be understood as a security layer in and of itself. Your defense-in-depth security strategy should always account for the following:

- Determined human attackers who are continually probing for flaws within your security technologies (and that flaws will always exist)
- Unwitting employees who find themselves on the receiving end of a cybercriminal seeking to accomplish their goals by going around the technical layers of an organization's defenses, targeting humans instead
- Employees who negligently or intentionally circumvent technical controls
- Employees who negligently or intentionally divert from the organization's policies, controls, and processes
- The interdependency between policies, controls, and processes that exist in the physical world and those of the organization's technology-based systems

- The ever-evolving ecosystem of mobile, IoT, and other new technology-based systems that your people will engage with
- The reality that digital data can easily spill into the physical world (e.g., printouts, whiteboards, conversations, and so on)

Thinking about this we can safely conclude that the human element of security will always be something that deserves intentional focus. And that's where security awareness training comes in. But it's time to push past the one-dimensional programs that have given security awareness training a bad name. Our goal is to change hearts, minds, beliefs, instincts, and behaviors. All of this means that we need to think broadly and incorporate practices from several disciplines that most security professionals have little experience or expertise in: topics such as marketing, public relations, communication theory, behavior design, culture management, and more.

Transformational programs break from the mundane mold that we've all seen for decades. That means if you decide to implement the concepts presented later in this book, you may be breaking new ground in your organization. Or, maybe you've started incorporating some of these practices already. If so, congratulations! My hope for you is that you'll be further challenged and encouraged to keep going deeper.

This is the point where I get to pretend to be Morpheus from the movie *The Matrix*. So, here's the challenge. My hands slowly open. In one hand, a blue pill. In the other hand, a red pill. . .

> *This is your last chance. After this, there is no turning back. You take the blue pill—the story ends, you wake up in your bed and believe whatever you want to believe. You take the red pill—you stay in Wonderland, and I show you how deep the rabbit hole goes. Remember: all I'm offering is the truth. Nothing more.*
>
> **Morpheus,** *The Matrix*

I see you are still here. Let's begin.

Outlining the Key Components and Tools of a Transformational Program

As we discussed at the beginning of this chapter, it's important to answer the "why" question before deciding on what your program will look like. You need to have an "eyes open" view of what your organizational drivers are because, for instance, if your goal is simply compliance, then you can happily close this book now and go to any one of the great vendors serving the security awareness market and purchase a subscription that will help you quickly achieve that goal. But, remember, you chose the red pill because you know that going the "security awareness simply for the sake of compliance" route is taking an extremely limited view of your responsibility as a security leader. We all know that compliance does not necessarily result in security. If you are already doing something because you need to be "compliant," then why not do more and have a real impact for your organization and people? Why not do something that is *transformational*?

Figure 2.2 represents my take on how each of the four "whys" we previously discussed map to a level of effectiveness in impacting an organization's human-based security risk.

Awareness programs that focus on compliance or simply sharing information are of inherently limited benefit. Such programs are either overly formulaic, thereby often becoming rote exercises that feel irrelevant and soulless, or focus on information sharing with the futile hope that presenting people with good information will result in those people automatically retaining and applying the information.

But awareness programs can achieve more. Much more. They can be *transformational*. Our awareness programs can be designed to shape behaviors, change the way employees think, modify their habits and beliefs, and even positively impact the social and cultural fabric of the organization. That may sound like a lofty goal achievable by only a select few willing to scale high mountains in search of gurus who miserly dispense secret wisdom; but, lucky for us, that isn't the case. The secrets of shaping behaviors and cultures stare us in the face every day; they are wielded by communications professionals, economists, psychologists, religious communities, political groups, professional designers, artists, storytellers, sociologists, and more. We just need to enter their worlds.

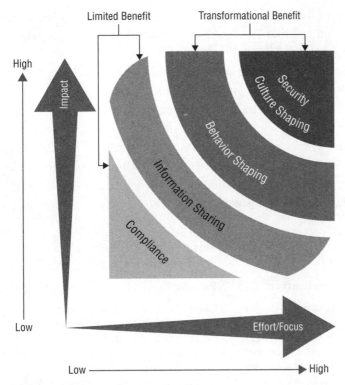

Figure 2.2: Your program's goal either will produce limited benefit or can be transformational for your organization.

Consider the groups I just mentioned. Each of them "sells" ideas and experiences with the goal of understanding how to motivate people toward specific beliefs and behaviors. And they each draw from millennia of research and experimentation that have helped shape and refine their practices. They hold the keys that will help us unlock the elements of human belief and behavior. That is the journey that we will undertake for the remainder of this book.

Let's flash back to the two statements that I introduced in Chapter 1 and introduced in Table 1.2: *the reality of human nature and security awareness programs.*

- "Just because I'm aware doesn't mean that I care."
- "If you try to work against human nature, you will fail."

When I presented that table in Chapter 1, I included the statement and the implication; then I promised that I'd introduce a column with the resolution in this chapter. Take a look at Table 2.1.

As you review the table, notice that the resolutions are all about connecting to the humanity of the situation. For the first statement, it's about finding the bigger "why," connecting with something that the learner will truly care about. For the second statement, the key is helping to support them and to realize that humans are wired in specific ways and that overcoming that innate wiring is difficult. We therefore need to either bow to the wiring or provide social support, motivation, and facilitating tools and practices that will help the learner "make the leap" to the new practice.

Table 2.1: Human nature and security awareness programs: statement, implication, and resolution

Statement	Implication	Resolution
"Just because I'm aware doesn't mean that I care."	Awareness doesn't lead to caring. And, if I don't care about something, I'm unlikely to go out of my way to engage with it.	Connect security awareness messaging to topics, situations, and outcomes that your audience will naturally find relevant and meaningful. In cases where the connection is less intuitive, you will need to help them "connect the dots." Don't neglect the power of emotion and story. The more human the ideas become, the better. Move away from abstract, security-centric information and connect the information to human-centric outcomes, purposes, and compelling visuals. I'll be discussing the nuts and bolts of how to do this in Chapter 3."

Statement	Implication	Resolution
"**If you try to work against human nature, you will fail.**"	Humans are wired in specific ways. We don't like to do things that are difficult, awkward, or require change.	When human nature makes performing secure behaviors difficult, you will need to either increase their motivation to perform the behavior (help them remember or understand why it is important), or you will need to find ways to make it easier for them by helping to facilitate the correct behavior. This can be accomplished with technology-based help or by "prompting" the correct behavior at the appropriate time. Even more difficult behaviors can begin to become easy and intuitive when repeated enough times. The goal is to create healthy security habits so that the behavior no longer becomes an exercise in logic but instead becomes engrained, effectively second nature. I'll be discussing how this is achievable in Chapters 4 and 5.

By now, you've undoubtedly noticed that we've gone much broader than anything that can easily be labeled "awareness." That's true. If you recall the four "whys" that I outlined at the beginning of this chapter, I mentioned that the first two of those (compliance and information sharing) produce inherently limited benefit. Awareness, generally defined, covers those first two "whys." But, to be transformational, you must move past awareness as it is typically understood.

So, why do we still use the term *awareness* to describe our programs? That's a great question. And you may or may not be satisfied with my answer; but, it's one that is true regardless of how you feel about it. In my time as an awareness practitioner and as a Gartner analyst covering security, I had a mantra that I'd repeat to anyone who would listen. In fact, I made it the title of a presentation that I used to give at Gartner Security conferences; it was "Move Beyond 'Awareness' to Security Culture Management."[6]

But, here's where the difficult to digest truth comes in. This is an "in-house" argument over semantics that is relevant only to the initiated. What I mean by that is that security leaders think this way only once they've been placed in a context that helps them see the conclusion. And here's why "awareness" has and will likely continue to be the term that the security industry will be forced to use despite all of the term's inherent limitations and baggage: *Google.*

We use the term *awareness* because that is the term that people use when they are looking for information about the practices and tools that are needed to engage end-user populations with security-related information and training. It's that simple. When most security leaders want to find information about how to change the security-related mind-set and behaviors of their end users, they still start with the search phrase *security awareness*, *security awareness training*, or some variant thereof. So, even forward-thinking vendors and security leaders wanting to educate others on the necessity of security behavior management or security culture management must start the conversation with security awareness or risk being a third-page Google result (equivalent to nonexistence).

So, let's not waste time arguing semantics. Instead, let's get on with the work of helping our employees and organizations be more secure. Our program—regardless of what we decide to call it—can be deep, dynamic, and transformational.

A Map of What's to Come

Up to now I've been teasing at several things, ranging from the idea of being able to accomplish something transformational with our awareness efforts, to some of what the underlying tactics will be to achieve that goal, to the fact that awareness itself is actually too narrow a definition for what we are trying to accomplish. And yet, I still haven't explicitly defined what I mean by *transformational.*

So, let's start with a definition, and then I'll add more context. The term *transformational* is obviously a form of the word *transform*. I love the way that this word is defined in the *Cambridge Advanced Learner's Dictionary & Thesaurus*.[7] Check it out. Resist the urge to skip over the definition simply because it is something that you already know.

transform verb [T] UK /træns'fɔːm/ US /træns'fɔːrm/
> **2B:** to change completely the appearance or character of something or someone, especially so that that thing or person is improved:

Now, read the example uses of the word that they provide:

- The reorganization will transform the entertainment industry.
- the power of art to transform experience
- Whenever a camera was pointed at her, Marilyn would instantly transform herself into a radiant star.

Why would I have you read a definition for a word that you already know and read sentences with that word in it that are probably similar to the types of sentences we each use every day? Answer: I want us to pause for a moment and ponder how the idea of transforming something applies in different contexts. Let's look at the definition again. To transform is, "to change completely the appearance or character of something or someone, *especially so that that thing or person is improved* [emphasis mine]." That is exactly what we are after! Now, look again at the way they apply the concept to multiple contexts/scenarios. Those examples portray the transformation of an industry, human experience, and a person's perception, emotions, and presence. Those are just examples that a dictionary provided to show how the word is used, but the examples do a masterful job at pointing toward what we want to do with our awareness programs. Imagine if we could do each of the following:

- Transform the way our end users think and approach situations
- Transform the way our end users react and behave when facing security-related challenges
- Transform the way that social structures within our organizations manage risk and foster secure thoughts and actions
- Transform the way that our executives model good security-related behaviors to others within our organizations
- Transform our security programs that are overly technology-centric to programs with a proper appreciation for the importance of the human layer
- Transform our old way of approaching security awareness from something that can seem disconnected and irrelevant to our employees to something that is highly relevant and engaging

■ Transform our methods that expect humans to think or behave in non-human ways to methods that recognize, and work with, human nature

■ Transform our understanding of what awareness programs can accomplish because—after all—we really mean something much broader and deeper

That type of transformation is our new goal. We want to transform each context, "especially so that that thing or person is improved."

Making your awareness program transformational means you are connecting it with humanity. So, that's where we are going for the rest of this book. Let's dive in and get an idea of what's in store.

Part 1 in a Nutshell

This chapter concludes the first section of this book, which (as you already know) was about making the case for why awareness programs are crucial. Humans are our last line of defense, and we need to equip them with the tools and discernment to make smart security decisions and to build good security hygiene. To do that, we must move past one-dimensional information-centric or compliance-driven programs and embrace strategies that account for the multidimensional realities of human nature.

Part 2 in a Nutshell

Part 2 of this book is all about the tools of transformation. In each chapter, I'll highlight some key thoughts, principles, and practices from a domain that specializes in influencing human thought, belief, and behavior. For convenience, I'm chunking the tools section into three core topics: communications, behavior, and culture. While each of these may seem distinct from the other, we'll quickly see that there is a lot of interaction between each of them. For example, we behave in specific ways depending on the input we receive (communication) and the context (of which culture is a part) that we use to filter that communication. Each of these areas is like an intricate gear interacting with one another to produce a complex result.

We'll take a journey through the worlds of marketing communications, public relations, and other professional communicators to get an idea of how they use words and visuals to shape the opinions and beliefs of those with whom they are communicating.

After that, we will look at the field of behavior science to get a grasp on how we can impact both the conscious and unconscious decisions that people make so that we can begin designing behaviors that are more secure and start extracting our security programs from situations where we are constantly frustrated because we expect our end users to act more like computers than like humans.

The third area we'll study is culture management. This gets into the complex social dynamics of organizations. We'll deal with issues around how to work with regionally diverse cultures, different divisional/departmental cultures, organizational roles, socioeconomic and age differences, and so on. The focus here is on how we build a sustainable security-conscious culture.

Lastly, we'll look at different tools that can be used as part of your program. This is where a lot of the more traditional awareness components (e.g., videos, posters, interactive learning modules, simulated phishing and social engineering testing, and so on) enter the picture. The difference here is that we will be talking about how to use each of these components in ways that fit within a larger framework that incorporates the principles of communication, behavior, and culture management. Therefore, we'll be using familiar components, but doing so in a way that will produce transformational results.

Part 3 in a Nutshell

Our last main section of the book is where we weave everything together. I'm including a whole chapter on how awareness fits within the context of life so that we can walk through a "journey map" of sorts and experience the program through the eyes of different groups of end users. Then we'll think about how each persona that we consider has different motivations, concerns, strengths, and weaknesses. Understanding and accounting for different personas and end-user segments will unlock a range of new possibilities for engagement.

After looking at awareness in the context of life, we'll be set to talk about actually beginning to create your security awareness training program. This is where it gets fun. I'll discuss everything you need to consider at the beginning, such as getting executive buy-in, dealing with pushback, and creating your justification, and then I'll get into campaign design, ambassador programs, metrics/reporting, and operationalization.

VOICES OF TRANSFORMATION

One of the great things about the field of security awareness is the passionate practitioners and vendors. At the end of Part 2 and Part 3 of this book, I'll be sharing many of their stories and perspectives. My hope in doing so is to expose you to a ton of unique and interesting perspectives that will help foster new ideas, encourage you, and perhaps ignite new passions.

Key Takeaways

- *Your "why" determines your "what."* Knowing the ultimate purpose and goal of your program is critically important because your "why" maps directly to the amount of impact your program will have. Security awareness programs whose goals are strictly set to meet a compliance mandate or to disseminate security-related information are of inherently limited benefit. To achieve transformational benefits, your goal(s) will need to include shaping end-user behavior and/or shaping of the organization's overall security culture.

- *Don't let the term "awareness" trip you up.* We know that the term *awareness* is not descriptive of the full scope of our programs, but it is the term that the industry has adopted. We can start our discussions using the term *awareness* and then shift the discussion to be more inclusive of the transformational tools and tactics that we'll be relying on.

- *Effective programs intentionally work with human nature rather than against it.* But, most security leaders don't have deep experience and expertise in shaping human thought, behavior, and belief; to overcome this, we must look at disciplines that specialize in doing so. Specifically, we can learn lessons from experts in the fields of communications, behavior, and culture management.

Notes and References

1. That isn't to say that the ideas that I'm presenting are new. In fact, several voices within the security industry have been saying many of the same things that I'm proposing for well over a decade now. Where possible, I'm

going to reference quotes from these pioneers and to always give credit where credit is due. And, despite these not necessarily being new ideas, the state of the industry is still extremely one-dimensional. My hope is that, in some small way, this project helps to reframe the way that we all approach security awareness programs.

2. https://www.csoonline.com/article/2131941/security-awareness/why-you-shouldn-t-train-employees-for-security-awareness.html

3. https://www.schneier.com/blog/archives/2013/03/security_awaren_1.html

4. Ibid.

5. https://www.schneier.com/books/secrets_and_lies/pref.html

6. You can find a webinar version of that presentation here: https://www.gartner.com/webinar/3391518

7. https://dictionary.cambridge.org/us/dictionary/english/transform

The Tools of Transformation

3

Marketing and Communications 101 for Security Awareness Leaders

More than 80% of security awareness professionals have highly technical backgrounds. That's great—they understand the problem—but that's bad because they're really bad at communicating the solution.

Lance Spitzner, Director SANS Security Awareness[1]

Have you ever watched someone trying to communicate with a person who doesn't speak the same language, but they hope that talking louder and slower[2] will somehow magically help? Yeah—Security awareness communications can feel like that.

We expect a lot of our employees when it comes to making secure decisions, protecting customer and organizational information, and behaving in a secure manner. Doing all of this can require a pretty complex collection of steps; and, while humans are generally pretty good at performing complex tasks that they've practiced and care about, they are not near as good at consistently performing complex tasks when they don't yet possess the required proficiency or motivation. But that hasn't stopped us as an industry from hoping that if we simply give people the right information, they will suddenly start acting in a more secure manner.

In Chapters 1 and 2, I introduced one of the fundamental problems that we must deal with: *even if someone is aware, that doesn't mean that they care.* Moreover, we can put out a ton of great information aimed at helping raise the awareness of our people, but we probably don't even know if our information dissemination has translated to understanding. And even if they understand and care, we can't guarantee that they understand to the extent that they'd be able to correctly apply the information in a different context than the way in which the information was first presented.

So, how do we deal with these disconnects? That's where a better understanding of communication techniques and the psychology of communication will help us.

THE ROLE OF COMMUNICATION

Forrester Research captured the essence of the critical role of communication techniques for effective security awareness in its research note "Harden Your Human Firewall."[3] Here's how authors Nick Hayes and Claire O'Malley put it:

> *Communication is the glue that binds and the means of delivery. Just as security professionals provide subject matter expertise, developing an effective campaign requires individuals with good communication skills, familiarity with learning concepts, and knowledge of a variety of tools and techniques. A commonality of winning security campaigns is that the security messages are personal, emotional, and relevant. Getting these messages across also requires a mix of media, materials, and examples that are relevant to your particular environment and organization's culture.*

The Communications Conundrum

Often, the first thing you think of when someone says "security awareness" is the communication aspect of the program: that aspect of ensuring that we've exposed our employees to certain security-related facts and practices. And, as we have already discussed, it is this function of the program that seems to consistently fall short of our hopes.

How is it that we continually fail at the quintessential defining feature of awareness? The answer is simple: most security awareness leaders aren't skilled communicators. The *2018 SANS Security Awareness Report* captured the reason well. Check it out[4]:

> *Consistent with last year's report findings, the 2018 report shows that a clear majority of awareness professionals come from a technical background with less than 20% of individuals coming from non-technical fields such [as] communications, marketing, legal or human resources. While technically skilled professionals have some advantages, in that they have a solid understanding of technology and human-related risks, this can also create a challenge. These same individuals often lack the skills to effectively communicate those risks and engage employees in a way that changes behavior.*

So, here is the crux of the issue. Most security awareness leaders are technical professionals who understand cybersecurity thoroughly but have a difficult time packaging the security facts and messages they want to convey into a format that the average, nonsecurity person will understand or care about. As the SANS report indicated, less than 20 percent of awareness leaders come from backgrounds inherently tied to skill sets related to training, influencing others, or communicating complex topics in understandable ways.

The phenomena of experts having difficulty communicating with "normal" people is well known. Ramit Sethi, author of *I Will Teach You to Be Rich* and founder of GrowthLab.com, captures the reason for this issue well. Ramit says that experts have difficulty in this context because they can't remember what it's like to be a beginner. Here's how he explains it; see if you can relate[5]:

> *Sometimes the very best are horrible teachers.*
>
> *That's because they just can't remember what it's like being a beginner!*
>
> *Go talk to Mariah Carey and ask her how to break into the business. She doesn't know! She's been a diva for so long—she requires that her music is played when she enters a room—that she has no idea what it's like to be a beginner.*
>
> *Love you, Mariah.*
>
> *Smart people have spent so many years working on something that they often forget what it's like to be a beginner.*
>
> *Like my computer science professor in college who once looked at my problem—which I was hopelessly stuck on—and he told me to "Harness the power of C."*
>
> *PLEASE DIE!!!*
>
> *As you get more and more advanced in your career (or relationship or business or pretty much anything), it becomes harder and harder to relate to true beginners. That's because you've built your skill on a series of increasing foundational blocks of knowledge—like building a skyscraper, first sketching it on paper, then with the concrete, then on and on.*
>
> *If you're a NYC real-estate developer and someone comes to you and asks what type of wood to use in their house, you'd stare at them blankly. 'Wood? Who the hell knows? I want to talk about complex financing to get this thing built.'*

*That's why not all smart people are great teachers. (But most great
teachers are smart.)*

Ramit Sethi, "Problems smart people have"

We see that being a security expert doesn't naturally translate to being an
expert on communicating security-related information to people outside of
the security field. So, what's to be done? Really, the answer is the same as with
any issue that we face professionally. We have four choices.

- **Ignore** the issue and hope for the best
- **Grow/learn** the skills that we lack
- **Hire** for the skills that we lack
- **Augment** the skills that we have by bringing in experts from outside
  (consulting with other teams and/or third parties)

The first choice is clearly unacceptable if we hope to improve our situation.
That leaves us with three remaining choices, all of which require that we gain
at least a base-level understanding of the skills and categories of skills related
to closing the communication gap. Let's do that now.

The Marketing Connection

I'm sure you've heard it said before that "we live in a marketplace of ideas."
This phrase, while simultaneously overused and slightly obtuse, contains a lot
of truth. The point is that we live in a world that is *filled with noise*. It is filled
with ideas in the form of messages, information, and stimulation all competing
for our attention. The effect of all this noise is that our brains now exist in a
state of hyper-vigilance, on guard and trying to battle sensory overload.

Effectively cutting through the noise and slipping past the brain's defenses
is no simple task. But it is possible. There is a science and an art behind how
to grab someone's attention. To do so, it's time to learn from the experts—the
people who are already bombarding all of us with the logos, slogans, jingles,
trendy websites, "must-have apps," stories, and ideas that shape many of the
decisions we make every day: marketers and advertisers.

MENTAL NOTE: THE SCIENCE OF ATTENTION

When speaking to marketers, psychologists, and user experience (UX) designers, I've heard several times that we are living in a society where we are facing a problem of diminishing attention. We've gotten to the point where people are ignoring things more and more each day. Right now, think about how many calendar reminders you've dismissed without reading them, text messages that you've glanced at and forgotten to reply to, or even system security warnings that you've received and swatted away before reading them.

As I mentioned, we live in a world where we are constantly being bombarded with sensory noise. The result of this noise is that capturing people's attention is difficult and is getting more difficult with each passing day.

In 1890, psychologist William James described the state of attention in Volume 1 of his work *The Principles of Psychology*.[6] James writes that "attention" is the

> *taking possession by the mind, in clear and vivid form, of one out of what seem several simultaneously possible objects or trains of thought, localization, concentration, of consciousness are of its essence. It implies withdrawal from some things in order to deal effectively with others, and is a condition which has a real opposite in the confused, dazed, scatter brained state which in French is called* distraction, *and* Zerstreutheit *in German.*

Notice that James defines *attention* as the opposite of *distraction*. Attention is intentional focus on one thing at the expense of other things that may be working in competition.

Attention is a limited resource; it can be focused or manipulated. In their book *The Invisible Gorilla*, authors Christopher Chabris and Daniel Simons discuss how our attention and perceptions often conspire against us. If you want a quick glimpse into how distractible we are and how easily attention can be manipulated, check out the video page on their website (http://www.theinvisiblegorilla.com/videos.html). For more examples, plug the following terms into your search engine or video sharing platform of choice:

- *Attentional blindness*
- *Inattentional blindness*
- *Change blindness*
- *Spotlight of attention*

Many aspects of a successful marketing effort or advertising campaign work because the creators of those campaigns leverage (either knowingly or unknowingly) the science of attention to their benefit. As security awareness leaders, we should be asking ourselves at all times what we are doing to manage attention.

It's no accident that marketers and advertisers are so good at getting our attention. They live in a Darwinian world where there is no survival for ineffective ideas and strategies or forgettable messages. And so, the domain of marketing exists in a state of continual evolution as technology and society change. Only the best products and messages are able to claw their way through the muck of societal noise to capture our attention, but those practices that prove effective pay off. Their brands and products are noticed. And the successful marketing and advertising tactics that survive are replicated and become part of the genetic make-up of new campaigns and variant strategies.

TRESPASSING INTO OTHER WORLDS

Throughout the next several chapters, I'm going to introduce and reference numerous domain-specific terms, models, and frameworks. This isn't because I want or expect you to adopt each of these. Rather, my goal in exposing you to concepts from non-security-related disciplines is to help provide a view into how others approach issues related to influencing human thought and behavior.

I love the way author Malcolm Gladwell describes this practice of incorporating cross-domain thinking in his course on writing (`https://www.masterclass.com/classes/malcolm-gladwell-teaches-writing`). Gladwell emphasizes "how important it is to trespass into foreign territories."[7] Doing so helps break our thinking out of the ruts that we all tend to find ourselves in and places us into new fields of ideas and expression.

When we allow the contexts of multiple disciplines to cross paths, we open the doors to new insights, and these insights can lead to breakthroughs.

As we continue through this chapter (and book), I'm sure you'll see a few themes keep popping up. Themes that are critical to the success of any communications endeavor; they are implied within many of the ideas and models that I'll share but should be teased out here for our purposes. I want you to see this list now so that you notice the themes more prominently as the ideas surface again and again. The following list is the way that I've personally interpreted and internalized the key takeaways from the communications disciplines:

1. **Understand** your audience.
2. **Craft/uncover/discover** something of value to sell or talk about.
3. **Capture** attention.
4. **Connect** with emotion/need/humanity.
5. **Embed** the message by making it compelling (finding a Trojan horse—
   e.g., stories, visuals).
6. **Follow through** by setting up the "next step" (in other words, telling
   them what to *do* and leading the behavior). This is also referred to as
   having a *call to action*.
7. **Evaluate** your impact. Establish a method of measuring the effectiveness of your efforts (e.g., metrics).

Figure 3.1 depicts these elements as a cycle that you can use to continually
innovate and improve your communications efforts.

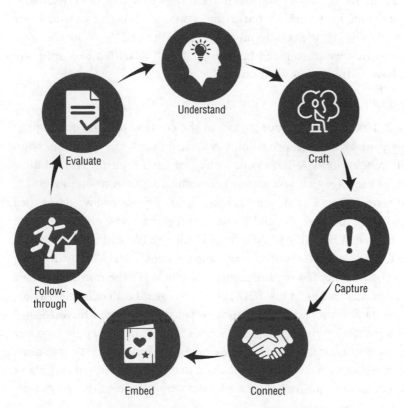

Figure 3.1: Seven key takeaways from the communications disciplines

Defining Marketing

The word *marketing* brings with it a lot of baggage. But, most of us haven't thought about it in depth. For that reason, it can be instructive to start with a basic definition. The American Marketing Association (AMA) defines *marketing* as follows[8]:

> *Marketing is the activity, set of institutions, and processes for creating, communicating, delivering, and exchanging offerings that have value for customers, clients, partners, and society at large.*

Let's start with the end of the definition. Notice that the definition is written in a way that makes it *customer-centric*; it says that the things being marketed "have value for customers, clients, partners, and society at large." In other words, the things being marketed are things that will benefit others. That's one of the big keys here. In marketing, a product doesn't exist solely for the purpose of existing; it exists to meet a real or felt need. So, now we come back to an idea that we introduced in Chapter 2 . . . but with a new spin. We once again have to figure out what our "why" is.

The Return of "Why"

In Chapter 2, I asked what's your "why" in the context of determining the purpose for your awareness program. Now, we can ask the same question but in a different context. What's your "why" for each security-related idea, instruction, or message that you want to communicate to your employees?

In his 2009 book *Start with Why*, author Simon Sinek described what he called the "Golden Circle." This is essentially a set of three concentric circles with the outer circle labeled WHAT, the middle circle labeled HOW, and the inner circle labeled WHY. Sinek's premise is that every company knows WHAT they do (what their product is), but very few organizations can state WHY their product exists. Sinek discusses these ideas in his TED Talk, *How Great Leaders Inspire Action*, and makes the statement, "People don't buy what you do. They buy why you do it."[9]

If we take the underlying thought of Sinek's statement and apply it to our security awareness training programs, we get something like, "People don't necessarily care about what we are asking them to do, but they might care about why we want them to do it." And, if we are honest with ourselves, that rings true.

NOTE   "People don't necessarily care about what we are asking them to do, but they might care about why we want them to do it."

Communicating from the WHY and out to the WHAT is extremely powerful; it evokes more instinctual and emotion-based thinking. This is important because we humans generally make decisions at a subconscious level, based on instinct and emotion and then we rationalize those decisions based on whatever logical reasons we can attach to the decisions *that we already made.*[10,11,12] What's the implication? Simple—if we expect our people to be swayed to action by our information and logic, we will achieve extremely limited results. But, when we connect with our people at an emotional level (speaking to the WHY), our chance of leading them to care increases dramatically. We help them achieve an "ah-ha!" moment.

In Figure 3.2, I've adapted Sinek's Golden Circle concept for security awareness.

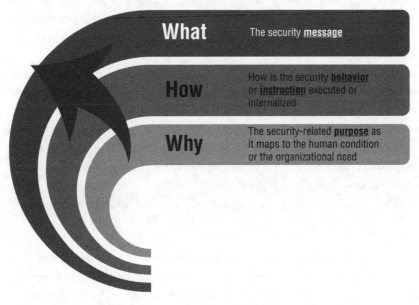

What — The security **message**

How — How is the security **behavior** or **instruction** executed or internalized

Why — The security-related **purpose** as it maps to the human condition or the organizational need

Figure 3.2: Security awareness leaders should start with "why."

In the context of security awareness:

- Your WHY is the purpose of the message or instruction as it relates to the human condition or the needs of your organization. This is the *customer-centric* aspect of our awareness messaging.

- Your HOW is a simple method that a person can follow in order to act on your message or instruction. It must have a clear connection to the WHY.
- Your WHAT maps to the actual security-related message, instruction, or program element.

Here's an example using concepts related to incident reporting as the intended behavior or message:

- **WHY:** We want our employees to work in a safe environment and to feel the sense of accomplishment and success that comes with being productive. Security incidents work against that; they frustrate employees by making systems unstable or unusable, and they cause big problems for the organization and potentially even our customers. Because we care about these things, we want our employees to know that they can and should always notify us of anything that is concerning.
- **HOW:** Create a variety of fast and simple methods to notify us of any suspected security-related issue. Because we know that some people will have anxiety in reporting issues, we need to find methods of eliminating that anxiety. We can have methods that support anonymous reporting and/or develop processes, policies, and messaging to ensure employees that reporting is encouraged and appreciated even when the report turns out to be a false alarm.
- **WHAT:** "See Something. Say Something. It's easy and safe. Here's how: *followed by a simple instruction.*"

You'll notice that I used a modified version of the old "See Something. Say Something." campaign message as an example. There are a few reasons for doing so. The first reason is simply because "See Something. Say Something." is well known. The phrase is used so often as to be ubiquitous. We all know that phrase, and to that extent, it's successful.

But even though people know the phrase, there are some key components that work against it, namely, anxiety on the part of the reporter and the lack of a known quick and simple method for reporting. So, for this campaign, the HOW must strive to achieve three elements: *quick*, *easy*, and *stress-free*. That's why I appended those two additional phrases, "It's easy and safe. Here's how." You might ask why I didn't word it as "It's easy and *anonymous*. Here's how." That really comes down to a judgment call on my part. The word *safe* seems to carry more immediate emotional impact than the word *anonymous*. So, I believe the word *safe* speaks more to the primal and instinctual need that someone may feel when they are dealing with what could be a stressful situation. And that's the part of the mind that I would want to target with this messaging.

With the example of "See Something. Say Something." many people do implicitly understand the WHY; they see it as helpful to the organization, other employees, or the community. So here, with the traditional "See Something. Say Something." campaign, the WHY isn't too bad. A sense of civic duty and altruism is inherent. But you'll see that I shifted it a bit as well to try to move it closer to the employee. That doesn't necessarily filter all the way down to the message itself, but it does two important things here.

- It helps inform the process for building the HOW.
- It will map to the overall cultural tone in any supportive messaging, such as executive videos, team meetings, and so on.

But, let's say you didn't like the fact that we omitted an explicit link to the WHY. We could tease it out a bit more with the addition of one word. We could modify the statement to "See Something. Say Something. It's easy, safe, & important. Here's how." By adding the idea of importance, we naturally draw the reader into an internal dialogue where they tie the word *important* to whatever meaning might be implied based on their personal understanding, context, and history.

MENTAL NOTE: THEORY OF MIND

The Importance of Understanding That Other People May View the World Differently

In cognitive science, there is an important concept known as *theory of mind* (ToM).[13] Central to the concept is the notion that a person should be able to recognize that different people may view and interpret information and situations differently depending on their background and immediate context. Relational and communicative problems can arise when someone has a deficit in ToM and therefore doesn't understand or appreciate that other people have different thoughts, beliefs, opinions, experiences, or values than themselves.

Here is a good description of ToM:

Theory of mind (ToM) is the ability to recognize and attribute mental states—thoughts, perceptions, desires, intentions, feelings to oneself and to others and to understand how these mental states might affect behavior. It is also an understanding that others have beliefs, thought processes and emotions completely separate from our own. Deficits in ToM may occur in people with Asperger's syndrome, autism, schizophrenia, sociopathy and other mental disorders.

Theory of mind is called a "theory" in that the mind is not directly observable. We never know for sure what is going on in the minds of other people—we can only make assumptions based on experiences with our own beliefs, emotions and perceptions.

Theory of Mind. Traci Pedersen. PsychCentral.com. https://psychcentral.com/encyclopedia/theory-of-mind/

I see a few parallels here. Please take this the right way: many security awareness programs don't account for the fact that their audience may have different thoughts, beliefs, values, or opinions than the person who creates the security message. In effect, the security team views their world in a way that lacks ToM and doesn't account for the different perspectives of their audience.

This is another example of why we need to uncover the "why." We need to—as much as possible—learn to see through our participant's eyes so that we can create compelling messages that will connect with them. I'll discuss the marketing practices of persona creation and audience or market segmentation a bit later in this chapter. When you read that section, I'm sure that you'll immediately notice how these marketing principles relate to many of the concepts inherent in ToM.

Breaking It Down

We began this section by looking at the tail end of the definition of the term *marketing* and exploring how it implies customer-centricity. Now that we have the appropriate mind-set, we are ready to consider the beginning section of the definition, which covers the mechanics of marketing. Here it is again with that section bolded:

Marketing is the activity, set of institutions, and processes for creating, communicating, delivering, and exchanging offerings *that have value for customers, clients, partners, and society at large.*

There is a lot packed into the beginning of that definition! Let's unravel it a bit by looking at a concept referred to as the "marketing mix." This is the collection of techniques and considerations that an organization should use to promote its products and services. One popular model used to determine marketing mix is known as the "7Ps,"[14] and it maps very well to the elements listed in the beginning of the definition of *marketing*. I'll be adapting this model to fit a security awareness context as we move forward, but, before I do so, let's take a look at the original model to get a feel. The 7Ps are comprised of the following:

1. **Product/service:** The thing being sold or charged for.
2. **Price:** The fee and associated pricing model.
3. **Place:** Where the customer can find the product. This is the store, website, or other distribution channel.
4. **Promotion:** How and where is the product or service being "talked" about? Advertising, word-of-mouth, press releases, endorsements, etc.?
5. **Physical evidence:** Proof of quality, design elements, packaging, online presence, company stability/relevance, etc.
6. **People:** Your internal people (such as your employees, management, culture, and customer service) and your external people (such as your customers, social influencers, and media).
7. **Process:** Your operational processes. The things you do to create, market, and support the product. Your processes help ensure consistency and predictability.
   It's important to note that an eighth P is often added to the mix: partners. This will become important to us as well. So, rounding out the model is
8. **Partners:** Other people or organizations that can become new channels for promoting and selling the product or services.

You are probably already starting to see several connections between these 8Ps and security awareness program strategy. But, let's make it explicit. Table 3.1 is a quick reference to help connect the dots.

Table 3.1: Connecting the 8Ps of Marketing to Security Awareness

8Ps That Comprise the Marketing Mix	Marketing Context	Awareness Context
Product/service	The thing being sold or charged for.	The security-related message or behavior that you are hoping to train.
Price	The fee and associated pricing model.	The time, effort, or sacrifice that the end user must put in as part of the training.
Place	Where the customer can find the product. This is the store, website, or other distribution channel.	Where does the training take place? How do end users receive the training? Examples include computer-based training (CBT) modules, videos, posters, in-person events, simulated phishing campaigns, and so on. How do your people encounter training within the context of their lives?
Promotion	How and where is the product or service being "talked" about? Advertising, word-of-mouth, press releases, endorsements, etc.?	Similar to Place. But, the distinction here is that there are certain activities, forums, or people used to support or advance the object of your training. Examples here would be events such as National Cybersecurity Awareness Month or an executive video talking about the importance of security to the organization.
Physical evidence	Proof of quality, design elements, packaging, online presence, company stability/relevance, etc.	These are the subtle and not so subtle cues that you provide (both intentionally and unintentionally) about the value and traits of your security message or the behavior that you are promoting. How do they encounter the artifacts of your messaging naturally throughout the day? And what is the experience they receive when they intentionally seek out security-related information or advice in your organization?

8Ps That Comprise the Marketing Mix	Marketing Context	Awareness Context
People	Your internal people (such as your employees, management, culture, and customer messaging) and your external people (such as your customers, social influencers, and media).	These are the people involved in creating your program, advocating your program, and who are on the receiving end of the training. It's important to think in terms of roles. For instance, how does your executive team support (or work against) your security messaging? What is the overall tone and direction of your organization's security culture? What is the overall tone that your security team takes when engaging with the broader organization? And, how are others outside of your security team supporting or working against your security-related messaging?
Process	Your operational processes. The things you do to create, market, and support the product. Your processes help ensure consistency and predictability.	This is your formal security awareness training plan and the methodologies (both intentional and unintentional) that you use to promote security-related messaging and behaviors. Understanding your process and being intentional about your plan, methodologies, and metrics is vitally important. Process is what helps you drive continual improvement so that you learn from your successes and challenges. Process is the key that unlocks consistency and sustainability.
Partners	Other people or organizations that can become new channels for promoting and selling the product or services.	The other methods that you've put in place that will work to propagate your message and reinforce behavior. Security liaison/champion/ambassador/advocate programs are a prime example. Used well, these groups can be a force multiplier for your program.

Even if you go no further in this book and simply decide to organize your program using the 8Ps, you will be on your way to creating goals and reaching audiences that are more clearly known, defined, and measurable. But, those organizing principles are just the tip of the iceberg. There's a lot more to uncover.

Crossing the Chasm

Your organization already has a certain amount of people who "just get it." They are the people who are already interested in security and want to do the right thing. (We'll talk about how to really make the most of these people in the chapters on behavior management and culture management.) But, how do you hit the tipping point where you are having a true impact on a wider population? This is known in the marketing world as *crossing the chasm*: moving from *innovators* and *early adopters* and to mainstream adoption.

Author Geoffrey A. Moore described the idea of crossing the chasm in his 1991 book *Crossing the Chasm: Marketing and Selling High-Tech Products to Mainstream Customers*. In his book, Moore plots five phases of adoption for products, services, and ideas across a bell curve. Each phase represents the group of people who will adopt the product, service, or idea. The five groups are *innovators*, *early adopters*, *early majority*, *late majority*, and *laggards*. Speaking to technology startups, Moore outlined a problem: a huge chasm exists between the *early adopters* phase and the *early majority* phase, one that very few startups ever successfully cross.

If you read Moore's work or listen to him in interviews, you'll notice that one of the key factors in being able to cross the chasm is to understand the different values of the audience. Specifically, the people who will adopt a product in the early phases have a different set of values and ideas than those who will adopt something in the early and late majority phases. So, it will come as no surprise that one of Moore's main points is that we need to get in touch with our customer's real and perceived needs.

Sound familiar? Again, it all comes back to what is important to the person being communicated to. There will be a group of employees in our organizations who will readily adopt and advocate for our security messages, values, and behaviors. These are the equivalent of Moore's *innovators* and *early adopters*. And there are others (*early majority*, *late majority*, and *laggards*) for whom we will need to do more work mapping to their needs[15] and what is most relevant to them so that we can design meaningful messages, guidance, training, and interventions.

Security leaders who want to cross the chasm with their awareness programs will need to become experts at understanding the diverse groups within their organization.

Embedding Your Messages

You may have already read *once or twice* in this book that information alone is of little value (he says, wryly . . . har, har). Information doesn't lead to caring or action. But this is a chapter on communication; communication is information based, and we still *do* have information that we need to share. So, what gives?

At the beginning of this section, I listed seven elements of a communication campaign that stands a chance at impacting our audience. Numbers three, four, and five were 3) *capture* attention, 4) *connect* with humanity, and 5) *embed* by making it compelling. These all work together and are interconnected. When used intentionally and skillfully, the following elements will grant those who wield them a superpower: the ability to more consistently create messages that people remember and care about.

In our lives as security professionals, we worry about software acting as a Trojan Horse, sneaking malware past our system defenses and on to vulnerable devices. What if I told you that I'm a big fan of Trojan Horses? It's true; but I'm a fan of a different kind of Trojan Horse. I'm a fan of finding Trojan Horses for the mind. Here's what I mean: When designed well, our messaging can sneak past mental defenses and noise. In other words, the way we design and deliver our messages can become a Trojan Horse.

Figure 3.3 illustrates four communication elements that I refer to as Trojan Horses for the mind.

A Trojan Horse Feels Like: The Power of Emotion

As I mentioned at the beginning of this chapter, people tend to make decisions based on emotion and then build a case for their decision based on logic. This is hugely important for us to grasp as we develop our security awareness messaging. I'll put it this way: People will experience emotion when interacting with our messages even if we don't intentionally put it there. So, we are at a disadvantage when we aren't actively engaged in bridging our audience to an emotion that will be helpful to our cause. When developing our messaging, we have to develop for both the information and the emotion that we want to convey with the message.

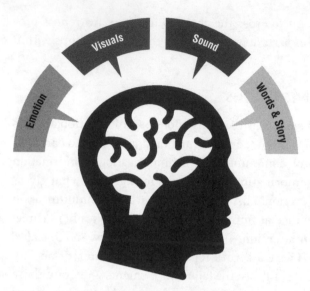

Figure 3.3: Trojan Horses for the mind

Think about the times in your life that are most memorable. Those are likely times when you experienced a heightened emotion. They are above or below your normal emotional baseline. This is one of the reasons that you can remember times of sadness, melancholy, or anger so much more vividly than general happiness. It's because we generally do a good job of living on the neutral to slightly happy side of the emotional bell curve. But times of extreme happiness, or even times of slight sadness or anger, will stand out within our memories because they are sufficiently different. And different is memorable.

Pixar explored the complexity of emotions in its movie *Inside Out*. The majority of *Inside Out* takes place in the mind of a young girl named Riley who is having difficulty adjusting to her family's recent relocation to a new city. Riley's mind is an interesting place populated by the personifications of five distinct emotions: Joy, Anger, Sadness, Fear, and Disgust. Up to this point in her life, Riley's predominant emotion, and the one who always wants to call the shots in her mind, is Joy. And Joy feels that her primary job and duty to Riley is to suppress negative emotions (most specifically, Sadness) and fill Riley's mind with joyful memories.

Over the course of *Inside Out*,[16] Joy is taken through a journey where she comes to realize that no one can (or should) be happy all the time. It takes contrasting emotions for happiness to be appreciated. The movie's resolution and emotional climax is when Joy decides that the best thing to do to help Riley is to allow Sadness to touch Riley's core memories, infusing them with a touch of sadness. For those of you who watched the movie, you can already remember the beautiful impact that this had. Yes, Riley's once purely Joy-filled core memories became infused with Sadness; but it was that Sadness that added even more beauty, and empathy, to Riley's memories.[17] Sadness gave Joy context, and the context and variety is what makes a purely joyful memory more meaningful.

Now, I'm not saying that I want you to make your security messages sad, or fearful, or angry, or anything like that (though data show that articles that agitate or inspire are more likely to go viral[18]). But what I *am* saying is that you owe it to yourself and your people to connect your security messages with emotions that will add context to, and enrich the meaning of, the information you are trying to get across. Once someone can intellectually and emotionally place themselves within the context of a situation, they are more likely to appreciate the meaning. And emotion allows the meaning to become rooted within the person's memory.

How can you make your messages more emotional? This, again, comes back to the WHY. Think about both the positive and negative outcomes of the security value or behavior that you are promoting. And do this across several levels. Think through (or, better yet, list) any positive and negative outcomes that someone may have if they internalize and act upon the information contained in your message. Once you've listed the positive and negative outcomes associated with the security value or behavior, link each of these outcomes to positive and negative emotions. What emotions can be discovered? What is the juxtaposition of emotions associated with the outcomes for someone who would follow your security message verses someone who doesn't? What stories emerge?

MENTAL NOTE: THE SCIENCE OF CURIOSITY

One of the most useful states we can induce within our audience is *curiosity*. Curiosity isn't an emotion; it's a *feeling,* like hunger or thirst. Specifically, it is hunger or thirst of the mind. Curiosity emerges when our interest is piqued by a stimulus (like a loud noise from the other room), and we lack sufficient data to fill in the knowledge gap caused by the stimulus (thus making you ask yourself what caused the noise).

You've probably heard the term *clickbait* before. *Clickbait* refers to many of the headlines that you see in your social media and newsfeeds. The headline is often written in such a way as to hint at some bit of information that will be provided in the underlying article, but the headline intentionally leaves out a critical piece of the puzzle. After reading the clickbait head-line, your mind nags you to fill in that piece of the puzzle; your mind feels like it needs the information. So, the only way to scratch the mental itch is to click the headline and engage with the content. An example would be:

> 5 Things You Need to Know About Security Behavior. #4 Will Change Your Program Forever!

Now your mind is drawn in. It's curious as to what the five things are, and it wants to know what program-altering information might be contained in #4. Heads up: I just created that headline as I was writing this section. So, you are left to your own devices to figure out how to scratch that mental itch. *You're welcome!*

This mental itch is called a *curiosity gap*. The reason that curiosity can be useful is because, when used well, curiosity motivates a person to seek out and engage information to fill the gap in their knowledge. In other words, they are feeding themselves rather than you force feeding them. That volitional aspect of the engagement makes a big difference in how they internalize the content.

The curiosity gap is also why Facebook, Twitter, Pinterest, LinkedIn, YouTube, and other addictive social sites will allow you to scroll down infinitely. These sites drive revenue through engagement, and the best way to keep you engaged is to keep you curious. So, you are always wondering if you'll find something interesting by scrolling down *just a bit more*. That's why you go to social sharing sites thinking that you are only going to check on one thing but find yourself still scrolling an hour later. *Argh!*

Here's another great example of the curiosity gap in action. This one comes from the 1997 autobiographical movie about Howard Stern, *Private Parts*. In this scene,[19] two employees of the radio station where Stern works are confronted with the effects of the curiosity gap. For those of you who haven't seen the movie, the character Pig Vomit is a network executive with whom Stern has a less than stellar relationship. Check out the conversation between these two employees, shown here, and see how they are confronted with, and confounded by, the power of the curiosity gap:

> **Researcher**: *The average radio listener listens for eighteen minutes. The average Howard Stern fan listens for—are you ready for this?—an hour and twenty minutes.*

Pig Vomit: *How can that be?*

Researcher: *Answer most commonly given? "I want to see what he'll say next."*

Pig Vomit: *Okay, fine. But what about the people who hate Stern?*

Researcher: *Good point. The average Stern hater listens for two and a half hours a day.*

Pig Vomit: *But . . . if they hate him, why do they listen?*

Researcher: *Most common answer? "I want to see what he'll say next."*

Curiosity is a powerful tool. Find interesting ways to use it in your messaging and events. Curious to learn more? Here are some great introductory articles:

- Is Curiosity a Positive or Negative Feeling? NPR. September 2017. https://www.npr.org/sections/13.7/2017/09/25/553443078/is-curiosity-a-positive-or-negative-feeling
- The Itch of Curiosity. Jonah Lehrer. August 2010. Wired. https://www.wired.com/2010/08/the-itch-of-curiosity/
- The Psychology and Neuroscience of Curiosity. Neuron. Volume 88, Issue 3, 4 November 2015, pages 449–460. https://www.sciencedirect.com/science/article/pii/S0896627315007679

A Trojan Horse Looks Like: Branding, Design, and Visual Elements

Think for a moment about all the great companies, products, media sites, and networks that you interact with daily. Now close your eyes and mentally scroll through five of them. Go ahead, I'll wait.

When you scrolled through each of those items in your mind, did you see their names as plainly printed words? Probably not. If you are like most people, you saw the logos of the companies when thinking about an organization or service; or if you were thinking about a specific product, like McDonald's chicken nuggets, your mind summoned forth an image of the product.

Here's another quick experiment using the same example. Which of the examples in Table 3.2 do you *feel* more connected to?

Table 3.2: Power of Visual Branding

Brand Name as Text		Brand Representation as Logo
Facebook	or	**facebook.**
YouTube	or	**You Tube**
CocaCola	or	*Coca-Cola*
Amazon	or	**amazon**.com®
Taco Bell	or	**TACO BELL**

Here's another interesting thing. Each of these brands are still just as recognizable using the simplified version of their logo. See Table 3.3.

Think about it. Images are basically a compression algorithm that the mind easily and readily uses to unzip bundles of data whenever presented with the image. Now consider what a brand and logo really is . . . it is a simple word, phrase, or symbol that encapsulates the values, products, services, and history of an organization or idea. Icons can serve this purpose as well; they can pack a complex meaning into a simple picture. And all of these complex ideas register in your mind as soon as you are presented with a simple logo or icon.

Table 3.3: Even Simplified Versions of Brand Logos Are Effective

Facebook Icon	YouTube Icon	CocaCola Icon	Amazon Icon	Taco Bell Icon

NOTE   Images are basically a compression algorithm that the mind easily and readily uses to unzip bundles of data whenever presented with the image.

MENTAL NOTE: REPETITION IS MAGIC

Remember that Britney Spears song that you hated the first few times you heard it? Then before you know it, the song is on auto-loop in your mind and you find yourself physically grooving to the music the next time you hear it. There's a reason for that . . . and that reason emerges in all forms of communication, from the way words are used to music to imagery.

Here's the reason: *familiarity breeds likability.* Cognitive scientists refer to this as the *familiarity effect* or the *mere-exposure effect.*[20,21]

People feel more relaxed and less on guard when they know what to expect. So, familiarity and consistency are key if you want someone to let their guard down. This is why we say things like, "I didn't like that (*fill in the blank*) at first, but now it's growing on me."

This is also why brands are consistent with their color choices, font styles, phrases, and so on. These choices become a part of their *brand identity.* They are essentially character traits and become a visible representation of the brand's products, services, values, history, and customer base.

One of the markers of a mature security awareness program is how seriously the program leaders take the value of consistency in the visual and textual components of their communication. These security leaders approach their awareness programs with an entrepreneurial mind-set and treat the branding aspects of the program with the same zeal.

As you can *see*, images carry with them a lot of power. The old adage "A picture is worth a thousand words" rings true because, in many ways, it *is* true. Here's a slightly more elaborate example. Consider the following few sentences:

> *You see a young boy. He's sitting in a chair near a window. Also,*
> *nearby is a reading lamp. The boy is reading a story about a sea*
> *monster attacking a pirate ship.*

There was a lot of intentional focus and mental processing that your mind had to do to parse and interpret the data in those few lines of text. But, if I put that scene into a simple sketch, such as that in Figure 3.4, your mind absorbs all of that detail in an instant. In fact, it absorbs, processes, and interprets *far more* data than what I wrote in the previous lines. Your mind instantly processes the context of the room that the boy is in, that there is also a desk nearby, details about the desk, the drinking mug that they boy has on a table in front of him, the size of the book he is reading, the length of his hair, and so on.

Figure 3.4: Images are the language of the mind.

It's super important for us to understand and appreciate the power of imagery. Resist the urge to skip ahead, thinking, "I already know this stuff." Yes, you *do* already know this, but it's an entirely different thing to slow down and appreciate the implications. To be human is to inherently understand the power of pictures. We think in pictures. We quickly and more readily absorb information that is image-based. The moment an image hits our retinas, our brain not only decodes the data in that image but also assigns any preconditioned emotional response. So, imagery is important if you want to evoke or enhance the emotional impact of your security-related messaging. Simple text-based security awareness messaging will always be less effective than messaging that includes well-thought-out and well-designed visual components.

NOTE Simple text-based security awareness messaging will always be less effective than messaging that includes well-thought-out and well-designed visual components.

A discussion about images and design wouldn't be complete without talking about the use of color. Colors serve a much greater purpose than just being pretty. Colors imply meaning, can evoke emotion, and help establish context. While there are some general rules of thumb that you can use when working with color, it's important to recognize that the intended meaning behind your color choices may not be interpreted the same by everyone in your audience; there are no hard-and-fast rules.

One of the best ways to think about how to use color is to see what already exists that is like what you want to communicate. Let's say you wanted to build messaging related to how employees can secure their home networks and help their kids make better security decisions. You may have already defined the practices and now you are trying to figure out how to package and promote the information.

If you aren't an experienced designer (or even if you are), this is where Google can be your friend. You don't have to understand color theory, have a degree in marketing, or have studied the psychology of color to create something that can be great. Just enter brand names or search terms related to family, kids, childhood, and so on, and look at the image results. In this example, you'd quickly notice that many of the colors commonly associated with family, kids, and childhood are yellow, orange, green, light blue, and sometimes purple. And after seeing these examples, you can piece together plausible reasons why these colors have become the cultural reference point for the scenarios that you want to relate to. Green is typically associated with life and growth. The orange and yellows can be reminiscent of the sepia tones that we associate with memory and nostalgia, and so on. That's a valuable starting place. In this Googling exercise, you may even come across examples of font styles and images that you may want to use in your messaging. This is way better than starting with a blank page and agonizing about how to begin.

WARNING: YOUR VISUALS CAN UNINTENTIONALLY PULL AGAINST YOUR MESSAGE

When developing your visuals, it's important to ensure that you aren't sending mixed messages. Visual design is a powerful and refined art that carries with it several patterns and principles second nature to professional designers. Examples of these are color associations that are now usual and customary for designers and viewers alike or concepts around visual framing and positioning, such as the rule of thirds.[22]

Even concepts rooted in the dynamics of interpersonal communication arise as critical when designing imagery to work with, rather than against, your intended message. Let's say you are trying to create a poster or slide coupled with a security message that really connects with humanity, so you decide to use a person's face as a key image. You've found the perfect face and expression, and now you are placing the text of your message to the side of that person. There will be way more impact if the person's gaze is directed *toward* your text than if their gaze points in another direction.[23] This is because of the concept of joint (or shared) attention.[24] Our focus is naturally drawn to where someone else is gazing or pointing. So, if the person in your poster is looking away from your text, the signal would be that your text isn't important or interesting.

A book like this can't possibly cover all critical areas or pitfalls of design. So, be sure to check out the additional resources section, below.

ADDITIONAL RESOURCES FOR DESIGN

If you want to take a deeper dive into color, and design principles in general, check out the following resources:

Books

- *Slide-o-logy* by Nancy Duarte
- *Superpowers of Visual Storytelling* by Laura Stanton and David LaGesse
- *Design Elements, Color Fundamentals: A Graphic Style Manual for Understanding How Color Affects Design* by Aaris Sherin

■ *Presentation Zen* by Gary Reynolds
■ *The Senses: Design Beyond Vision* by Ellen Lupton (Editor)

Web Links

■ *Advertising Psychology: 27 Psychological Tactics to Improve Any Advertisement* by Nick Kolenda (https://www.nickkolenda.com/advertising-psychology/)
■ *Impact of Color on Marketing* by Satyendra Singh (https://doi.org/10.1108/00251740610673332)
■ *Color Psychology: How Color Meanings Affect Your Brand* by Nicole Martins Ferreira (https://www.oberlo.com/blog/color-psychology-color-meanings)
■ *Psychology of Color in Logo Design* by the Logo Company (https://thelogocompany.net/blog/infographics/psychology-color-logo-design/)

A Trojan Horse Sounds Like: The Power of Sound and Music

By now I'm sure that you are starting to arrive at the conclusion that the messages we create are like individual data elements. Those data can be transmitted in different ways (printed words, images, and video to name a few). We all think of those methods when it comes to getting information to people. But, one of the most powerful communication methods that advertisers, storytellers, and teachers have used for millennia to make messages stick is *sound*.

Have you ever been watching a children's television program and heard the sound of a little chime as a key word was being used or a key fact was mentioned? That's another great example of how sound can be used to convey meaning and help to embed information. In that example, the sound is acting as a signal to our brains that the information being presented at that time is different (more important) than the rest. Because our mind is cued to the difference, it then treats the information differently, thereby aiding memory.

Now, think about the music that was popular during your high school and college years. Chances are that you can remember the lyrics, melody lines, guitar solos, and musical hooks for dozens (if not hundreds) of songs that you never consciously tried to memorize.[25] What happened? The music acted as a carrier wave for the information (lyrics). And so, even when you don't want to remember the lyrics from that Spice Girls song, your brain happily trots them to the front of your mind whenever prompted whether you *really, really want* it or not.

In our messages, presentations, custom videos, and other communications formats, we do ourselves a favor by remembering the power of sound and music. I'm not suggesting that you create a security-centric version of "The Alphabet Song" or "Uptown Funk," but let me know if you do!

> **NOTE** I'm not suggesting that you create a security-centric version of "The Alphabet Song" or "Uptown Funk," but let me know if you do!

A Trojan Horse Says: The Power of Words and Story

Given everything I've said about how sound and visuals can be more effective than words, it may be surprising that I have another section here titled "The Power of Words and Story." Well, there is no getting around it. When trying to communicate, most of the time we will need to use words, especially when communicating complex or nuanced concepts.

When combined with sound and images, words can be added with great impact and effectiveness. Think about the power of a well-produced advertisement or public service announcement that mixes imagery with just the right music and sound design and a compelling voiceover. Those ingredients all come together to create a sum much greater than their individual parts.

But even without the support of great sound and visuals, words can be used in compelling ways; master orators and storytellers have been doing so since the beginning of humanity. What's the secret? Well, again it comes back to many of the elements that we've already discussed in this chapter: *emotion*, *imagery*, and *sound*. Words that move us the most and that have the greatest impact are usually words that have been *intentionally crafted* to do so. Great speakers and storytellers evoke emotion and create vivid mental imagery and landscapes solely through the sound and rhythm of words.

A PERSONAL NOTE ON CHOOSING WORDS

Even in the writing of this book, I've spent countless hours working and reworking my choice of words. By training, I'm an extremely formal writer. I naturally produce prose that is complex and dense. In contrast, my goal with this book is to make the writing straightforward and easy to read. Doing so requires me to have greater empathy for my reader (you) and for me to set aside my desire to convince you that I'm smart or qualified by the words and phrases that I use. It requires me to practice what I'm preaching . . . and that's a good thing.

If your job is to help craft the specific messages and text for your awareness program, you owe it to yourself to get your hands on a copy of (and read) *Language Intelligence: Lessons on Persuasion from Jesus, Shakespeare, Lincoln, and Lady Gaga* by Joseph J. Romm. At just 230 pages, Romm presents a masterclass on the power of words "to convince people of something by moving them both intellectually and emotionally, at both a conscious and unconscious level." Doesn't that sound like something we need to be able to do as awareness leaders? Romm's book covers the punch that comes with using short words, straightforward prose, and repetition. He also covers the power of engaging the mind through irony, foreshadowing, and metaphor.

You should never take words for granted. Most of your messages will be text based (even if delivered orally via video, learning module, or in-person presentation). Educating yourself on how to craft powerful prose will make your messaging more memorable and ring with greater clarity.

There's another power that words grant us, and this is a superpower: the ability to *tell stories*. I'm sure that you already know the benefits of telling a good story even if you don't realize that you do.

For instance, would you be more interested during a 60-minute lecture on the complexities of cellular biology and immunoresponse delivered by a PhD who specializes in cancer research? Or, would you have greater interest in listening to a story about an epic battle between forces where lives hang within the balance and enemy forces continue their onslaught, multiplying and ravaging the land that they are invading despite the harrowing efforts of the defending forces? But now, we see a glimmer of hope . . . .

I'm sure that you've already realized that these are two ways of presenting the same facts. But the second example is naturally more engaging. It transcends mere facts and language, connecting directly to the mind by teasing us with tension, emotion, mental imagery, and anticipation. That's what a good story does. That's why your security messages will always be more effective when wrapped in story.

Stories can transform the most boring of fact sets into edge-of-your-seat emotional experiences that have measurable impacts in both your mind[26] and body.[27] Consider this:

> *Paul Zak, director of the Center for Neuroeconomics Studies at Claremont Graduate School, found that reading simple, humanistic stories changes what is in our blood streams. Taking blood samples of subjects before and after reading a story about a father and*

his terminally ill son, Zak, found their blood levels contained an increase of cortisol and also oxytocin after reading the story. Called the human bonding or empathy chemical, oxytocin is also released by breastfeeding mothers.

Once they had read the story, subjects were then asked to donate money to a cause for ill children. Eighty percent of the subjects complied. Imagine anything that would cause 80 percent of subjects to do as they were asked.

Michelle Weldon, "Your Brain on Story: Why Narratives Win Our Hearts and Minds"

We'll discuss storytelling more throughout this book. But, if you'd like to do more research now, here are a few good resources:

Books

- *Long Story Short: The Only Storytelling Guide You'll Ever Need* by Margot Leitman
- *Resonate: Present Visual Stories that Transform Audiences* by Nancy Duarte
- *StoryTraining: Selecting and Shaping Stories That Connect* by Hadiya Nuriddin
- *Unleash the Power of Storytelling: Win Hearts, Change Minds, Get Results* by Rob Biesenbach
- *Wired for Story: The Writer's Guide to Using Brain Science to Hook Readers from the Very First Sentence* by Lisa Cron

Web Resources

- *The Analogies Project: Finding the Hidden InfoSec Story* (https://the-analogiesproject.org/)
- *The 22 Rules of Perfect Storytelling, According to Pixar* by Jared Keller (https://mic.com/articles/101740/the-22-rules-to-perfect-storytelling-according-to-pixar)
- *The Science of Storytelling: What Listening to a Story Does to Our Brains* by Leo Widrich (https://blog.bufferapp.com/science-of-storytelling-why-telling-a-story-is-the-most-powerful-way-to-activate-our-brains)
- *Why Your Brain Loves Good Storytelling* by Paul J. Zak (https://hbr.org/2014/10/why-your-brain-loves-good-storytelling)

TROJAN HORSES: REAL-WORLD EXAMPLES

Before we end our conversation on Trojan horses, let's look at a few real-world examples. I'll give you one from the security industry and a couple others that come from mainstream marketing.

CVE-2014-0160: A Security Branding Story

Let's try an experiment. Read the following identifier: *CVE-2014-0160*. Now close your eyes and try to recite it back to yourself. You could probably do it, but that's mostly because you read it immediately before I asked you to recall it. But, do you think you'd correctly recall the identifier CVE-2014-0160 an hour from now? Or tomorrow? Now tell me if you think you can remember this name: *Heartbleed*.

This is an example of how savvy branding and design thinking helped make a security-related story go viral in April 2014. Those of us who were in the security industry back then probably remember hearing about the Heartbleed Bug. The vulnerability was a big deal. It impacted the integrity of OpenSSL, an open source implementation of SSL and TLS. These are the protocols that allow systems to pass information back and forth to each other in a cryptographically protected session. OpenSSL is used widely by even the largest Internet-based companies around the world. And the danger posed by the bug was grave.[28]

> *The Heartbleed Bug is a serious vulnerability in the popular OpenSSL cryptographic software library. This weakness allows stealing the information protected, under normal conditions, by the SSL/TLS encryption used to secure the Internet. SSL/TLS provides communication security and privacy over the Internet for applications such as web, email, instant messaging (IM) and some virtual private networks (VPNs).*
>
> *The Heartbleed bug allows anyone on the Internet to read the memory of the systems protected by the vulnerable versions of the OpenSSL software. This compromises the secret keys used to identify the service providers and to encrypt the traffic, the names and passwords of the users and the actual content. This allows attackers to eavesdrop on communications, steal data directly from the services and users and to impersonate services and users.*
>
> *heartbleed.com*

Properly known as CVE-2014-0160, the vulnerability known as Heartbleed didn't enter the world with a sexy name. Security vulnerabilities are cataloged using a system that assigns each vulnerability a unique Common Vulnerabilities and Exposures (CVE) number like the one given (in other words, something unremarkable, unmemorable, and definitely *not* sexy).

But one of the engineers credited with discovering the bug felt that a simple CVE number assignment would fail to bring enough attention to the criticality of the issue. It needed something different to cut through the noise. It needed a *brand*, complete with catchy name and killer minimalist logo of a bleeding heart. By the way, the engineer worked at a company called Codenomicon; with a company name like that, you know that they are fond of attention-grabbing names.

The following excerpt is taken from an interview that *Fast Company* conducted with Leena Snidate, the Codenomicon graphic designer who created Heartbleed's striking logo (see Figure 3.5).

> . . .*a Codenomicon engineer came up with the name Heartbleed– inspired by a tangentially related piece of software called Heartbeat– and quickly thereafter, Codenomicon registered Heartbleed.com, designed sleek FAQs explaining the bug, and accompanied it with a logo by Codenomicon designer Leena Snidate.*
>
> *"This huge vulnerability needed a striking mark," Snidate explains over email. "The colour choice was immediate for me–deep blood red."*
>
> *Deep blood red. Because it's talking about a heart that's bleeding. Heartbleed is not a clever logo, no, but it's not going for clever. Its power is in sheer, bold literalness–the visual equivalent of talking slowly to a slack-jawed luddite audience that has no clue what the hell CVE-2014-0160 means. And in that regard, it's perfect for its purpose of welcoming the masses to Heartbleed.com and assuring us, yes, you've come to the right corner of the Internet, you idiot. In return, Codenomicon is forever associated with being the solution to what will likely go down as one of the greatest security oversights in Internet history. Plus they get a halo effect to, not just their peers in the security community, but all of the laypeople who barely under-stand what's even going on in the first place.*
>
> *Why the Security Bug Heartbleed Has a Catchy Logo by Mark Wilson* (https://www.fastcompany.com/3028982/why-the-security-bug-heartbleed-has-a-catchy-logo)

Figure 3.5: Marketing-based thinking helped drive awareness for the Heartbleed bug.

The Heartbleed Bug goes down in history as the first vulnerability to receive the full branding treatment. And the resulting news coverage and widespread *brand awareness* are a testament to the effectiveness of that strategy.

Google: *Jess Time* **and** *Dear Sophie* **(Making Technology Personal)**
When you think of an Internet browser, what comes to mind? Probably the ability to transmit or receive information over the Web. You want speed, stability, and reliability. You might think about shopping, browsing, banking, and news. But, remember the secret of communications and marketing that we keep coming back to? Making someone care about a message or product all comes down to finding a WHY. And that should be rooted in something related to emotion and the human condition.

Google understands this well. Its 2011 *Dear Sophie*[29,30] and 2012 *Jess Time*[31,32] commercials are great examples. Many Internet-based companies might have tried to make one of the following points:

- Our technologies put the world's information at your fingertips.
- Our technologies help you connect faster, smarter, and cheaper.
- Our technologies serve the Web to you, one byte at a time.

But, Google's pitch for Chrome is about all of that and none of that at the same time. Google wanted to show how the Chrome platform is less about enabling people to connect with services and more about facilitating real, meaningful *person-to-person* connections.

Dear Sophie depicts a new dad, Daniel Lee, using Gmail, YouTube, Google Maps, and other Google services to create an online scrapbook through a series of emails to his newborn daughter, Sophie, chronicling their shared life together. Through the use of video, animated screen captures, sound, music, and printed words, the commercial is incredibly effective in driving home Google's ultimate point: "The Web is what you make of it."

Google continues to show how their technology enables meaningful human interactions in their follow-up commercial, *Jess Time*. This commercial showcases Hangouts, Calendar, and Gmail as a father and daughter help each other cope with all of the changes, questions, and home sickness that arise from the daughter's recent move to college. Google then makes it even more emotional by slowly revealing that both father and daughter are also working through the grief and adjustment associated with losing a mother and wife. The result is a striking testimony for the power of storytelling in marketing—a commercial that connects with viewers on multiple levels. Their point? Chrome isn't about connecting impersonal, far-flung *computers* to each other. It's about connecting the *hearts and lives* of far-flung *people* to each other.

Get the Right Message to the Right Person at the Right Time

There are a few other concepts that are important when working to embed your message: *audience segmentation*, *personas*, and *communication channels*. Audience segmentation and personas are all about understanding how to contextualize the relevant aspects of your message in ways that will best resonate with different groups/populations that you want to reach. And communication channels are different forms of messages or different vessels that can carry your message to your audience.

A good communication strategy will find ways of putting your message in front of your audience and will do so in ways that are relevant to their lives and their modes of work and play. How do you do that? Become a detective. Remember the "five Ws and one H" information-gathering questions we learned to ask in our early schooling years? Start by brainstorming these basic questions:

- **Who**: *Who* are you speaking to?
- **What**: *What* makes that audience member unique? What's their WHY?

- **When**: *When* is the best time to get the message to your audience?
- **Where**: *Where* should your audience receive the information?
- **Why**: *Why* should the recipient care and why do you need to get their attention in the first place?
- **How**: *How* will the information be delivered to your audience? This is the device that they will receive the message on (such as computer, mobile device, poster, etc.) as well as the format that the message will take (such as email, video, interactive learning module, handout, etc.).

Audience Segmentation and Personas

You'll notice that, in the introduction to this section, I used the word *contextualization* when describing the concepts of audience segmentation and personas. This is all about finding relevant points of connection between our message and the lives of our audience. It means that we need to see our message within the context of their lives and how they view and interact with the world around them.

If you and I were watching a crime drama together, we'd likely see a scene where a brilliant criminologist walks in and starts rattling off specific traits about the unsub (unknown subject) that committed the crime. You already know the word that we use for this process (in both its positive and negative connotations): *profiling*. The criminologist creates a profile of the criminal so that the police can get an understanding of who they are going after. And that's what we need, an idea of the type of person that *we* are going after.

Building audience segments and personas is like profiling in reverse. You first think about the entirety of your organization's employee population, and then you find ways to break it down by different *types* of people; this can be by region, job type, age groups, and so on. These are known in the marketing world as *segments*, groups of people within a larger population.

Once you have carved out some segments, you need to dig a bit deeper. You need to work to uncover what makes each segment tick. For instance, you will want to know about any distinct motivations, fears, relevant job duties, systems, and technologies that the segment uses, job-specific terminology that they use, history of security issues and successes, and so on. Then you tailor your message to any WHYs inherent to that segment.

MARKETERS ENGAGE CUSTOMERS BY USING BIG DATA, BEHAVIOR SCIENCE, AND PERSONALITY SCIENCE. AND SO SHOULD WE.

When developing campaigns, many modern marketing campaigns use a combination of behavior science and personality science. We'll have a detailed discussion of behavior science in the next chapter. Personality science is relatively new and has been misused in some very public ways in recent years (see "Facebook crossed a thin line between creepy intrusion and everyday targeting." https://mashable.com/2017/05/02/facebook-ad-targeting-by-mood/#QmczKXWC8iqQ).

While some companies may have struggled with finding the most ethical ways to leverage the vast amounts of data available about users, you should be considering how to use this type of data for your awareness campaigns.

You likely already have a wealth of relevant information about your employees that you collect using tools such as employee monitoring systems, security information and event management (SIEM), endpoint protection platforms (EPP), web proxy data, and training databases. That data, in many ways, holds the secrets to having a nuanced view into how and why each specific employee may not follow a specific security practice. The data from these tools also hold the keys to help you find the right messages, interventions, or alternate behaviors that can be prescribed (even *auto-prescribed*) on a user-by-user basis.

When defining the different segments of your user population, it can be helpful to categorize them in ways that are easy to remember and describe. This is where the idea of personas comes in. Remember the example I used earlier about how a criminologist builds a profile? Building personas is a lot like that process, but it is building a profile for one of your *segments*. Here's how Ardath Albee, CEO of Marketing Interactions and author of *Digital Relevance* describes the idea[33]:

> The first thing you need to understand about personas is that they are not representative of a real person. Buyer personas are a composite sketch of a segment of your target market designed to help brands align with these specific buyers' needs and priorities to build engagement that results in a profitable relationship.

Because buyer personas are focused on role, needs, priorities and objectives, a single persona could represent a range of titles. Role must take precedence over title.

Ardath Albee, CEO of Marketing Interactions

So, your personas are well-thought-out profiles of the different types of users that exist within your organization. Like a criminologist, you want to understand your subject's motivations, character traits, job duties, questions, fears, and social influences so that you can focus your efforts for maximum impact.

Figure 3.6 provides an example of a persona template that might be used for marketing.

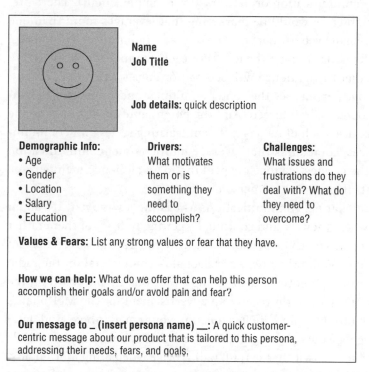

Figure 3.6: Personas transform "targets" into people.

Notice how having all that information consolidated in a poster-like form helps to humanize the target audience. Personas attach emotions, drives, needs, struggles, and preferences to otherwise abstract roles; they allow you to view your product, brand, or message through another person's eyes.[34] As the term indicates, a *persona* can help us see and treat our audience in a more personable way: as *people*, not targets, not roles, not problems, not generic end users, and not any other *impersonal* term.

We'll develop some security awareness-related personas in Part 3 of this book as we think about security awareness in the context of life.

Channels of Communication

A fundamental marketing practice is to do whatever you can to maximize the chance that your message will reach your intended audience. That means casting a wide net. To do so, marketers employ a tactic called *multichannel marketing* (aka multichannel communications).

Understanding multichannel communication is simple enough. A *channel* is one mode of communication or delivery (for example, email). Therefore, multichannel marketing would be marketing that leverages more than one channel such as email, web banner ads, YouTube ads, radio ads, television ads, and physical billboards. You get the idea. For each channel added, there is a greater chance that the audience will see and/or engage with the content. Additionally, if one person sees the content multiple times in multiple channels, then the content is reinforced. And the potential of repetition isn't the only benefit. Because each of us has different learning styles and communication preferences, companies that leverage multichannel communication methods have the greatest chance of speaking to an audience member in a way that is most effective for that person.

Think of multichannel communications as casting a wide net. It's about finding people where they are and continually getting in front of them rather than hoping that they will come to you. This is why you'll see an advertisement for McDonald's on TV and then hear a McDonald's commercial on the radio as you drive to work, potentially also seeing a McDonald's billboard on the way. While at work, you might receive an advertisement for the McDonald's McRib sandwich (*available for a limited time!*) in your email inbox. And, later that day, you might be out driving and receive a digital coupon on your mobile device whenever you are within a certain radius of a participating McDonald's. Powerful stuff! What communication channels can you leverage for your awareness materials?

THE DIFFERENCE BETWEEN MARKETING AND PUBLIC RELATIONS

As security professionals, we don't always appreciate the variety of disciplines represented within the communications field. As an example, I'm sure you hear the terms *marketing* and *public relations* (PR) all the time . . . and maybe in the same breath. But, have you ever given thought to the distinction between those two disciplines? Let's consider the purpose for each.

For the most part, *marketing* is *product-centric*. The target audience is the group of people who will be consuming products and services. And so marketing is about building and positioning the products and services based on real or perceived customer needs.

Public relations has a subtle difference. The focus of public relations is on positioning the organization in the best possible light. It is about shaping public opinion positively and working to minimize any negative opinions. Here's how the marketing company, HubSpot describes public relations[35]:

> *A PR professional works with an organization, company, government, or individual to cultivate a story that portrays that client's reputation, idea, product, position, or accomplishment in a positive light. So, in a sense, you can think of PR professionals as storytellers. Unlike advertisers, who tell stories through paid methods, PR professionals tell their stories through unpaid or earned media.*
> *HubSpot blog by Caroline Forsey*

When building your awareness programs, there will be communication efforts that fall within the realm of marketing, and there will definitely be public relations aspects of the program.

Your "public," in this case, is your organization as a whole, but it will also need to specifically account for executives, stakeholders, and different divisions and departments. In business-speak, this is the *political* part of managing your program. And, in this respect, your PR efforts will be multifaceted.

Use marketing practices to package and promote your brand and security awareness information and content. And use public relations practices to promote the overall importance and efficacy of your program, shape opinion, get buy-in, and position your program within the context of the interests of the larger organization.

Campaigns: If You Aren't Reinforcing, Your Audience Is Forgetting

Security awareness should always be an ongoing campaign, not just an event.

One of the main mistakes I've seen security leaders make over and over is that they tend to approach security awareness as a once- or twice-per-year activity. That approach is ineffective. It simply doesn't work; marketers know this. And, if those security leaders were to be honest with themselves, they know it, too.

Our opinions and behaviors aren't generally swayed by hearing information once. We learn and change through repetition. So, marketers seek to influence us as often as possible so that they have the best chance at getting us to purchase their product or service.

Have you ever played the game where someone throws a ball or balloon in the air and everyone's job in the room is to keep it afloat by giving it an upward smack before it drops to the floor? If so, you have a good idea of what a marketer's task is when it comes to promoting their product, service, or idea. They have to keep it afloat; they can't let it drop. Security awareness programs should have that same mind-set. Our mission is to keep the ideas in the air and off the floor.

Adopting an ongoing campaign mind-set is the only way to do this. We'll be discussing how to craft campaigns in Part 3 of this book. And our campaign methods will be designed around marketing concepts that leverage customer segmentation, persona development, multichannel communication, and more.

Tracking Results and Measuring Effectiveness

If something is worth doing, it is worth measuring to determine its effectiveness. Marketing practices tend to generate a lot of data. And that data is used to track the impact of each campaign and tactic. Typical marketing dashboards display a number of data elements. What is the marketing manager looking for? *Engagement*. To be more specific, they're looking for *engagement* and *movement*.

The marketing manager will be looking at things like these:

- Page views (for sales collateral, blogs, newsletters, and ads)
- Document downloads (for whitepapers, brochures, etc.)

- Web forms completed (for things like registration to webinars, product evaluations, or anything behind a registration wall)
- Requests to speak to a salesperson or company representative (enough said!)
- Web traffic by device type
- Demographic/firmographics for engaged versus unengaged prospects
- Relative effectiveness of each channel
- And what effect do all of these have on actual *sales* (conversions)?

In addition to these, the marketing manager may conduct surveys or commission third-party research to get an idea of how their brand and products are perceived by prospective customers. When it comes to measuring the effectiveness of our information delivery, these marketing-based statistics can be a great place to start.

Know When to Ask for Help

In this chapter, we covered a ton of information, and I've pointed you to several additional resources. I hope you feel a bit more connected to topics related to marketing, communications, and design. But, take this information for what it is: *a starting place.* I've exposed you to many key ideas and the reasons why those ideas work or are relevant to our security awareness programs.

As with all areas in life, it is important to know when to ask for help, and there are (at least) three great ways to augment your skill set:

- Through the robust security awareness vendor community that has already created a wealth of ready-to-use resources and tools
- By leveraging your internal marketing and public relations (aka corporate communications) teams
- With a combination of the previous two options

I've always been a fan of getting your organization's marketing or public relations departments directly involved in your program. There are lots of good reasons to do so; namely, the more you can involve other teams in creating some key aspects of your program, the more buy-in they feel. In addition to getting professional-grade work done for some of your design and communication elements and learning design directly from professionals, you win additional advocates within your organization.

Key Takeaways

- *Get in touch with your audience's WHY.* Understanding your audience is the key to crafting meaningful messages. There is no one-size-fits-all security message. It is our job to understand and care about our audience enough to contextualize it (make it personally relevant to them).
- *Connect by using emotion.* Emotion is probably the single most important resource we can tap into. If we can connect our message with something emotional, then we will have succeeded in making the message feel relevant.
- *Take advantage of Trojan Horses.* You need every advantage possible to make your messages stick. Simple text-based security awareness messaging will always be less effective than messaging that includes well-thought-out and well-designed visual components. Words alone are always of limited value when compared to what you can accomplish using words plus compelling imagery and sound.
- *Understand and appreciate the nuances of your audience.* Build campaigns that target segments and personas. Your messages need to target the right people, with the right message, at the right time, on the right device. This all comes back to understanding and appreciating who you are speaking to.
- *Make it ongoing.* Repetition is key. Repetition is key. Repetition is key. If there is something worth saying to your people, then you need to say it over and over. Your audience is drowning in other stimuli. Even if you have an engaging message, you will need to repeat it often or risk getting drowned out in the noise of life.

Notes and References

1. https://www.forbes.com/sites/taylorarmerding/2018/10/16/lance-spitzner-how-to-secure-the-human-operating-system/#28ae9f26ed59
2. In researching this particular phenomenon, I learned that it has a name: *translation by Volume.*" The things you learn when writing a book! See https://tvtropes.org/pmwiki/pmwiki.php/Main/TranslationByVolume.
3. *Harden Your Human Firewall* by Nick Hayes and Claire O'Malley (https://www.forrester.com/report/Harden+Your+Human+Firewall/-/E-RES122800)

4. *2018 SANS Security Awareness Report* (https://www.sans.org/sites/default/files/2018-05/2018%20SANS%20Security%20Awareness%20Report.pdf)
5. *Problems smart people have* by Ramit Sethi. (https://growthlab.com/problems-smart-people-have/)
6. The Principles of Psychology (https://en.wikipedia.org/wiki/The_Principles_of_Psychology)
7. *Malcolm Gladwell Teaches Writing, Lesson 8* (https://www.masterclass.com/classes/malcolm-gladwell-teaches-writing)
8. https://www.ama.org/AboutAMA/Pages/Definition-of-Marketing.aspx
9. *How Great Leaders Inspire Action* by Simon Sinek (https://www.ted.com/talks/simon_sinek_how_great_leaders_inspire_action#t-271891)
10. Ibid.
11. *Neuroscience Confirms We Buy on Emotion & Justify with Logic & Yet we Sell to Mr. Rational & Ignore Mr. Intuitive* by Michael Harris (http://insight-demand.com/neuroscience-confirms-we-buy-on-emotion-justify-with-logic-yet-we-sell-to-mr-rational-ignore-mr-intuitive/)
12. If you are interested in a couple very accessible books on how the logical and emotive/instinctual areas of our brain govern decision-making, pick up *Thinking, Fast and Slow* by Daniel Kahneman and *Blink* by Malcolm Gladwell.
13. *Theory of Mind* (https://en.wikipedia.org/wiki/Theory_of_mind)
14. "How to use the 7Ps Marketing Mix" by Annmarie Hanlon (https://www.smartinsights.com/marketing-planning/marketing-models/how-to-use-the-7ps-marketing-mix/)
15. And potentially even finding where security messaging can be skipped entirely and a more secure behavior can be facilitated via technology.
16. *At the end of "Inside Out," why did Joy give Sadness the core emotions?* by Jeff Saporito (http://screenprism.com/insights/article/at-the-end-of-inside-out-why-did-joy-give-sadness-the-core-emotions)
17. *Inside Out - Sadness Saves Riley - Ending Scene (HD)* (https://www.youtube.com/watch?v=y2CJ46XkwxA)
18. *Deep Feelings: A Massive Cross-Lingual Study on the Relation between Emotions and Virality* by Marco Guerini and Jacopo Staiano (https://arxiv.org/abs/1503.04723v1)

19. *Quotes, Private Parts* (https://www.imdb.com/title/tt0119951/quotes/qt0468488)

20. *Mere-Exposure effect* (https://en.wikipedia.org/wiki/Mere-exposure_effect)

21. *Familiarity Breeds Enjoyment. Why forced familiarity with novel experiences enhances enjoyment in life* by Raj Raghunathan (https://www.psychologytoday.com/us/blog/sapient-nature/201201/familiarity-breeds-enjoyment)

22. *Rule of Thirds* by Darren Rouse (https://digital-photography-school.com/rule-of-thirds/)

23. Unless maybe you wanted to communicate that someone was ashamed or embarrassed. In those cases, you could have the person averting their eyes or casting them down for dramatic effect. But these are exceptions to the rule.

24. *Joint Attention* (https://en.wikipedia.org/wiki/Joint_attention)

25. I can't even begin to count the number of times that a song has come on the radio and my wife knows and sings every word and phrase perfectly. Then, as the lyrics pause, she'll smile and say, "These words are where my math facts should be."

26. *A novel look at how stories may change the brain* (https://esciencecommons.blogspot.com/2013/12/a-novel-look-at-how-stories-may-change.html)

27. *Your Brain on Story: Why Narratives Win Our Hearts and Minds. Our craving and connection to story is so much more than a haphazard preference* by Michele Weldon (https://psmag.com/social-justice/pulitzer-prizes-journalism-reporting-your-brain-on-story-why-narratives-win-our-hearts-and-minds-79824)

28. Heartbleed home page (https://heartbleed.com)

29. *Google Chrome: Dear Sophie* (https://adage.com/creativity/work/dear-sophie/23153)

30. *Google Chrome Dear Sophie* (https://www.youtube.com/watch?v=zhPklt9nYas)

31. *Google Jess Time* by Duncan MacLeod (http://theinspirationroom.com/daily/2012/google-jess-time/)

32. *Google Chrome: Jess Time* (https://www.youtube.com/watch?v=PbGhHaUpv5E)

33. *Buyer Personas* by Ardath Albee (https://marketinginteractions.com/buyer-personas/)

34. *The Complete, Actionable Guide to Marketing Personas* by Kevan Lee (https://blog.bufferapp.com/marketing-personas-beginners-guide)
35. *What Is Public Relations? The Definition of PR in 100 Words or Less* by Caroline Forsey (https://blog.hubspot.com/marketing/public-relations-definition)

Additional Reading

Allie Decker. *The Ultimate Guide to Storytelling. Learn how to develop your storytelling skills to elevate your brand and connect to your audience.* (HubSpot blog), https://blog.hubspot.com/marketing/storytelling.

Ashley Welch. *Psychologists identify why certain songs get stuck in your head.* (CBS News, 2016), https://www.cbsnews.com/news/psychologists-identify-why-certain-songs-get-stuck-in-your-head/.

Ben Parr. *Captivology: The Science of Capturing People's Attention.* (HarperOne, 2015).

Bernadette Jiwa. *Difference: The one-page method for reimagining your business and reinventing your marketing.* (CreateSpace Independent Publishing Platform, 2014).

Brian G. Peters. "6 Rules of Great Storytelling (As Told by Pixar)." https://medium.com/@Brian_G_Peters/6-rules-of-great-storytelling-as-told by pixar-fcc6ae225f50.

Bronwyn Fryer. *Storytelling That Moves People.* (Harvard Business Review, 2003), https://hbr.org/2003/06/storytelling-that-moves-people.

Daniel Kahneman. *Thinking, Fast and Slow.* (Farrar, Straus and Giroux, 2011).

Jonah Burger. *Contagious: Why Things Catch On.* Reprint edition. (Simon & Schuster, 2013).

Jonah Lehrer. *The Itch of Curiosity.* (Wired, 2010), https://www.wired.com/2010/08/the-itch-of-curiosity/.

Joseph J. Romm. *Language Intelligence: Lessons on persuasion from Jesus, Shakespeare, Lincoln, and Lady Gaga.* (CreateSpace Independent Publishing Platform, 2012).

Is Curiosity a Positive or Negative Feeling? (NPR, 2017), https://www.npr.org/sections/13.7/2017/09/25/553443078/is-Malcolm Gladwell. *Blink: The Power of Thinking Without Thinking.* (Back Bay Books, 2007). curiosity-a-positive-or-negative-feeling.

Nancy Duarte. *Resonate: Present Visual Stories that Transform Audiences.* (John Wiley and Sons, 2010).

The Psychology and Neuroscience of Curiosity. Neuron. Volume 88, Issue 3, 4 November 2015, pp. 449–460, https://www.sciencedirect.com/science/article/pii/S0896627315007679.

Why Does Music Aid in Memorization? A Memory Expert on How Songs Get Stuck in Your Mind. (The Wall Street Journal, 2013), https://www.wsj.com/articles/why-does-music-aid-in-memorization-1388458293.

4

Behavior Management 101 for Security Awareness Leaders

Security needs to be viewed through a wider lens. Beyond technology invest-ments, security begins and ends with people: their behaviors, motivations, and habits.

Deloitte Insights[1]

Let's start with a question that I asked back in Chapter 1: *Do you care more about what your employees* know, *or what they* do? When it comes to the security of our organizations, actions speak louder than words. And actions speak louder than mere head knowledge. After all, it doesn't matter if your employees can verbally recite all the hallmarks of great password management if they never put that knowledge into practice. And even when your people read your flyers, posters, and newsletters on how to spot a phishing email and pass your phishing training module with flying colors, it's all worthless if they fall for a phishing attack during the hustle and bustle of real life. Actions—not head knowledge—will determine whether your organization is breached.

> **NOTE** Actions—not head knowledge—will determine whether your orga-nization is breached.

As humans, we all struggle with behaviors. Our bodies sometimes just behave on autopilot, without consulting the logical/reasoning part of our minds. Think about times when an object—let's say a pen—has started to roll off your desk and your arm seemed to quickly reach over and try to catch the pen before it falls to the floor, maybe even knocking over your coffee mug along the way and causing a bigger mess than if you did nothing. What happened? Many times, you didn't consciously decide to try to catch the pen. Your mind quickly processed the situation and made the decision to intervene without consulting your logical self.

We are dealing with what I like to call the *knowledge-intention-behavior gap*. People may have the knowledge they need to make a wise decision, and they may even have the intention to make wise choices, but even the right knowledge and intentions don't naturally translate to their associated and implied behaviors.

Here's an example of the *knowledge-intention-behavior gap* that I'm sure you can relate to. Each year many people make New Year's resolutions. They want to lose weight, eat healthier, save more money, and so on. But the unfortunate truth is that most people don't keep those resolutions *even though they are new behaviors that the person wants to do and believes will be in their best interest.* Of the people that make New Year's resolutions, more than 27 percent give up within one week,[2] and more give up each week following. Even more discouraging is that the success rates for people who keep their resolutions are also impacted by their age. Roughly 38 percent of people in their 20s are able to keep their resolution, but that number drops dramatically, to just 16.3 percent, for people older than 50.[3] This is significant. We're talking about behaviors that people genuinely want and intend to embrace, but the pace of life, effort involved, and other factors work against the behavior, and the person falls back into their old patterns and habits.

When it comes to the human side of security, you must treat the *knowledge-intention-behavior gap* as a fundamental law of reality that affects any behavior that you hope to encourage or discourage. As security leaders, we need to stop expecting to make people more secure by simply exposing them to more information. Information will always have its place, but for a person to act on information, you must first somehow navigate them into a context where they are able to intentionally reason through the situation that they are in. That's difficult.

NOTE   When it comes to the human side of security, you must treat the *knowledge-intention-behavior gap* as a fundamental law of reality that affects any behavior that you hope to encourage or discourage.

Like instinctively grabbing for the pen falling from the table, most of the security-related actions your people take on a day-to-day bases are reactive; so, they are not likely going to decide to stop and do the hard work of reasoning through their situation. Instead, your people will almost always do what is easiest, what is habitual, what is quickest, or what is most like what they've done in the past.

> ## THE THREE REALITIES OF SECURITY AWARENESS
>
> At the risk of over-repeating myself, I'm going to list three statements that I've written a number of times so far. Let's call these the *three realities of security awareness*:
>
> - Just because I'm *aware* doesn't mean that I *care*.
> - If you try to work *against* human nature, you will *fail*.
> - What your people *do* is way more important than what they *know*.
>
> Keep these in mind as you design your program.

This chapter is all about trying to work with the realities of human nature so that you can build secure behaviors. When you embrace behavior management as a central goal and methodology for your awareness program, you've stepped into the *transformational* zone. I'll cover a lot of theory and different models for behavior and why people do the things they do. Heads-up: Don't be surprised when you start thinking about how the principles of behavior management are useful not only within the security context but across multiple areas of your business and personal life.

Your Users Aren't Stupid, They're Human

Over the course of your security career, I'm sure that you've had one or two instances where you've felt extremely frustrated with the end-user community. After all, you've given them all the information they need to follow security policies and best practices, but they just don't. You've told them why good password management is important, but they still choose passwords like *123456* or *password*.[4] And you've been telling them not to blindly click links or download attachments from emails, but your people still do it. The same is true across the entire spectrum of security-related behaviors — from tailgating to insecure data disposal to oversharing on social media, and more. All too often, your employees' behavior is at odds with the information you've given them.

So, why are your users still making poor security choices despite all the information you've given them? Are they stupid? Is training worthless? What's going on here? There are several reasons why. But I'll boil it down to one simple phrase: *your users aren't stupid; they're human*.

This takes us back to the *knowledge-intention-behavior gap*. Here's the issue: When a behavior is hard, or even just unfamiliar, people generally won't do it despite their knowledge or good intentions. I'm betting that you can even think of areas in your own life where you too aren't fully implementing the security-related behaviors that you know are best and that you recommend to others. Congratulations, you are human!

BJ Fogg, founder of the Stanford University Behavior Design Lab, succinctly describes the problem with getting humans to perform specific behaviors in the following quote.[5]

Take a second to consider the truth of that statement. And resist the urge to feel offended by the bluntness of the quote.

- **We are *lazy*:** We humans generally don't like to do anything more than is required to accomplish a task. When something takes a lot of effort, our interest in doing it decreases dramatically. When things are hard, we want to avoid those things or find tools that will help us accomplish those things more easily.
- **We are *social*:** Our thoughts and actions are influenced greatly by the people around us. We feel the pressure to conform. And we learn by watching and imitating those around us. We desire a sense of belonging and approval and will avoid the discomfort associated with being an outsider.
- **We are creatures of *habit*:** We like to do things in the same way that we've done them in the past. Our bodies and minds reinforce this by creating habits (patterns of behavior that become automatic). Breaking a habit is difficult because the habitual behavior is deep-seated and can even be comforting to us.

MENTAL NOTE: LAZY BY NATURE?

Is it fair to say that humans are lazy by nature? How can we say humans are lazy considering all the difficult things we see people do, like running marathons, participating in extreme sports, or even just doing high-school math?

When people do hard things such as these activities, it's because they derive some sort of reward for it or avoid some greater pain. The reward can be feeding an intrinsic motivation, to fit in with their peer group, to impress others, and so on. The avoided pain can be associated with things like negative social pressure or fear of bad grades.

Even people considered high-achievers are usually only high-achievers in areas of their lives where they are highly motivated. In other areas, these high-achievers have strictly middle-of-the-road or even subpar performance. It is well recognized that a law or *principle of least effort*[6,7] exists and

> *. . . applies to cognitive as well as physical exertion. The law asserts that if there are several ways of achieving the same goal, people will eventually gravitate to the least demanding course of action. In the economy of action, effort is a cost and the acquisition of a skill is driven by the balance of benefits and costs. Laziness is built deep into our nature.*

Daniel Kahneman, *Thinking, Fast and Slow*, p. 35[8]

So, if this is the reality of human nature and if working against human nature is a recipe for failure, how can you get people to make better security decisions? The good news is that you can design your security awareness program with these realities in mind. In fact, you should design the *entirety* of your information security program and related policies around the realities of human nature.

Thinking, Fast and Slow

We aren't just wired to be lazy in our physical behaviors. We are lazy even in the way we think and process information. Nobel Prize–winning psychologist Daniel Kahneman[9] describes this problem. Well-known for his research and findings related to human judgment and decision-making, Kahneman is one of the founders of a field that we now call *behavioral economics*.

Behavioral economics is concerned with the "effects of psychological, cognitive, emotional, cultural, and social factors on the economic decisions of individuals and institutions and how those decisions vary from those implied by classical theory."[10] In other words, behavioral economists are interested in understanding why people make bad decisions in spite of the data they have available to them.

One of the main principles underlying Kahneman's work is that humans use mental shortcuts in their decision-making. *Lots and lots* of mental shortcuts. Essentially when posed with a difficult situation or problem, our mind offers up a substitute question that is easier to answer, and then our mind solves for the simpler, substitute question. This substitute question is referred to as a *heuristic* (a "mental shortcut" or "rule of thumb"), and these heuristics account for about 95 percent of our thinking.

Heuristics are good in many ways because they help people process information quickly and efficiently. If not for heuristics, people would get bogged down fully analyzing each and every situation they encounter. But heuristics are also the root cause of several problems that lead people to make poor decisions.

In his 2013 book *Thinking, Fast and Slow*, Kahneman outlines two systems that drive the way the mind processes information: *System 1* and *System 2 thinking*.[11]

System 1 Thinking

System 1 thinking is fast, emotion-driven, and intuitive.

Remember the examples with images and logos that we used in the previous chapter? System 1 thinking is what allowed you to immediately process all the information about the boy reading the book, including his surroundings, posture, and so on. System 1 thinking is also in play when our mind immediately associated logos with companies. System 1 thinking is extremely helpful in those cases. However, System 1 thinking can lead us astray.

Here's an example of where System 1 thinking can work against us. Take a quick look at the different lines in Figure 4.1 and pick out which is the longest.

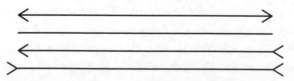

Figure 4.1: System 1 thinking example, part A

If you are like most people, you chose the second or last line as the longest. But neither is correct. In fact, all the lines are the same length. Figure 4.2 helps to make this clear by explicitly pointing out the endpoints of each line.[12]

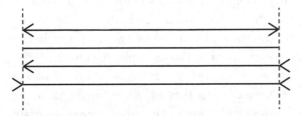

Figure 4.2: System 1 thinking example, part B

That's just one example. Remember 95 percent of our thinking is governed by System 1. That means there are tons of chances every day where our heuristic-driven thinking leads us to poor decisions.

From a security standpoint, there are two major implications[13] related to System 1 issues. First, your people naturally employ System 1 thinking when building their security habits. This is why people gravitate toward algorithms when they are faced with the challenge of choosing a password. They want something that is easy and memorable, so they choose something based on their current password, passwords they've used in the past, or something that they have an emotional connection with (like the name of their spouse or child coupled with a significant date).

The second security-related implication of System 1 thinking is that attackers are good at weaponizing our heuristic thinking against us. Social engineering, specifically phishing, is a perfect example. System 1 thinking is what drives users to instinctively and impulsively click anything that shows up in their inbox. And even savvy, trained end users can fall victim to weaponized System 1 thinking when a crafty attacker helps the heuristic by embedding comforting cues within a malicious URL.

Here's an example. Let's say that one of your well-trained users receives a phishing email. This email is purportedly from a well-known and trusted bank informing the user that she needs to check her account because of suspicious activity. Helpfully, the email contains a Go to My Account button. Because our hypothetical user is well-trained, she knows to hover over the link and verify that the URL is not malicious. And, in this case, she spots the name of the bank in the URL . . . *click*.

There are several System 1–based landmines here. First, the email is purportedly coming from a trusted source. Second, there is the emotion attached to "suspicious activity" with the user's account. But, the truly devious tactic here is that the URL was crafted to exploit the user's heuristic in a sophisticated way. Of course, the name of the bank was in the URL; the attacker placed the bank's name at a location within the URL that the user would immediately see without taking notice of the true domain. For example, the attacker URL could be `https://secure.trusted-bank.verifyacctsite.com/customer-security-verification/`. Notice how in this example, the bank name (`trusted-bank`) is front and center. Additionally, the other user subdomain is simply named "secure" and the actual domain is `verifyacctsite.com`. Additionally, the location on the site that the user will be navigated to is intended to feel comforting, `/customer-security-verification/`.

MENTAL NOTE: RELATING TO THE SYSTEM 1 THINKING OF A NONSECURITY PRACTITIONER

I'm assuming that the majority of people reading this book currently work within the cybersecurity field. Because you live, eat, and breathe security concepts all day, it can be difficult to relate to how a nonsecurity professional's System 1 might lead them astray with phishing emails that seem blatantly obvious to you.

Here's a non-security-related System 1 exercise for you. Don't spend a lot of time on this. Instead, just listen to your intuition as you think about this problem:

A bat and a ball cost $1.10.
The bat costs $1 more than the ball.
How much does the ball cost?

As you read that, your mind solved the problem with relative ease. Or at least that's what it felt like. What number came to mind? For many people, the number that comes to mind is 10¢. But that's not the correct answer. Here's how Kahneman describes what's happening in your mind:

> The distinctive mark of this easy puzzle is that it evokes an answer that is intuitive, appealing, and wrong. Do the math and you will see. If the ball costs 10¢, then the total cost would be $1.20 (10¢ for the ball and $1.10 for the bat), not $1.10. The correct answer is 5¢.

> *It is safe to assume that the intuitive answer also came to the mind of those who ended up with the correct number—they somehow managed to resist the intuition.*
>
> Daniel Kahneman, Thinking, Fast and Slow. p44

You just felt the tension and frustration that comes with realizing that your System 1 can easily lead you astray. In this example, System 1 offered you an easy answer by solving for a simpler question than the one that was posed to it. Now here's the thing . . . in virtually all things related to security, your users' System 1 is "helping" them solve complex security questions by offering up questions and answers that are simpler, leading to answers and behaviors that are, unfortunately, wrong.

The phishing example I provided in this section is pretty simple from an attacker's perspective. Extremely crafty attackers may seek to lay even more System 1 landmines by making use of what are called *evil twin* or *doppelgänger* domains. These are domains that, at first glance (or even second glance), can look nearly identical to a domain that an attacker wants to impersonate. This can be done with font manipulation, using non-ASCII characters to simulate standard characters, using number substitution for letters (like the number 1 in place of a lowercase L), letter substitution for numbers, putting letters together to visually simulate another letter (like placing a lowercase r next to a lowercase n to simulate a lowercase m), and the list goes on. In all these scenarios, System 1 is an attacker's friend.

System 2 Thinking

System 2 thinking is slower, more methodical, logical, and deliberate.

In contrast to impulsive, quick System 1 thinking, System 2 is deliberate. It is much slower, more deliberate, and intentional. Look at the following:

$$15 \times 32 = ?$$

That feeling you got when looking at this math problem gives you a good feel for what System 2 thinking is. You look at the problem and, to engage it, you need to slow down and intentionally reason through it. You know that you can do it, but you will decide if you want to spend the energy on it.

I'm sure that you can immediately see our problem as security practitioners. For people to exhibit good security behaviors or make good security decisions, either we have to build behaviors that naturally rely on System 1 or we have to get people to slow down and intentionally engage in System 2 thinking.

But, there's another complicating factor. Getting someone to engage in System 2 thinking won't always lead to good security decisions. Context is key. Continuing with the example of phishing, we face another System 1 versus System 2 problem. Even when someone is actively engaging in System 2 thinking, their mind is usually trying to solve for a nonsecurity issue. They are looking at the email within a business context or an urgency context or a curiosity context, and so on. In the same way that you become temporarily unaware of what's going on around you when you are focusing on a task, your users can be fully engaging with the pretext behind a malicious email using System 2 thinking and effectively become blind to the security issues (they miss the Gorilla[14]) because of the issues associated with selective attention.[15]

When it comes to security behaviors around something like phishing, we (as an industry) are good at saying, "Stop and think before you click" in an effort to encourage System 2 thinking. But the problem with that statement is that someone must be primed to enter System 2 before they can apply the advice, and they need to enter System 2 within the right context. That means that we need to find ways to bridge this type of advice into a more automatic, System 1 type of pattern.

To build a program that works with human nature, you must account for the fact that 95 percent of the time your users are acting on autopilot, leveraging System 1 thinking. You'll explore ways of doing so throughout this chapter. In the meantime, take a look at the following resources if you'd like to explore these topics in greater depth.

NOTE To build a program that works with human nature, you must account for the fact that 95 percent of the time your users are acting on autopilot, leveraging System 1 thinking.

Books:

- *Thinking, Fast and Slow* by Daniel Kahneman
- *Predictably Irrational, Revised and Expanded Edition: The Hidden Forces That Shape Our Decisions* by Dan Ariely
- *The Invisible Gorilla: How Our Intuitions Deceive Us* by Christopher Chabris and Daniel Simons

Web Resources:

- *Brain Tricks: This Is How Your Brain Works* (https://www.youtube.com/watch?v=JiTz2i4VHFw)
- *Our Brains: Predictably Irrational* (https://www.ted.com/playlists/74/our_brains_predictably_irrati)
- *An Introduction to Behavioral Economics* (https://www.behavioraleconomics.com/resources/introduction-behavioral-economics/)
- *Heuristics and Biases: The Science of Decision Making* by Steve Dale (http://www.stephendale.com/2018/07/29/heuristics-and-biases-the-science-of-decision-making/)
- *Oh, Behave! What Information Security Can Learn from Behavioural Economics* (https://www.tripwire.com/state-of-security/security-awareness/oh-behave-what-information-security-can-learn-from-behavioural-economics/)
- *Deep Thought: A Cybersecurity Story* (http://www.ideas42.org/wp-content/uploads/2016/08/Deep-Thought-A-Cybersecurity-Story.pdf)

Working with Human Nature Rather Than Against

Whenever there is a gap between your security policy and the reality of your users' behavior, it is probably because you are expecting people to behave in ways that don't align with human nature. That's a recipe for failure. Our security policies and procedures need to account for the fact that people are humans, not computers.

In all things related to the human side of security, you need to account for the complexities of human behavior and decision-making, the realities of life and competing priorities, the stresses, time crunches, and different contexts of life that your people find themselves in each day.

The *us* versus *them* mentality that all too often comes from security professionals as they think about how they differ from the end-user community isn't helpful. Instead, let's recognize that we are equally human, and our humanity brings with it inherent strengths and weaknesses each of which manifest differently depending on the context in which a person is placed.

If you are a security professional, you likely bring a security-centric mind-set to everything you do. In the same way, a finance professional, marketing professional, or product manager brings with them the mind-set and skills that are distinctive to their role. In other words, we all view the world through a set of filters, and those filters color everything about the way we see, process information, and behave. So, in every situation you enter, among *your* primary thoughts is the security implications behind things; and among the primary thoughts of your *end users* is almost certainly something *other* than security. They are solving for a different problem.

Now, let's be gut-level honest with ourselves. We security folk are generally hypocritical in our condemnation of end-user behavior. Think through the last month of your own life. How many times have you done the following?

- Created a password that is substandard because you were in a hurry?
- Logged in to an existing system that still uses a substandard password and you didn't take the time to change to a better password?
- Had the opportunity to set up one of your accounts to use multifactor authentication but didn't take the time?
- Swatted away a security notification without fully reading it?
- Walked away from your computer without locking your screen thinking that you'd be right back but then got distracted?
- Left your laptop or mobile device in plain view within your automobile?
- Connected to a public WiFi hotspot because you needed to get something done?
- Downloaded a relatively unknown or unvetted piece of software from the Internet because you were trying to solve a problem?
- Tailgated or allowed someone to follow you through an access-controlled door?
- Left papers with sensitive information on your desk or in a publicly accessible area?
- Blindly accepted permissions for an application?
- Accepted permissions for an application that were outside of what you'd normally accept, but you "needed" the app or were curious about it?
- Blindly clicked a link within an email on your desktop computer?
- Blindly downloaded a document within an email on your desktop computer?
- Blindly clicked a link within an email on your mobile device?
- Blindly downloaded a document on your mobile device?

- Used a USB drive to transfer documents?
- Sent email and documents from your corporate email account to a personal email account so that you could get more work done off-hours?
- Scrolled through a policy and clicked the "I understand and acknowledge" button without reading the policy?

You get the idea. Most people—even security professionals—have done one or more of the things on that list within the recent past. Why? I'm pretty sure you know. The answer is all about context, pressure, and convenience. When people are rushed, inconvenienced, or overwhelmed, they feel compelled to circumvent best practices and policies and default to what is easiest, fastest, and just gets the job done.

Adding complexity to the situation, even the best security habits and behaviors don't travel well between contexts; for example, you might have fantastic security habits on a traditional computer, but once you are on your mobile device, all of those habits and behaviors go out the window. The mobile device's form factor and interfaces are different, making things like "hovering over a link" or verifying the legitimacy of an email's sender much more difficult. To make that worse, we use our mobile devices in completely different contexts of life than when we are on a more traditional computer. We use our mobile devices in cars (sometimes even while driving), at restaurants while simultaneously participating in conversations with other people, and during meetings surreptitiously while pretending to pay attention to other things in order to respond to emergencies or to quickly get things done as they arise. In other words, our mobile devices are with us during the busyness, messiness, and distractions of life—the very times when we are most apt to let down our guards and make mistakes.

If we, as security professionals, are susceptible to behavioral compromise, we need to be understanding of our people's tendency to do the same. It's basic human nature.

So, what should you do? Working *with* human nature requires a multi-pronged strategy that includes both technology and behavioral guardrails. We aren't going to go too deeply down the technology rabbit hole right now, but I'll make this statement: Building technology-based guardrails that encourage secure behavior is less about purchasing security technologies and more around adopting a mind-set that is aware of human nature as you select and implement each and every piece of technology that your users will interact with. You are looking for technologies and tools that will naturally encourage the right behaviors or will facilitate the behavior for the user. For instance, if you are worried that users might forget to encrypt documents before sending, then your email and collaboration systems should do that for them, thus skipping the step that will require your users to 1) know how to correctly perform the action, 2) spend time performing the action, and 3) care enough to perform the action.

> **NOTE** Working *with* human nature requires a multipronged strategy that includes both technology and behavioral guardrails.

If you use this mind-set across the technologies that you purchase and the policies you create, you'll be well on your way to creating a security program that is working with human nature. The remainder of this chapter, and this book, is about building human-aware, *behavior*-based guardrails.

The Nuts and Bolts of Shaping Behavior

Driving specific security behaviors requires us to be extremely intentional in two areas: we must define the specific behavior that we want to encourage or discourage, and we have to spend time understanding the subcomponents of the behavior. If your goal as a security awareness leader is *to build a security awareness program that will help employees to make better security decisions*, that's great. Those are good aspirational starting points. However, to design for real change, in a practical way, you need to get clear on the exact behaviors you want people to do. You can use these questions to get more specific:

- What precise behaviors, if adopted, would have the most security benefit for our organization?
- Is this a group of behaviors, or is this a single behavior?
- Is this a behavior that we have the appetite to take on right now?

After listing the behaviors that you are considering working with, you can narrow the list to the top few that would benefit your organization and that your organization would have the appetite to focus on in the near term. As an example, if you wanted to focus your efforts toward shaping only three security behaviors over the next year, you might know right away that you want to focus on behaviors related to phishing and password management. Then you might think about behaviors related to tailgating, secure document disposal, incident reporting, etc., as your third. In all things you are asking 1) if the behavior will have a positive impact, and 2) if you have a chance, in your current organizational situation, of adequately focusing on the behavior.

The Fogg Behavior Model

Remember BJ Fogg from the "three truths about human nature" quote that I used at the beginning of this chapter? It's time to go deeper into his work.[16] BJ Fogg is the father of the field we call *Behavior Design*. His primary work, the *Fogg Behavior Model*, provided many of the ground-breaking insights used by web and mobile application designers who have built technologies that encourage high levels of ongoing user engagement. Many of Silicon Valley's giants are former students of BJ and readily cite his model as being a critical ingredient in the secret sauce of achieving high user engagement.

Of course, with great power comes great responsibility.[17] Understanding the keys to getting someone to perform a specific behavior has both positive and negative implications. Highly addictive apps that provide absolutely no societal value (or even *negative* societal value) leverage the Fogg Behavior Model or a derivative thereof. Luckily, BJ Fogg's motives and the thrust of his work is on using Behavior Design to help solve for many of society's biggest problems like helping people make healthier lifestyle choices and building positive habits.

One thing you can be struck by when presented with the Fogg Behavior Model is how elegant it is—simple and powerful at the same time. See Figure 4.3.

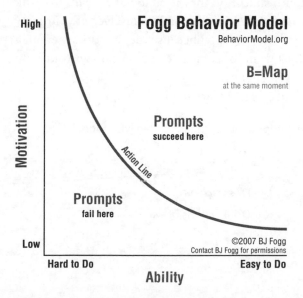

Figure 4.3: Fogg Behavior Model

Behavior happens when three things occur at the same time: *Motivation*, *Ability*, and a *Prompt* to do the behavior. This is represented as B=MAP. For any specific *behavior (B)*, a person's *motivation (M)* to perform the behavior can range from being *low* to *high*, and the person's *ability (A)* varies from being *easy to do* to being something that is *hard to do*. Additionally, no behavior happens without a *prompt (P)*. A *prompt* can be any of several things from simply asking the person to perform the behavior, to the person having an intrinsic drive to perform the behavior, to a computerized message, a cue within the person's immediate context, and so on. The *Action line* within the model depicts the relationships between ability, motivation, and prompts. Prompts that happen above the action line (in areas where there is sufficiently high motivation and the behavior is sufficiently easy to do) will succeed every time. Prompts occurring below the action line will fail because there is not sufficient motivation to perform the behavior, because the action is too difficult to do, or both.

A Nonsecurity Example

Let's unpack this with a nonsecurity example so you can see the model at work. If I want someone to perform the behavior of drinking a nice, tall glass of water, three things need to happen at the same time. The person must *want* to drink the water (have enough *motivation* to do it), they need to have the *ability* to drink the water (the water needs to be where they can get to it and you can't have taped their mouth shut), and they need to be *prompted* to drink the water (either they are thirsty and naturally avail themselves of your tasty water or you offer it to them and they accept it because they are thirsty enough to drink it or because they don't want to seem rude and turn down your kind offer of freshly poured liquid sustenance).

Table 4.1 shows how it might look if I were to break that down.

Table 4.1: Understanding the components of the Fogg Behavior Model (nonsecurity example)

Fogg Behavior Model Component	Description
Behavior (B): What is the specific behavior you're designing for?	Drink a glass of water.

Fogg Behavior Model Component	Description
Motivation (M): What types of things might motivate someone to perform the **B**?	■ They could be thirsty or have just eaten a spicy meal. ■ They might want social acceptance (everyone else is doing it). ■ They might want to avoid offending the person, offering them water. ■ They believe that there are positive health benefits associated with staying hydrated. ■ Etc.
Ability (A): What types of things must someone already be able to do or know to successfully perform the **B**?	■ A glass of water is available to the person or can be obtained with little effort. ■ The person's mouth is not taped shut. ■ The person is not asleep or otherwise incapacitated. ■ Etc.
Prompt (P): What types of things can cue the B?	■ The person notices that they are thirsty or is reacting to the spicy meal. ■ Someone offers the person a glass of water. ■ The person receives a prompt from a health app reminding them to drink. ■ Etc.

This example, absurd as it is, shows both the simplicity and the power of the model. The Fogg Behavior Model can be used to troubleshoot behaviors that aren't happening as well. For example, is someone not drinking your water? First check if they've been prompted to have some water. If they are being prompted, then explore what's going on with ability and motivation. If they don't drink your water, it's either because they don't have the ability to drink it (check to see if their mouth is taped shut) or because they simply don't want it (maybe they are full or just don't like water and are holding out for fruit juice).

A Security-Related Example: Password Management

Let's turn to a more serious, security-related example. If you want a person to choose a good password, you need to look at three things.

- Does the person have the motivation to choose a good password?
- Does the person have the ability to choose a good password?
- Is the person being prompted to create a good password *at a time that coincides with the person's motivation and ability being at the right levels*?

Table 4.2 shows the Fogg Behavior Model components for this example.

Table 4.2: Understanding the components of the Fogg Behavior Model (security example)

Fogg Behavior Model Component	Description
Behavior (B): What is the specific behavior you're designing for?	Choose a good password.
Motivation (M): What types of things might motivate someone to perform the **B**?	■ They understand and appreciate the value of choosing a good password. ■ They feel empowered by choosing a good password. ■ They feel more secure by choosing a good password. ■ They are afraid that their current password has been (or might be) compromised due to its simplicity. ■ They feel pressure to create a better password because the organization is monitoring password strength. ■ Etc.
Ability (A): What types of things must someone already be able to do or know to successfully perform the **B**?	■ The person has the required knowledge of how to construct a password that is both strong and memorable. ■ The person has tools that will help them construct a password that is both strong and memorable. ■ The person has tools that will choose a strong password and remember that password for them. ■ Etc.

Fogg Behavior Model Component	Description
Prompt (P): What types of things can cue the B?	■ The person just feels like changing their password.
	■ The person receives notification that it is time to change their password.
	■ The person is locked out of their account because they forgot their current password.
	■ The organization issues a forced password reset.
	■ The person receives a security tip that has advice on how to create and remember a good password.
	■ The person forgot their current password and is about to perform a password reset.
	■ The person receives a notification that their account was breached and hackers may have accessed the password.
	■ Etc.

Before I break this down further, it's time to face a hard truth. If the only time you train users on how to create and remember good passwords is during a once-per-year security awareness training, you are wasting your time. It's that simple. For anyone not immediately about to change their password, the information feels irrelevant, and it will soon be forgotten. Any increased motivation or ability they received during the training will decay as time passes.[18,19] So, ask yourself, how many of the users who participate in your annual training are going to change their password on that day? Answer: it's likely a *really, really, really* small number . . . .

MENTAL NOTE: THE DECAY OF KNOWLEDGE

Information and training that is not frequently used is quickly forgotten.

To understand the problem of knowledge decay as it relates to corporate training, the *Wall Street Journal* interviewed Eduardo Salas, a professor of organizational psychology at the University of Central Florida and an expert on the dynamics of corporate training programs. The following exchange should serve as a wake-up call for security leaders:

WSJ: How big of a problem is skills decay?

DR. SALAS: The American Society for Training and Development says that by the time you go back to your job, you've lost 90% of what you've learned in training. You only retain 10%. If you don't use the skills very quickly, you will have big decay very quickly. That's why you need to reinforce, you need to assess. If you learn something and you don't have the opportunity to practice, eventually you are going to lose it.

WSJ: Training sessions often seem like cram sessions, full of information and facts. Are there effective ways to help employees retain all this information?

DR. SALAS: Companies need to teach employees how and where to access facts. If you are inundated with facts and concepts, you will forget 90% of it. What training ought to do is help you get access to that information—databases, manuals, checklists—when you need it on the job. They cannot memorize everything.

The Wall Street Journal[20]

Now, let's look at password management with a Behavior Design lens. Looking at Table 4.2, you can probably already see a few things here that are significant and maybe even a bit troubling. First, there's not much that's compelling in the way of the *motivation* factors. With *motivation*, we might hope that there will be enough intrinsic or extrinsic *motivation* to overcome the difficulty of the task, but sufficient *motivation* is *not* guaranteed. And, creating a password that is both strong and memorable can feel difficult, so, on the *ability* front, there really aren't too many ways to ensure that the person has the *ability* at the time they are *prompted* to do the behavior. So, with the example of password management, there are a lot of things that can break down. There is significant tension between the desired *behavior* and the required *motivation* and *ability*.

What can you do? Don't give up. There are a few behavior-related concepts and tools that we can use in our quest to design for this behavior! Let's quickly take a look at those tools, and then we'll tackle this specific behavior (password management) in the section on designing and debugging behaviors.

The Problem with Motivation

Of all the factors related to getting people to perform specific behaviors, motivation is the most difficult to account for. Motivation is transient; it changes from moment to moment. The difficulties associated with motivation are one of the major reasons for the *knowledge-intention-behavior gap*. People's motivations are fleeting and don't always result in the desired behavior.

If someone has all the information they need and they just don't care, they are unlikely to be motivated enough to perform a desired behavior. And even when someone has the knowledge they need *and they generally do care*, there is no guarantee that they will be motivated enough *at that specific moment* to perform a desired behavior.

The motivation problem is why we see so much effort in the marketing and communications world to focus on influencing the emotions of a target audience. It's all about trying to shape motivation. I discussed many of these marketing and communications tactics in the previous chapter. Now let's take a quick look at a few of the tactics that behavioral scientists leverage. I'm sure that you'll notice quite a bit of bleed over between the two disciplines, and you'll notice these themes pop-up again in Chapter 5 as I discuss culture management.

Nudge Them in the Right Direction

I want to draw a clear line here. The concept that I'm about to discuss is not part of the Fogg Behavior Model, but it can be useful to understand and have at your disposal as you build your program. Let's talk about *nudge theory*. Here's a quick definition[21]:

> *"A nudge, as we will use the term, is any aspect of the choice architecture that alters people's behavior in a predictable way without forbidding any options or significantly changing their economic incentives To count as a mere nudge, the intervention must be easy and cheap to avoid. Nudges are not mandates. Putting fruit at eye level counts as a nudge. Banning junk food does not."*
>
> **Richard H. Thaler and Cass R. Sunstein.** *Nudge: Improving Decisions About Health, Wealth, and Happiness,* **p. 6.**

So, *nudges* use psychological ploys, implemented at the point of behavior, to subtly encourage desired behaviors and can be used to target motivation, ability, or both. While nudges themselves are small, their impact on behavior, and society, can be huge. Because of this, Britain, the United States, and other governments and nongovernment organizations around the world have formed groups (also known as *nudge units*) dedicated to nudging their citizens to make better decisions ranging from making healthier lifestyle choices to saving for retirement to embracing diversity and inclusion in the workplace.[22]

A particularly famous example of nudging comes from what might seem to be an unlikely place: a public men's bathroom.[23] If you've ever been inside a men's room, you may have noticed that the areas under the urinals are usually extremely unsanitary—*scarily* so. Without getting too graphic, there is often a lot of liquid on the floors around the urinals, and that liquid is *not* water. Men heading to the urinal often have to do a risk assessment as they approach.

Urinal designers have been trying to find a solution for problems associated with "splashback" and, well, just poor aim, for decades—everything from funky-shaped urinals, to urinals stretching down to the floor, to floor mats, and more. But, as it turns out, there can be a quick-and-dirty (sorry for the pun) method that goes a long way (sorry, again) toward helping with this. The famous fix for this emerged from Amsterdam's Schiphol Airport in the 1990s. What was it? They etched the image of a fly into the ceramic of the urinals. They gamified urination, and the issues associated with bad aim and splashback were reduced by around 80 percent.

Klaus Reichardt, inventor of the waterless urinal, said the following when discussing the Schiphol Airport urinal nudge: "Guys are simple-minded and love to play with their urine stream, so you put something in the toilet bowl and they'll aim at that. It could be anything. I've seen a golf flag, a bee, a little tree. It just happens that at Schiphol it's a fly."[24] Figure 4.4 shows the fly in action.

Figure 4.5 shows another example of the humble nudge: using nudges to encourage recycling. Have a look at the figure now and see if you can identify the nudging elements before you continue reading.

What nudging elements did you spot in Figure 4.5? Would they work on you?

Figure 4.4: Example of nudge theory: improving bathroom sanitation
https://commons.wikimedia.org/wiki/File:Nudge_Toilet_1.jpg

Figure 4.5: Example of nudge theory: encouraging recycling

What I like about the previous example is that you can see a few different nudge elements simultaneously.

- Yes, this is happening at the point of behavior. Someone is about to discard waste.
- The words being used (*landfill* and *recycle*) describe the ultimate destination for the waste, giving the person a timely reminder as to the end result of their behavior. And I think we can all agree that the word *landfill* carries with it more implied meaning than a descriptor like *trash*.
- The photo below the word *landfill* speaks volumes. A garbage truck is disgorging its contents into a landscape filled with waste. It practically screams, *"This is where your stuff is going! Do you really want to add to all of that waste?"*
- The photo below the word *recycle* is pristine, almost glowing. It shows the types of items that can be recycled, and they are all clean and shiny. So, the person is given a clue as to what can/should be recycled as well as the visual cue that they are making the "clean" decision.

Once you understand the principles behind nudging, you'll notice examples all around you of where organizations and governments are using nudges to try to encourage the behaviors that they find desirable or to discourage behaviors that they find undesirable. You can, and should, be thinking about how nudging can be used as part of your security awareness program.

NOTE You can, and should, be thinking about how nudging can be used as part of your security awareness program.

EVERYBODY CAN NUDGE

Nudges sometimes have a cleverness to them that can be intimidating at first. Certainly, learning about the heuristics and biases that shape our behavior (e.g., endowment effect, loss aversion, status quo bias, etc.) or hiring a behavioral science consultant can improve and accelerate your nudging efforts. But it would be a mistake to create the impression that nudging is only for experts. Much of it is very intuitive. If, for example, you want to encourage collaboration in your team, equip a meeting room with some basic tools that make co-creation easy. This is a nudge, simple, intuitive, effective.

Small Is Beautiful: Using Gentle Nudges to Change Organizations,
Forbes Online[25]

Nudging Toward Better Security: Two Examples

A great security-related example of nudging is the use of password strength meters. While the actual effectiveness of any particular password strength meter lies solely in the algorithm and password creation rules behind the meter (and most are implemented poorly), the nudging aspects should practically jump off the page when you look at Figure 4.6.

Figure 4.6: Password strength meters are a great security example of nudge theory in action.

Another security-related example of nudging can be as simple as putting a reminder poster about secure document disposal over an area in your office that has both a regular trash can and a locked shredding bin nearby. The prompt to do the secure behavior is happening at the point of behavior and serves as a gentle nudge in the direction of security.

Books

- *Inside the Nudge Unit: How Small Changes Can Make a Big Difference* by David Halpern
- *Nudge: Improving Decisions About Health, Wealth, and Happiness* by Richard H. Thaler and Cass R. Sunstein

Web Resources

- *Behavioral Insights Team EAST Framework* (https://www.behavioura-linsights.co.uk/publications/east-four-simple-ways-to-apply-behavioural-insights/)
- *Choice Architecture (Behavioural Economics)* (https://www.tutor2u.net/economics/reference/choice-architecture)
- *Choice Architecture 2.0: How People Interpret and Make Sense of Nudges* by Job Krijnen (http://behavioralscientist.org/choice-archi-tecture-2-0-how-people-interpret-and-make-sense-of-nudges/)
- *Nudges* (https://www.economicshelp.org/blog/glossary/nudges/)
- *Nudging: A Very Short Guide* by Cass R. Sunstein (https://dash.har-vard.edu/handle/1/16205305)

DARK PATTERNS: WEAPONIZED NUDGES

Given the power of nudging, you probably won't be too surprised to learn that there are some unscrupulous people seeking to weaponize nudges and use them against us. These weaponized nudges are called *dark patterns*, and they are generally used to nudge us toward whatever agenda the person or organization leveraging the nudge has as opposed to the good of the person being nudged.

Dark patterns sometimes also take the form of what I'd call *anti-nudges*. In other words, a dark pattern could be used to make something that is good or beneficial for us more difficult to find or harder to achieve. For example, many people struggle to find and decipher the security and privacy settings within many popular social media platforms.

One particularly devious dark pattern gets employed on mobile devices where an advertisement makes it look like there's a speck of dust or a hair on the screen.[26] You try to blow it off to no avail. Then, when you go to wipe it off with your finger, you accidently tap the ad. This has also been done in apps that have subscription options. You go to wipe away the dust or hair and *bam* . . . you've just been billed for the subscription.

From a security awareness standpoint, I think there are a few interesting things to consider about dark patterns. Attackers will use dark patterns to trick your users into performing behaviors that benefit the attacker; that's probably self-evident. But what may not be so self-evident is that you can teach your employees how to detect dark patterns in mobile apps, websites, and other contexts that are not necessarily security related, and then remind them that phishers and other attackers leverage those same types of schemes against them in a security context.

For more information about dark patterns, see the following resources:

- *DarkPatterns.org* (https://darkpatterns.org/)
- *How to Notice and Avoid Dark Patterns Online* by Susie Ochs (https://lifehacker.com/how-to-notice-and-avoid-dark-patterns-online-1827734449)
- *WTF if Dark Pattern Design* by Natasha Lomas (https://techcrunch.com/2018/07/01/wtf-is-dark-pattern-design/)
- *Dark Patterns: inside the interfaces designed to trick you* by Harry Brignull (https://www.theverge.com/2013/8/29/4640308/dark-patterns-inside-the-interfaces-designed-to-trick-you)
- *The Year Dark Patterns Won* by Kelsey Campbell-Dollaghan (https://www.fastcompany.com/3066586/the-year-dark-patterns-won)

Frames: Why Context Is Everything

Here's something interesting, useful, and potentially disturbing. We've all had the experience of "discussing" an issue with someone and feeling like not only do they have an entirely different opinion about the issue than you, but they must live on another planet. You may have even tried to argue with that person, presented them with facts, figures, and anecdotes that "prove" your side of the issue. And it ends with your friend saying something like, "Well, that's all good, but I just don't believe that" or "Let's just agree to disagree."

What's going on here? You've run into the edge of someone's *frame* (aka their worldview) for the issue that you were discussing. Each of us has our own frame that we carry around with us and use to filter and interpret the world around us. That means that our frames have a direct influence on our behaviors because our behaviors and decisions are shaped by our reactions to the world and unfolding circumstances. And we are constantly interpreting the world and unfolding circumstances through the lens of our frames. If that all sounds a bit circular, you're right. In many ways, our frames are self-reinforcing.

Religion, politics, the region of the world and country that someone is raised in,[27] personal history, education, and many other factors play into the frames that people have. Many of the frames we all have are created over long periods of time and are deeply rooted. And frames are so powerful because they operate via System 1 thinking.

Because frames are so deeply rooted, you can't expect people to give them up easily. That's why people argue in circles for hours about politics, religion, climate change, and other topics; these are *worldview* issues. Susan Bales, founder of the FrameWorks Institute (a nonprofit focused on increasing meaningful discourse around important social and scientific topics by helping to *reframe* the discussions), has a quote that is worth taking to heart. Bales says, "When the facts don't fit the frame, the facts get rejected, not the frame."

Some frames can also be constructed extremely quickly; for example, when someone sets the context for a meeting, they've just created a frame, and your mind sets interpretive filters for the conversation accordingly. And when a social engineer dons the disguise of a janitor when skulking about an office environment, the social engineer is exploiting the frame of "janitor"—a person who can pass with near invisibility through most office environments.

So, in everything, our mind evaluates the information presented to it through its own preconstructed frames and the frames built in the contexts of the moment. Figure 4.7 provides some examples of the combinations of preestablished frames working and more moment-by-moment, transient frames.

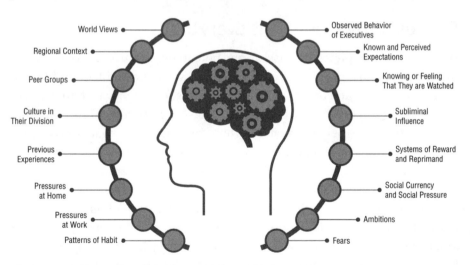

Figure 4.7: Everything is interpreted through context.

NOTE In everything, our mind evaluates the information presented to it through its own preconstructed frames and the frames built in the contexts of the moment.

You may have seen the example of the following psychological word puzzle in which the spaces are removed from between the words within a phrase. Here is the resulting set of letters:

GODISNOWHERE

The idea is that the reader's experience or current *frame* of mind will greatly influence how they segment the phrase. If the reader is a person of faith and is feeling encouraged or positive, then the phrase would be interpreted as, "God is *now here*." If the reader is not a person of faith or is feeling discouraged by events of life, then the interpretation of the phrase would likely be, "God is *nowhere*." See Figure 4.8.

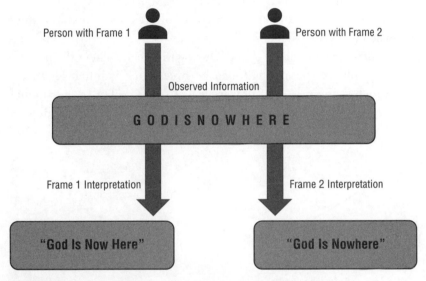

Figure 4.8: Example of frames as interpretive filters

MENTAL NOTE: PRIMING

Here's an example of how immediate context dictates (and can be manipulated to dictate) how your mind interprets what it observes. Have a look at this ambiguous word fragment:

S _ _ P

If we were discussing cleanliness earlier or even if I'd asked you a question about something that you are ashamed about, your mind would be *primed* to think along those lines. And, if I then ask you to suggest letters to complete the word fragment, you'll likely complete it as S<u>OA</u>P.

However, if we'd discussed something like automobiles, roads, traffic, or if you'd recently seen a photo representing those ideas, and I present you the same set of letters (S _ _ P), you'd be more likely to complete the word as S<u>TO</u>P.

You can see that the ideas of framing and priming are similar in that they are both factors that shape thought and behavior based on how the mind interprets context. Want to see how far the idea of priming can be pushed?

I'm sure that you've been in a breakroom before where people pay for their coffee using the honor system, dropping a suggested payment into a collection box. In 2006, researchers at Newcastle University conducted what is now a famous experiment[28] in which they posted a photo of a pair of eyes above an "honesty box." The experiment was conducted over several weeks, and they rotated between a poster of eyes one week, a poster of flowers the next week, then a week with a poster of eyes, and so on. You might be surprised at what they found. During the weeks where the poster of eyes was displayed, people paid nearly three times as much for their drinks than when the poster of flowers was displayed. This experiment demonstrates how even mere cues of being watched can greatly influence human behavior (see Figure 4.9).

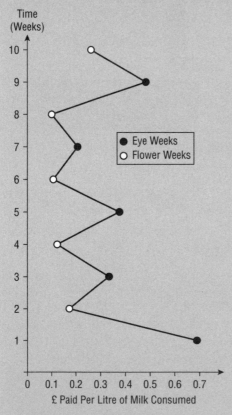

Figure 4.9: The Newcastle University experiment

What—you might ask—does all this framing stuff have to do with security behavior? Well, a lot. You need to be aware that your people walk around with, and view the world through, different frames, and the odds are good that their frames influence the way that they view and interact with your awareness materials and training efforts. This goes back to the idea of theory of mind (ToM) that I raised in Chapter 3. If your awareness messaging and program aren't designed with an understanding of other people's perspectives and frames, then you are setting your program up for trouble.

Now, here's the part that can be encouraging. We can use frames to further our security awareness goals. This is known as *framing*, which is the process of constructing a new frame, and it can be done in a variety of ways. Remember the examples that I gave earlier where someone is setting the context of a meeting or when a social engineer puts on the disguise of a janitor? That's what I am talking about: the ability to setup a new frame using language, visuals, context, or other cues.

Here's a quick example of framing in action[29]:

I give you $50.00 and present you with two options.

- **Option 1:** You keep $20.
- **Option 2:** You lose $30.

Did you feel that tug in your mind as you considered the two options? You probably thought, *I don't want to lose $30!* But I'm sure you've already figured out that both answers are the same. It's simple subtraction: $50 minus $30 equals $20. Either way, you still have $20. But there is more emotion attached with the idea of loss and you can't help but feel the aversion.

Some often-cited framing examples come from the worlds of healthcare and advertising. See these frame pairs for examples:

- **Frame 1 – Medicine:** Treatment A has a 10 percent mortality rate.
- **Frame 2 – Medicine:** Treatment A saves 90 out of 100 lives.

In this medical example, people are naturally drawn to Frame 2 because the phrase "mortality rate" in Frame 1 naturally evokes fear. Frame 2 feels optimistic and conveys more of a sense of safety.

- **Frame 1 – Food Advertising:** 93 percent lean ground beef
- **Frame 2 – Food Advertising:** 7 percent fat ground beef

With this food advertising example, people are drawn to Frame 1 because the term "lean" conveys a sense of health and positivity whereas Frame 2's reporting of "fat" is highlighting the negative.

As you can see, the way you frame your messages will have a great impact on how people perceive the message. This is why you have to be super intentional when it comes to communicating with your employees and your stakeholders. The frame will guide the interpretation and will have a significant impact on motivation. How are people interpreting your messages?

When you are seeking executive support for your security awareness program, you need to be intentional about how you frame your communication. And when you are building campaigns for your employees, you need to be intentional about how you frame your communication. Framing will be a critical part of how you justify, deliver, and report on your security awareness program. You'll revisit the concept of framing your messages in Part 3 of this book.

NOTE Framing will be a critical part of how you justify, deliver, and report on your security awareness program.

For more information on frames and framing, see these resources:

- *FrameWorks Strategic Frame Analysis and free eWorkshop* (https://www.frameworksinstitute.org/sfa-overview.html)
- *The Framing Effect Shows How Simple Word Swaps Can Secretly Trick Your Brain* by Ashley Hamer (https://curiosity.com/topics/the-framing-effect-shows-how-simple-word-swaps-can-secretly-trick-your-brain-curiosity/)
- *Building Cybersecurity Awareness: The need for evidence-based framing strategies* by Hansde Bruijn and Marijn Janssen (https://www.sciencedirect.com/science/article/pii/S0740624X17300540)

MENTAL NOTE: COGNITIVE BIAS

Our minds are a bit quirky. We aren't as rational as we think we are. Rather, our System 1 thinking is easily led astray by heuristics and several of what psychologists and behavioral economists call *cognitive biases*. Framing and *priming* effects, as well as the *mere exposure* effect discussed in Chapter 3, are just a few examples of the over 100 cognitive biases that have been cataloged.

The following are a few other interesting cognitive biases[30]:

- *Confirmation bias*: The tendency to search for, interpret, focus on, and remember information in a way that confirms one's preconceptions.
- *Dunning–Kruger effect*: The tendency for unskilled individuals to overestimate their own ability and the tendency for experts to underestimate their own ability.
- *IKEA effect*: The tendency for people to place a disproportionately high value on objects that they partially assembled themselves, such as furniture from IKEA, regardless of the quality of the end result.
- *Restraint bias*: Overestimating one's ability to show restraint in the face of temptation.
- *Sunk cost fallacy*: The phenomenon where people justify increased investment in a decision, based on the cumulative prior investment, despite new evidence suggesting that the decision was probably wrong. This is also known as Irrational Escalation.

With more than 100 being cataloged, there are more cognitive biases than you can easily remember. However, these biases can be grouped into a few different categories.[31]

- Decision-making and behavioral biases
- Biases in probability and belief
- Social biases
- Memory errors

If it feels like your executive team just doesn't "get it" or your employees continually exhibit viewpoints and priorities that feel alien to you, then you are likely dealing with one or more cognitive biases. And the reality is that these biases exist not only in the person (or people) you are communicating with but you as well.

It's important to acknowledge and account for cognitive biases in everyday life and in our awareness programs. This can also get into some of the struggles that the program manager will have whenever developing a business case.

In your program, consider these two things:

- Some information might be more readily accepted when it plays into an existing cognitive bias within your audience.
- There will be times when you need to find ways to help your audience *debias* (the process of actively working to avoid falling into cognitive biases) so that they can think more clearly about your information

Here are more resources on cognitive bias:

- *Common cognitive biases when assessing risk* (https://res.cloudinary.com/yumyoshojin/image/upload/v1/pdf/risk-culture-2018.pdf)
- *Every Single Cognitive Bias in One Infographic* by Jeff Desjardins (https://www.visualcapitalist.com/every-single-cognitive-bias/)
- *List of Cognitive Biases* (https://en.wikipedia.org/wiki/List_of_cognitive_biases)
- *58 cognitive biases that screw up everything we do* by Gus Lubin and Shana Lebowitz (https://www.businessinsider.com/cognitive-biases-2015-10)

Here is information on debiasing:

- *Cognitive Bias Mitigation* (https://en.wikipedia.org/wiki/Cognitive_bias_mitigation)
- *Debiasing and Corporate Performance* (https://traviswhitecommunications.com/2017/05/23/debiasing-and-corporate-performance/)
- *A Guide to Debiasing: How to Mitigate Cognitive Biases in Yourself and in Others* (https://effectiviology.com/cognitive-debiasing-how-to-debias/)
- *A User's Guide to Debiasing* by Jack B. Soll, Katherine L. Milkman, and John W. Payne (http://www.opim.wharton.upenn.edu/~kmilkman/Soll_et_al_2013.pdf)
- *Outsmart Your Own Biases* by Jack B. Soll, Katherine L. Milkman, and John W. Payne (https://hbr.org/2015/05/outsmart-your-own-biases)

Designing and Debugging Behavior

Now that we've discussed a few methods for upping your odds in areas where the motivation factor will be challenging, let's get back to the Fogg Behavior Model. The goal of this section is to expand your understanding of the model so that you can begin to use it as a tool in your campaign planning. What I really want you to get out of this section is a sense of how easily the model can help you structure your thinking about specific behaviors, how that maps to different target groups in your organization, and how it will force you to be realistic and intentional with your go-forward tactics.

Being Intentional with Target Groups

Remember the discussion of segmentation in Chapter 3? Here's an insight that BJ Fogg shared when I attended his Behavior Design Bootcamp: You can use the Behavior Model as a segmentation framework. Let me explain. In the Fogg Behavior Model (B=MAP), there are four combinations of *motivation* and *ability* that can be present at the time of *prompting*. Table 4.3 lists the cases that can exist and their associated outcomes.

Table 4.3: Outcomes arising from different combinations of motivation and ability within the Fogg Behavior Model

Conditions Existing at the Time of *Prompt*	Outcome
The person has sufficient *motivation* and sufficient *ability*.	When prompted, the person will perform the behavior.
The person has sufficient *motivation* but lacks sufficient *ability*.	When prompted, the person will want to perform the behavior but will be *unable to do so*. This can lead to feelings of frustration, incompetence, disillusionment with the task, etc.
The person lacks *motivation* but has sufficient *ability*.	When prompted, the person has the ability to do the behavior *but doesn't feel like it at the time (doesn't care)*. Repeated prompting will likely lead to aggravation and agitation.
The person *lacks* both motivation and *ability*.	When prompted, the person isn't *able* to perform the behavior and is *apathetic* about it.

As you can see, of the four possible combinations of motivation and ability, there is only one that will result in the person performing the behavior. This can be a hard truth to grapple with. But, if you are focusing on behavior as part of your awareness program, you will need to face this truth and find ways to work within that reality. In essence, your people's thoughts for each condition at the point of prompting are shown in Table 4.4.

Table 4.4: Different combinations of motivation and ability within the Fogg Behavior Model from a target person's perspective

Conditions Existing at the Time of Prompt	Target Person's Perspective
Motivated and able	"Yes, I'll do that now."
Motivated but lacking ability	"I'd be willing to do that, but I can't. Help me."
Unmotivated but able	"I can do that, but I don't feel like it right now."
Unmotivated and lacking ability	"Huh? Oh . . . nope. I can't, and I don't want to."

Account for these different groups and perspectives as you design your campaigns. There is a segment of people who will naturally perform the behavior that you are hoping for. That group will be the easiest to design for. But, what about the other segments? Let's look at each of these cases in the "Debugging Behaviors" section.

Debugging Behaviors

How do you ensure that you have the best chance possible that your people will perform the behavior that you are designing for? The answer is within the Fogg Behavior Model formula. *Behavior* happens when three things converge: *motivation*, *ability*, and a *prompt* to do the *behavior*. So, when you are designing for a behavior, you need to intentionally consider aspects of *motivation*, *ability*, and *prompting*. Similarly, when people aren't performing the desired *behavior*, you need to evaluate aspects of *motivation*, *ability*, and *prompting*.

No Behavior Happens Without a Prompt

Even if someone has sufficient motivation and ability, they won't do the behavior unless prompted. Don't leave prompting to chance; design for it. If people aren't performing the desired behavior, the first question to consider is if they are, in fact, being prompted. If so, are they aware of the prompt? If you've got nonexistent or ineffective prompts, then you may immediately be able to get people who are both motivated and able to do the behavior once you find an effective prompt and prompt them.

What will, or could possibly, prompt for the behavior? Prompts can be any of the following:

- **Intrinsic** (coming from a desire/motivation within the person)
- **Extrinsic from the environment** (signs or other context-based cues)
- **Extrinsic from technology** (email, mobile notification, text message, location-based reminders, and so on)
- **Extrinsic from other people** (for example, a phone call, meeting, in-person visit, group event, or social pressure and expectations)

Since no behavior happens without a prompt, you can't skip this part and hope for the best. Instead, as you are designing for your behavior, go through a process of listing all possible prompts that may cue the desired behavior and decide which prompts can realistically be relied on. In the same way that good marketing and communications campaigns leverage multiple channels, you should design your behavior management campaigns to leverage a multiplicity of prompts across different channels. We will flesh out some specific prompts in greater detail in Part 3 of this book.

DEALING WITH PROMPT FATIGUE

So, here's a problem. People are becoming more and more inundated with prompts every day. There are so many emails, calendar reminders, advertisements, news sources, and app notifications happening at any given time that it is increasingly difficult for any prompt to be effective. And even if a prompt is initially effective, the effectiveness will likely decrease (or become invisible) over time as other prompts clamor for attention. Sadly, your users will soon begin swatting away most prompts in the same way that you swat away calendar appointments, app update requests, security warnings, and all of the other daily pop-ups that compete for attention.

This situation is what we might call *prompt fatigue*. How do you deal with that? I really see only three ways.

- Decrease dependence on any one specific prompt by generating a multiplicity of prompts. Using a variety of types or styles of prompts, especially if they can be delivered via unexpected channels, combined with occasionally using prompts containing embedded encouragement, will make it harder for the person's mind to adjust to the prompt and see it as noise that should be ignored.
- Where possible, transfer external prompts to internal prompts so the person just feels the urge to perform desired behaviors at the right time. This is obviously difficult, if not impossible, for many behaviors.
- Establish the behavior as the cultural norm so that social pressure helps to cue and reinforce the behavior. This takes intentional work but is possible; I'll discuss how in Chapter 5.

Is There Sufficient Ability to Perform the Behavior?

If the person is being prompted and still doesn't do the behavior, in Fogg's Behavior Design you then move to the next step: you focus on ability.

If I asked you to go lift a 300-pound barrel of rocks, you probably wouldn't do the behavior. You probably wouldn't even try. Why? After all, I've prompted you by asking. And you might even have the desire to lift it. But, if you are like most people, you just don't have the ability, and no amount of additional prompting, encouragement, scolding, or expressing my disappointment at your inability to lift heavy objects will help. It would only leave you frustrated at me, the situation, and maybe yourself. That's not helpful.

So, in this example, you lack the *ability* to lift the barrel of rocks. The only way for you to be able to lift the 300-pound barrel is to do one of the following:

- Get stronger
- Use tools to assist with the weight
- Have another person help you lift the weight
- Make the task smaller by letting you remove rocks from the barrel in amounts of weight that you can manage

Isn't it a bit funny that we can all read, understand, and agree that this situation is true and that the listed options are also true, but somehow the security policies, procedures, and awareness programs of most organizations don't account for this reality?

To your end users, most security-related behaviors feel daunting, like the mental equivalent of having to lift a heavy barrel of rocks. Many security leaders ignore this reality and just continue on while hoping that the situation will magically improve (behavior geek fact: The act of ignoring a difficult truth is a cognitive bias known as the *ostrich effect*[32]).

If you want a specific security-related behavior in your organization to improve, you need to tackle the behavior head on. So, what can you do? Here again, the principles of Behavior Design can guide us. Your options are the same as in the earlier barrel of rocks example.

- Train them (strengthen their ability) so that the behavior is no longer difficult, onerous, or scary
- Provide them with tools that assist with the behavior
- Help them accomplish the behavior
- Make the behavior easier or smaller

There's one additional bullet point that I *could* put here if I really wanted to rock your world: *You have the option to do the behavior for them.* That's right. There will be groups of behaviors that, in the end, should be done automatically and without having to bother the end user. If you are relying on your end users to think about encrypting documents, attaching certificates to emails, remembering to enable VPN services, and so on, then it's time to take a good hard look at automating those behaviors. Doing so will free you, and your users, to focus more intently on the groups of behaviors that *can't* be automated.

Security leaders who decide to work within the realities of human nature will do anything within reason to make security-related behaviors easy for their users. You owe it to your users to be realistic about how difficult each security-related behavior is, or can *feel*, to them. For difficult behaviors, evaluate options that will make the behavior easier and less daunting. Doing so will increase the number of people who perform the behavior when prompted.

Is There Sufficient Motivation to Perform the Behavior?

If someone doesn't do a behavior when they are prompted *and* they have the ability, then Behavior Design tells us to move to the next step: you focus on motivation.

Motivation is complex. It changes dramatically from person to person, and from moment to moment within each person. And, as I mentioned earlier in the chapter, motivation is the most difficult element of the equation to solve for. That's why we spent an entire chapter on marketing strategies, working with emotion, storytelling, and other communications tactics. And that's why we tackled topics like nudge theory, framing, and cognitive biases in *this* chapter. And, that's also why methods of working with motivation will become a central theme in Chapter 5. So, while motivation is the most difficult to solve for and motivation can never be guaranteed, I hope that you will be encouraged by the number of tools that you have at your disposal for working with motivation.

From a Behavior Design perspective, your debugging efforts will get a lot more bang for the buck when focusing on the *ability* and *prompt* elements. In many ways, there is a give-and-take relationship at play in how *prompt* and *ability* elements interact with *motivation*. That's because if someone feels like a task is daunting, then they will naturally feel less motivated to tackle the task. But a person may be willing to perform the behavior if they feel like they have the possibility of being successful. Similarly, prompts can be given in ways that are encouraging or discouraging.

Design "Power Prompts" Wherever Possible

Given the interplay between prompting and motivation and the effect that ability and motivation have on each other, there is one last bit of advice that I'd like to give here: design *power prompts* any time you can. Let me explain.

You've probably been the recipient of a *power prompt* before. The way I define it, a *power prompt* is a prompt that the user receives that *also* contains something intended to *increase motivation*, make the behavior *easier*, or *both*. Social media platforms like Facebook and LinkedIn are masters at this. They want you to engage with their platform as directly as possible. So, of course, they send you prompts (in the form of notifications) to try to entice you. And they do this for as many reasons as they can get away with. Someone posts to your timeline: they send a prompt. Someone sends you a direct message: you get a prompt. Someone posts a picture and tags you in it: you get a prompt. There's a news story or other bit of activity that might interest you: (guess what?) you get a prompt.

Now here's the "power" part. The prompt isn't just a notification that tells you about the item. It's packed with power because, in addition to being a prompt, it does two things.

- The prompt *sparks motivation*. Facebook, LinkedIn, Twitter, and others won't send you a full copy of the post or message that they are notifying you about. Remember the *curiosity gap* discussed in Chapter 3? By giving you just enough information to make you curious, the notification creates an itch in your mind just begging to be scratched.
- The prompt makes engaging with the platform *easier* than opening a browser and navigating to the site or deciding to open the app on your mobile device. It does this by embedding a link (or some other clickable bit of content) that you know will take you directly to the post or message.

How are you currently prompting your users? I bet that you can immediately find ways to incorporate a just-in-time motivational boost, a way to make the task easier, or both.

Password Management Example, Continued

Now that we have unpacked the Fogg Behavior Model and seen one way to apply Behavior Design, let's revisit the password management example from earlier in this chapter. As a refresher, Table 4.5 shows how we mapped password management to the Fogg Behavior Model.

Table 4.5: Example of the Fogg Behavior Model applied to password management

Fogg Behavior Model Component	Description
Behavior (B): What is the specific behavior you're designing for?	Choose a good password.
Motivation (M): What types of things might motivate someone to perform the **B**?	■ They understand and appreciate the value of choosing a good password. ■ They feel empowered by choosing a good password. ■ They feel more secure by choosing a good password. ■ They are afraid that their current password has been (or might be) compromised due to its simplicity. ■ They feel pressure to create a better password because the organization is monitoring password strength. ■ Etc.
Ability (A): What types of things must someone already be able to do or know to successfully perform the **B**?	■ The person has the required knowledge of how to construct a password that is both strong and memorable. ■ The person has tools that will help them construct a password that is both strong and memorable. ■ The person has tools that will choose a strong password and remember that password for them. ■ Etc.

Fogg Behavior Model Component	Description
Prompt (P): What types of things can cue the B?	■ The person just feels like changing their password.
	■ The person receives notification that it is time to change their password.
	■ The person is locked-out of his/her account because they forgot their current password.
	■ The organization issues a forced password reset.
	■ The person receives a security tip that has advice on how to create and remember a good password.
	■ The person forgot their current password and is about to perform a password reset.
	■ The person receives a notification that their account was breached and hackers may have accessed the password.
	■ Etc.

Designing for the Behavior

I've discussed some of the issues related to the behaviors associated with password management. Let's flesh them out and work through some of the design and debugging patterns.

You already have plenty of information on how to create and remember good passwords. This isn't a new behavior that you are trying to introduce. So, we don't need to spend time brainstorming or debating the specifics associated with creating and remembering good passwords. But you can learn *a lot* by working through the segmentation/targeting and debugging processes.

Thinking Through Behavior Groups

Remember, as you design for the behavior, you need to think through your approach to four distinct populations (see Figure 4.10).

Group 1: People who have sufficient motivation and sufficient ability

Group 2: People who have sufficient motivation but lack ability

Group 3: People who have low motivation but sufficient ability

Group 4: People who are lacking in both motivation and ability

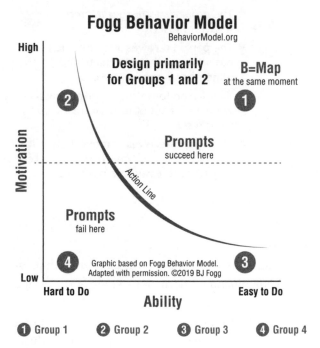

Figure 4.10: Thinking through behavior groups with the Fogg Behavior Model

Group 1: Sufficient Motivation and Sufficient Ability   Group 1 is a no-brainer (though with this behavior, it will likely be a small group). You just need to prompt them, and they will do the behavior. But you need to ensure that your prompts will be received by the group and are effective. So, you still don't want to take prompt design for granted. Use more than one style of prompt across multiple channels, if possible, such as email notifications, intranet banners, desktop popup notifications, etc.

Group 2: Sufficient Motivation, Lacking in Ability Group 2 gets a bit more complicated. You've got people who have sufficient motivation, but they lack the ability to create and remember a good password. This is likely the majority of your organization. They want to do the right thing, but they feel like the process is scary or cumbersome, or they simply don't know how. With this group, your job is to find ways to make creating and remembering a good password easier. And there are only a few ways to do so. Remember the *barrel of rocks* example and how that applies to security? I mentioned four (well, actually five) options.

- Train them (strengthen their ability) so that the behavior is no longer difficult, onerous, or scary
- Provide them with tools that assist with the behavior
- Help them accomplish the behavior
- Make the behavior easier or smaller
- Do the behavior for them

Here's how that would look. I can both train them and help them accomplish the behavior if I place just-in-time training on the password change page. The training would be timely and relevant and thus more easily remembered. This could be a combination of information (how to do it) and training (ways to practice, including real-time feedback). I could also include a just-in-time tool, like a password strength meter to help nudge people into the behavior, while also providing a bit of motivation. Of course, there are ways we might make this even easier, but I'm saving those for our discussion of Group 4.

Group 3: Lack of Motivation, Sufficient Ability Group 3 consists of people who have the requisite ability but lack motivation. We've discussed the inherent difficulties in addressing motivation. Your Group 3 people, in this scenario, are likely pressed for time, have too much on their mind, or just don't feel like they can be bothered. For this group, you should consider tactics such as nudging, creating social expectations, and so on. Your best bet here would be to take a multifaceted approach. Use a combination of nudges and power prompts to increase motivation. The prompt should be positive, be encouraging, and remind them that the behavior is easy. The prompt can also include a link to the password change page that includes all of the nudges and tools that you set up for Group 2. So now, the behavior is easy, fast, and the person feels supported and encouraged. This increases the likelihood that they will engage.

Group 4: Lack of Motivation and Lack of Ability   Group 4 is difficult. They lack motivation and they don't have the ability to perform the behavior even if they did. If you want to get them to perform the behavior, you'll have a lot of work and possible frustration ahead. Your options are to simultaneously dramatically decrease the effort involved in the task, provide training support, and encourage (or threaten) them until they do the behavior. Or, you can go with a combination of two other options by giving them a password manager (like 1Password, Dashlane, KeePass, or LastPass) that can automate the creation of strong passwords and will remember the password on their behalf.

Debugging the Behavior

The debugging cycle for this behavior is exactly as outlined earlier. If your people aren't performing the behavior, walk through each element of the Fogg Behavior Model in reverse. Here are the types of questions to ask:

- Prompt:
    - Are we prompting for the behavior? If not, prompt for the behavior.
    - If so, are the prompts designed effectively?
    - Have the prompts become "invisible" through overuse?
    - Are the prompts occurring through an optimal channel?
    - Can we create a power prompt?
- Ability:
    - Is the behavior still too hard?
    - Is there any way to make the behavior easier? Perhaps through tools, additional training, additional automation, etc.?
    - Is this behavior even something most humans can do consistently?
    - Is there a time that the behavior *feels* easier or more achievable than other times?
    - Can we embed something within the prompt that will reduce the real (or perceived) time, complexity, or effort required to do the behavior?

- **Motivation:**
    - What factors might enhance or erode emotion at the time of behavior?
    - Are their times when someone may feel more naturally motivated to do the behavior?
    - Is there a way to make the behavior feel more meaningful?
    - Are their social, environmental, or other factors that can be leveraged to provide intrinsic or extrinsic motivation?
    - Can we place a motivational boost within the prompt?

Designing for the Larger Issue

With password management, you may have already identified another potential problem that we will face: Our method of designing for this behavior (leveraging the password change page) is limited in scope. The design is sound and illustrates nicely how you can provide information, training, tools, and encouragement all as close to the point of behavior as possible. But here's the problem: This design will work only for passwords in your organization that can be changed via your password change page. There is a larger problem that you need to consider.

Most of your people are trying to juggle nearly 200 passwords across business and personal accounts.[33] This means that even your Group 1 people are only likely to be both motivated and able to exercise good password management within a small subset of their passwords. I'd argue that, when it comes to the *full scope* of password management (managing nearly 200 passwords), most of us would fall into Group 4. The way to design for this case is to provide the tool—a password manager—that will do the hard work and, in addition, provide training and encouragement to create a single, strong yet easy-to-remember password to be used to authenticate to the password manager.

Is suggesting a password manager a cop-out? I don't think so; here's why. The use of a password manager here is working within the realities of human nature. It recognizes the complexity/ability issues inherent with having to securely create and remember dozens or hundreds of passwords. It reduces the behavior to a manageable set of passwords (or even a single password) that must be manually created and remembered by the user. And so, that overall reduction of complexity can enhance the significance/motivation that the user feels when faced with manually creating a password if, for some reason, the user can't use the password manager in that situation.

THINKING ABOUT PEOPLE WHO JUST CAN'T BEHAVE

You'll have questions about what to do with people in Groups 3 and 4 over and over again. These are the people who are not motivated to do the behaviors that you are seeking or are both unable and unmotivated.

Since you are designing for behaviors that are critical to the security of the organization, it's probably difficult to consider that while you might be able to help address issues related to ability, motivation will always be your biggest hurdle. All this begs the question: what should you do with the people who are persistent in their unwillingness and inability to behave?

Most importantly, realize that *can't* and *won't* are two different things. People who can't do the behavior are facing an ability issue; you can focus on making the behavior easier by providing more frequent training, providing tools and help aids, and all the other tactics we discussed.

But, if someone *won't* perform the behavior, that's ultimately a motivation issue. If you can't make the behavior meaningful or use positive motivational methods, you may be forced to use negative pressure (tell them they are just required to do it, or else . . .), use social pressure (the group doesn't fully accept the person's behavior), and so on.

If there are large groups of people consistently in Groups 3 and 4, then you need to take a good hard look at potential problems related to policy expectations, technology choices, training effectiveness, as well as the culture and contexts that the people are operating in.

Habits Make Hard Things Easier to Do

One powerful way to deal with problems related to ability is to, wherever possible, train and reinforce the behavior you want until it becomes a habit. Habits work as heuristics and, because they are automatic, are governed by System 1. The keys to building habits are to make the behavior as small and easy to do as possible and to reinforce in ways that evoke a feeling of success.

A lot of research on habit formation has been done in OR over the past few years. For a good primer in how to leverage habits for yourself or to get some gems that you can transfer to your awareness program, check out the following resources:

■ *Video: Why Tiny Habits Give Big Results* (https://www.youtube.com/watch?v=g56aKi-z05w)

- Cue-action-reward (CAR) model as described in Dalton Combs and Ramsay Brow's eBook, *Digital Behavior Design* (https://docs.boundless.ai/digital-behavioral-design/boundless-mind-digital-behavioral-design.pdf)
- *Hooked: How to Build Habit-Forming Products* by Nir Eyal

MENTAL NOTE: REWARD AND REINFORCEMENT

One of the biggest secrets to habit formation is how the feeling of success makes people want to repeat the behavior. Here's how BJ Fogg describes the effect[34]:

> *When someone feels successful, this is where the magic begins. Very simply, change leads to change, and people will shift their identity in a positive way. A driver who is improving his or her behavior, and feels successful in the changes—even if they're small and incremental—is more likely to accumulate more and more good driving behavior.*

> BJ Fogg. Lytx Inc. Press Release

Additionally, psychologists and behavior scientists have discovered some facets about reward that are both interesting and counterintuitive. Specifically, providing rewards on an unpredictable, variable schedule is more potent than providing a reward every time a behavior is performed, or even every second, fifth, or tenth or any predictable pattern.

Variability of reward derives its power from a release of dopamine in the brain that occurs whenever something pleasant happens to us. When you reward someone for doing something right, dopamine is released, and the person experiences two things: the pleasure of the reward and a craving to find another reward. But this breaks down when the reward is the result of simple cause and effect. Nir Eyal, author of the book *Hooked: How to Build Habit-Forming Products*,[35] describes the process.[36]

Humans . . . crave predictability and struggle to find patterns, even when none exist. Variability is the brain's cognitive nemesis and our minds make deduction of cause and effect a priority over other functions like self-control and moderation.

If you've ever asked someone a question while he or she was engrossed in a video game, only to receive a mumbled "sure, ok, whatever," you've seen this mental state. Players will agree to almost anything to get rid of distraction and keep playing. Variable rewards seem to keep the brain occupied, removing its defenses and providing an opportunity to plant the seeds of new habits.

Bizarrely, we perceive this trance-like state as fun. This is because our brains are wired to search endlessly for the next reward, never satisfied. Recent neuroscience has revealed that our dopamine system works not to provide us with rewards for our efforts, but to keep us searching by inducing a semi-stressful response we call desire.

Nir Eyal, *Variable Rewards: Want to Hook Users? Drive Them Crazy*

Thinking About Guardrails

As I mentioned at the beginning of this chapter, wherever possible, you should consider how you can build "guardrails" around the behavior that you want. What I mean by that is that you are looking for as many ways as possible to channel people into the desired behavior. Where possible, the guardrails should not feel restrictive, forced, heavy-handed, etc. In fact, the ultimate goal to keep in mind when designing these guardrails is for them to not even be consciously noticed.

Building guardrails will require a combination of Behavior Design, nudges, social pressure, environmental factors (context and framing), and the tools and technologies that your people are using. All these things come together at the point of decision and guide behavior.

"One of the big lessons from behavioral economics is that we make decisions as a function of the environment that we're in."

Dan Ariely, Behavioral Economist[37]

Tracking Results and Measuring Effectiveness

I'm going to say something obvious here, but it needs to be said. Some behaviors will be easier to track than others. That's why tracking for click rate on simulated phishing emails is such a popular metric. Not only is phishing the primary way that an attacker will try to exploit your people, but you can also simulate the event and easily track your organization's behavioral preparedness. So, it's both easy to track and highly important to know. But what about other behaviors?

Here is a general framework of how you can approach measuring behaviors:

1. **Define the behavior** that you've designed for and want to track.

2. **Define the overall security-related outcome** that you are associating with the behavior. For example, if you are designing for safer web browsing, an outcome might be "Greater system stability through the reduction of malware infections." For some behaviors, there may be multiple outcomes that you can list.

3. **Pinpoint where the behavior happens**. For example, if you are designing for secure document disposal, then one location where that will happen (or not) will be the shredding bins in your office.

4. **Discover what provides evidence of the behavior**. An example of this would be that the number of pounds of paper per week in shredding bins increases over time as you roll out your behavior management campaign. Or, if you've designed for users to create better passwords, you could intermittently run a password audit tool against your Active Directory servers.

5. Where possible, **track engagement with the prompt**. For behaviors that are prompted with an electronic notification, measure the prompt's effectiveness by tracking the number of instances where your users dismiss or ignore the prompt without taking action, versus the times that they take action.

What about behaviors that are more difficult to track? There are a few ways to get some directional information on these. One well-worn method might be to conduct a survey. However, that is a last resort because you are measuring someone's knowledge or honesty at that point rather than the actual behavior. Usually a few minutes of brainstorming will help uncover a workable method for getting at least a directional indictor for the behavior.

Here's an example. It can be difficult to track the effectiveness of a behavior campaign around tailgating. But you likely have a few methods at your disposal to get at least some information. If your organization uses proximity cards for entry, then you can mine the data from your proximity logs. For employees who have log entries for which the only explanation is that they somehow materialized within the building (i.e., the proximity card was read in an internal door without the person having "badged in" through an external door), then you have a data point. If you don't have the ability to use that method, then you can use a low-tech method like stationing people to surreptitiously monitor doors and simply keep track of the number of tailgating instances they see. If your campaign is effective, then you should see a reduction of tailgating instances over time.

If you find that your behavior management campaign is producing positive results, that's great! It's then time to ask yourself if there are tweaks you can make to your Behavior Design that will produce *even greater* results. And, if your behavior management campaign isn't producing the results you'd hoped for, it's time to go through the debugging process. Remember the Fogg Behavior Model (B=MAP), and use it as a guide for debugging. Are your prompts effective? Is the action easy enough? Where might there be challenges associated with motivation?

Key Takeaways

- *Treat the knowledge-intention-behavior gap as a fundamental law of reality.* When it comes to the human side of security, you must treat the knowledge-intention-behavior gap as a fundamental law of reality that affects any behavior that you hope to encourage or discourage. Your users may have the knowledge they need to make a wise decision, and they may even have the intention to make wise choices, but even the right knowledge and intentions don't naturally translate to their associated and implied behaviors.
- *People aren't as rational as they think they are.* Ninety-five percent of human decisions and behavior is governed by System 1 thinking. Account for heuristic thinking when developing policies, selecting technologies, and designing awareness training campaigns.
- *Where possible, use power prompts.* Up the possibility that your users will do a behavior when prompted by incorporating motivation in the

prompt, embedding something in the prompt to make the behavior easier, or both. The prompt should be positive, be encouraging, and remind them that the behavior is easy.

- *Motivation is the most difficult aspect of behavior to design for.* Motivation is transient. It changes from moment to moment. Nudges, power prompts, framing, and related tactics combined with making the target behavior as easy to do as possible will enhance your likelihood of eliciting the desired behavior.
- *Place tools and training as close to the point of behavior as possible.* Doing so can have the effect of enhancing ability and motivation simultaneously.

Notes and References

1. *Toeing the line: Improving security behavior in the information age* by Joe Mariani, et al. (https://www2.deloitte.com/insights/us/en/focus/behavioral-economics/improving-security-behavior-in-information-age.html)
2. *New Year's Resolution Statistics* (https://www.statisticbrain.com/new-years-resolution-statistics/)
3. *Ibid.*
4. *List of the Most Common Passwords* (https://en.wikipedia.org/wiki/List_of_the_most_common_passwords)5. Tweet from BJ Fogg (https://twitter.com/bjfogg/status/53486588944056321
6. *The Principle of Least Effort: Definition and Examples of Zipf's Law* (https://www.thoughtco.com/principle-of-least-effort-zipfs-law-1691104)
7. *Principle of Least Effort* (https://en.wikipedia.org/wiki/Principle_of_least_effort)
8. *Thinking, Fast and Slow* by Daniel Kahneman
9. https://www.nobelprize.org/prizes/economic-sciences/2002/kahneman/biographical/
10. *Behavioral Economics* (https://en.wikipedia.org/wiki/Behavioral_economics)
11. System 1 and System 2 terminology was first coined by Keith Stanovich and Richard West, and the model is used widely in the field of psychology.
12. This is a version of the Müller-Lyer illusion (https://en.wikipedia.org/wiki/M%C3%percentBCller-Lyer_illusion).

13. Actually, there is also a third and fourth implication. Third: You—as a security awareness leader—are likely to take mental shortcuts when deciding how to structure messages and campaigns. Fourth: Technology professionals take shortcuts during selection and implementation of tools.

14. *The Invisible Gorilla: How Our Intuitions Deceive Us* by Christopher Chabris and Daniel Simons

15. *How We Use Selective Attention to Filter Information and Focus* by Kendra Cherry (https://www.verywellmind.com/what-is-selective-attention-2795022)

16. Many of the insights in the sections referencing the Fogg behavior model come from a combination of me long being a devotee to his work and my participation in BJ's Behavior Design Bootcamp. You can learn more about BJ Fogg by visiting his site (https://www.bjfogg.com/), and you can learn about the Fogg behavior model at http://behaviormodel.org.

17. Quote from Ben Parker in the 2002 movie adaptation of *Spiderman* (https://en.wikiquote.org/wiki/Stan_Lee)

18. *Decay Theory* (https://en.wikipedia.org/wiki/Decay_theory)

19. *Forgetting Curve* (https://en.wikipedia.org/wiki/Forgetting_curve)

20. *So Much Training, So Little to Show for It: An expert on corporate programs reveals why they often are a waste of time and money* by Rachel Emma Silverman (https://www.wsj.com/articles/SB10001424052970204425904578072950518558328).

21. *Nudge: Improving Decisions About Health, Wealth, and Happiness.* by Richard H. Thaler and Cass R. Sunstein

22. *Nudging grows up (and now has a government job)* by Bob Holmes (https://www.knowablemagazine.org/article/society/2018/nudging-grows-and-now-has-government-job)

23. *Have you been nudged?* by Lucy Hooker (https://www.bbc.com/news/business-41549533)

24. *Aiming to Reduce Cleaning Costs* by Blake Evans-Pritchard https://worksthatwork.com/1/urinal-fly)

25. *Small Is Beautiful: Using Gentle Nudges to Change Organizations* by Carsten Tamn. (https://www.forbes.com/sites/carstentams/2018/02/22/small-is-beautiful-using-gentle-nudges-to-change-organizations/#6c03c345a8d0)

26. *Sneaky Mobile Ads and What Marketers Learned* (https://www.spigot.com/sneaky-mobile-ads-and-what-marketers-learned/)

27. In fact, Geert Sofstede, professor emeritus of Organizational Anthropology and International Management at the University of Maastricht, the Netherlands famously refers to the cultures of our upbringing as "The Software of the Mind." You can read more in his book *Cultures and Organizations: Software of the Mind* by Gert Jan Hofstede, and Michael Minkov.
28. *Cues of being watched enhance cooperation in a real-world setting* by Melissa Bateson, Daniel Nettle, and Gilbert Roberts (https://doi.org/10.1098/rsbl.2006.0509)
29. This example appears in *Thinking, Fast and Slow* (p. 365).
30. *List of Cognitive Biases* (https://en.wikipedia.org/wiki/List_of_cognitive_biases)
31. *List of Cognitive Biases* (https://rationalwiki.org/wiki/List_of_cognitive_biases)
32. *The Ostrich Effect: On the Danger of Burying Your Head in the Sand* (https://effectiviology.com/ostrich-effect/)
33. *Password Exposé report* (https://blog.lastpass.com/2017/11/lastpass-reveals-8-truths-about-passwords-in-the-new-password-expose.html/)
34. *Coaching for Success Makes Big Difference in Changing Behavior, Expert BJ Fogg Says* (https://www.prnewswire.com/news-(releases/coaching-for-success-makes-big-difference-in-changing-behavior-expert-bj-fogg-says-300223791.html)
35. *Hooked: How to Build Habit-Forming Products* by Nir Eyal
36. *Variable Rewards: Want to Hook Users? Drive Them Crazy* by Nir Eyal (https://www.nirandfar.com/2012/03/want-to-hook-your-users-drive-them-crazy.html)
37. *Mental depletion complicates financial decisions for the poor* (https://www.pbs.org/newshour/economy/mental-depletion-complicates-financial-decisions-for-the-poor).

Additional Reading

Behavioral Insights Team EAST Framework, https://www.behaviouralin-sights.co.uk/publications/east-four-simple-ways-to-apply-behavioural-insights/.

Hansde Bruijn, Marijn Janssen. *Building Cybersecurity Awareness: The need for evidence-based framing strategies*. Government Information Quarterly

Volume 34, Issue 1, January 2017, pages 1–7, https://www.sciencedirect .com/science/article/pii/S0740624X17300540.

Job Krijnen. *Choice Architecture 2.0: How People Interpret and Make Sense of Nudges*. Behavioral Scientist, http://behavioralscientist.org/ choice-architecture-2-0-how-people-interpret-and-make-sense- of-nudges/.

Harry Brignull. *Dark Patterns: inside the interfaces designed to trick you*. The Verge. Aug 29, 2013, https://www.theverge.com/2013/8/29/4640308/ dark-patterns-inside-the-interfaces-designed-to-trick-you.

Deep Thought: A Cybersecurity Story. Ideas42, http://www.ideas42.org/wp- content/uploads/2016/08/Deep-Thought-A-Cybersecurity-Story.pdf.

Stephen Wendel. *Designing for Behavior Change: Applying Psychology and Behavioral Economics*. (O'Reilly Media, 2013).

Jeff Johnson. *Designing with the Mind in Mind: Simple Guide to Understanding User Interface Design Guidelines*. (Morgan Kaufmann, 2014).

Dalton Combs and Ramsay Brow. *Digital Behavior Design*, https://docs .boundless.ai/digital-behavioral-design/boundless-mind-digital- behavioral-design.pdf.

Steve Krug. *Don't Make Me Think, Revisited: A Common Sense Approach to Web Usability (3rd Edition) (Voices That Matter)*. (New Riders, 2014).

EAST: Four Simple Ways to Apply Behavioural Insights, https://www.behav- iouralinsights.co.uk/publications/east-four-simple-ways-to- apply-behavioural-insights/.

Chris Nodder. *Evil by Design: Interaction Design to Lead Us into Temptation*. (Wiley, 2013).

FrameWorks Strategic Frame Analysis and free eWorkshop, https://www.frame- worksinstitute.org/sfa-overview.html.

Ashley Hamer. *The Framing Effect Shows How Simple Word Swaps Can Secretly Trick Your Brain*. (Curiosity, 2018), https://curiosity.com/topics/ the-framing-effect-shows-how-simple-word-swaps-can-secretly- trick-your-brain-curiosity/.

Steven D. Levett, Stephen J. Dubner. *Freakonomics: A Rogue Economist Explores the Hidden Side of Everything*. (William Morrow Paperbacks, 2009).

Steve Dale. *Heuristics and Biases – The Science of Decision Making*. Communities and Collaboration, http://www.stephendale.com/2018/07/29/ heuristics-and-biases-the-science-of-decision-making/.

Nir Eyal. *Hooked: How to Build Habit-Forming Products*. (Portfolio, 2014).

David Halpern. *Inside the Nudge Unit: How Small Changes Can Make a Big Difference*. (Ebury Press, 2015).

An Introduction to Behavioral Economics. BehavioralEconomics.com, https://www.behavioraleconomics.com/resources/introduction-behavioral-economics/.

Christopher Chabris, Daniel Simons. *The Invisible Gorilla: How Our Intuitions Deceive Us.* (Harmony, 2011).

Nudge: Improving Decisions About Health, Wealth, and Happiness. Richard H. Thaler and Cass R. Sunstein (Penguin Books, 2009).

Nudges. Economics Help Blog, https://www.economicshelp.org/blog/glossary/nudges/.

Cass R. Sunstein. *Nudging: A Very Short Guide.* Harvard University's DASH repository 37 J. Consumer Pol'y 583 (2014). https://dash.harvard.edu/handle/1/16205305.

Oh, Behave! What Information Security Can Learn From Behavioural Economics. Tripwire, https://www.tripwire.com/state-of-security/security-awareness/oh-behave-what-information-security-can-learn-from-behavioural-economics/.

Dan Ariely. *Predictably Irrational, Revised and Expanded Edition: The Hidden Forces That Shape Our Decisions.* (Harper Perennial, 2010).

Stu Sjouwerman. The Seven Deadly Social Engineering Vices Updated. KnowBe4 Blog, https://blog.knowbe4.com/the-seven-deadly-social-engineering-vices-updated.

Daniel Kahneman. *Thinking, Fast and Slow.* (Farrar, Straus and Giroux, 2013).

BJ Fogg, Doug Abrams. *Tiny Habits: The Small Changes that Change Everything.* (Eamon Dolan/Houghton Mifflin Harcourt, 2020).

Kelsey Campbell-Dollaghan. *The Year Dark Patterns Won.* Fast Company. December 21, 2016. https://www.fastcompany.com/3066586/the year-dark-patterns-won.

5

Culture Management 101 for Security Awareness Leaders

The importance of a strong cybersecurity culture cannot be understated. It transcends technologies, processes, and even people. It is bigger than security awareness. Security culture becomes ingrained everywhere you look and touch. It is aligned with the objectives of the business. Everybody doesn't just practice security, they also own it.

Dan Kaplan, Trustwave[1]

It's flashback time. Early in the previous chapter, I used a quote from BJ Fogg stating that, "Humans are lazy, social, and creatures of habit." Throughout that chapter, and in previous chapters, I've referenced the social components of belief and behavior. Here is where the rubber really meets the road: *culture*. A positive security culture is a force multiplier for behaviors, beliefs, and messages; it represents a critical social component that will either work for you or work against you. And the ability to shape the security-related aspects of your organization's culture represents the pinnacle of our journey into transformational security awareness.

NOTE   A security culture lives and breathes within *every* organization. The question is how strong, intentional, and sustainable is your security culture, and what do you need to do about it?[2]

MENTAL NOTE: THINKING ABOUT THE SEMANTICS OF CULTURE

Here's an interesting question posed by consultant, podcast host, and author, Bruce Hallas. Bruce asks, "Are we looking for a security culture; or are we looking for an organizational culture that values security?"[3]

This question is brilliant because it teases out an important subtlety: The way we think about these phrases can take us toward different goals and can evoke different emotional responses. For some, the phrase *security culture* can sound staunch, restrictive, and militaristic; and for some organizations, such as banks, security tech companies, and military divisions, this may work fine. But, for other types of organizations, the phrase *security culture* may feel like it implies a security for the sake of security approach.

There is often also a fundamental gap between IT and security (collectively) and the rest of the organization. In many organizations, the security team is physically located in lower-class/visibility areas (such as lower levels of a building, the basement, least glamourous offices, and so on). There is the expectation from the C-suite that this stuff just works, but there's limited interaction and no "seat at the table." It is literally and figuratively a different world that creates a culture of disconnect: *us versus them*.

When you say that you want an "organizational culture that values security," there is a different *feel*. This phrase subtly conveys that the organization understands and appreciates the value that security brings, that security supports the organization's goals, and vice versa. This approach (or even just using the phrase "organizational culture that values security"), in many organizations, may gain acceptance more readily.

Could it be that both phrases mean the same thing? Absolutely. And I imply both interpretations when I use the phrase "security culture." But the important thing that I take from Bruce's question is that there is definitely a different interpretive *feel* to each phrase. That *feel* links to a mental *frame* that may either aid or impede your efforts.

Awareness and behavior don't happen in a vacuum; they are impacted by all the other "stuff" happening in and around your people's lives. Culture can be either your biggest ally or your biggest foe. All the great work you do with messaging and behavior can be degraded or undone if the overall culture of your organization isn't reinforcing your values or, even worse, if the organizational culture runs contrary to the values you are hoping to foster. As the Peter Drucker saying goes, "Culture eats strategy for breakfast."[4]

All the great work you do with messaging and behavior can be degraded or undone if the overall culture of your organization isn't reinforcing your values or, even worse, if the organizational culture runs contrary to the values you are hoping to foster.

DEFINING *CULTURE*

Here is a thought-provoking description of culture from Human Synergistics International, a consultancy focused on helping organizations build healthy and sustainable cultures. They define culture as follows:

the shared norms and expectations that govern the way people approach their work and interact with each other. Such norms and expectations shape how organizational members believe they are expected to behave in order to fit in, get things done, and at times simply survive.

Human Synergistics International[5]

Culture is the codification of the beliefs, behaviors, and values of a particular people group. So, in a security context, your security culture is the codification of the *security-related* beliefs, behaviors, and values of your organization and each subgroup within your organization (such as divisions, departments, regions, age groups, and so on). The power of culture lies in the fact that humans are social creatures. Group behaviors, beliefs, and values become self-reinforcing. The group establishes a *social norm* that is strengthened by expectations, pressures, and rewards. And people within the group identify with the different artifacts that make up the culture. A healthy security culture exists when your organization's security-related beliefs, behaviors, and values have been codified *into social expectations*.

NOTE   The power of culture lies in the fact that humans are social creatures.

Ideally by now you've noticed a theme to this book: that we owe it to our people and our organizations to look at security through a very human lens.

That's what culture management requires. If you want to shape the security aspects of your organization's culture, you'll need to become an anthropologist or sociologist of sorts. You'll need to understand the people and their current customs, behaviors, beliefs, drivers, and more. And you'll need to understand and appreciate *why* your people currently do *what* they do and what emotions or issues may arise as you work to influence their security behaviors. Will they feel that something is hard, scary, challenging, or (just maybe) exciting? And, probably the most important factor in culture management is that you need to genuinely care about your people and see them as humans, not as objects to be "fixed."

Managing your security culture requires an approach that works with the realities of human nature and social dynamics. Your efforts to shape culture should be adaptive and multilayered to proactively engage, influence, and manage the mind-set and behaviors exhibited by the various population groups within your organization. This is done by weaving together elements of innovative training; the active use of psychological, behavioral, and social triggers; and technology-based guard rails for when users step out of bounds. When done effectively, your culture-shaping efforts become a force multiplier for the influence of your security team by helping to embed security values and behaviors throughout your organization.

I've heard many security leaders mention that the topic of culture seems a bit amorphous, and they don't know where to begin. My goal here is to help make these concepts much more concrete for you. We've got a whole chapter to dive into the drivers that shape culture. Let's do that now.

Security Culture Is Part of Your Larger Organizational Culture

One of the biggest traps security leaders fall into is believing—*or hoping*—that by simply focusing on the right things, the organization will naturally begin to shift toward a more security-focused mind-set. Unfortunately, that's not true. The larger organizational culture can move with the force of a hurricane and easily overshadows and overpowers security-related cultural elements unless those security-related elements are woven into the larger culture.

NINE OUT OF TEN ENTERPRISES REPORT GAPS BETWEEN THE
SECURITY CULTURE THEY HAVE AND THE ONE THEY WANT

*Only 5 percent of organizations today believe that no gap exists bet-
ween their current and desired cybersecurity culture. A full third see
a significant gap. These firms have yet to experience how a strong
cybersecurity culture will impact operations or create brand loyalty
and a competitive advantage. While many organizations recognize
that gap, they don't know which practices or programs to institute—
and they generally lack a cohesive management plan.*

2018 ISACA/CMMI Institute Cybersecurity Culture Report[6]

Weaving security-related elements into your organizational culture can be
a challenge. People do the things they do and possess the values they possess
for specific reasons. Their beliefs and behaviors have been shaped by the environment around them. And the overall culture of your organization tends to
be self-referencing, self-reinforcing, and self-protecting. The influence that
most security teams can bring to bear is often dwarfed by the sheer size of the
rest of the organization. Let's suppose Figure 5.1 represents the size of your
security team in relation to the overall size of your organization.

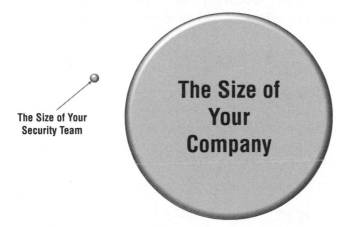

Figure 5.1: Security teams face issues of scale and gravitational influence.

When you see it in perspective, it becomes clear why influencing the entirety of your organization is so difficult. You face issues related to scale and gravitational influence. In short, it's difficult for a small object to affect the direction of a much larger object. Figure 5.2 sets our challenge before us.

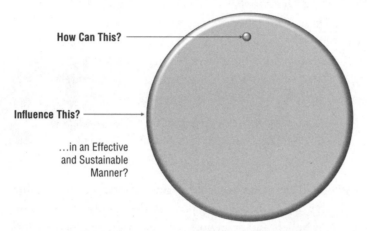

How Can This?

Influence This?

…in an Effective and Sustainable Manner?

Figure 5.2: Security teams need a force multiplier.

If you are continually frustrated because your employees "just don't get it" despite the training you provide, then you are likely facing a culture challenge and need a force multiplier. And, if you've spent years developing your workforce to exhibit a certain security-related behavior but then lost ground, it is likely that you face a culture issue and need a force multiplier.

WHY SHIFTING CULTURE CAN BE DIFFICULT

Bruce Hallas (mentioned in the introduction of this chapter) is the founder and chief strategist at Marmalade Box, a UK-based security consultancy that focuses on helping organizations manage human factor risk through awareness and behavior management programs, culture shaping, and staff training. I love how Bruce describes this issue in his book, *Rethinking the Human Factor: A Philosophical Approach to Information Security Awareness Behaviour and Culture.*[7]

> *In systems there is an innate tendency always to move towards equilibrium. When equilibrium is lost, the system tries to restore it using feedback loops. In biology this regulating process is called*

> *homeostasis. If the same applies in large organizations, any rapid change will conjure up counteracting forces. The bigger the change, the bigger the counteracting force. This creates a no-win situation.*
>
> For every action, there is an equal and opposite reaction.
>
> *Newton's Third Law*
>
> *If this is the case, rather than fighting the status quo, maybe we should accept it and instead find ways to lever it to our advantage. If we know how our end users think and behave, we can find ways to influence them to do what is right without resentment, coercion, bullying, or bribery.*
>
> *While not completely dismissing the idea of pursuing a specific infosec culture, I would suggest that rather than trying to impose infosec values on an existing cultural model, recognizing disparate culture values and working with them, would be a more effective option. Of course, we can only do that when we clearly understand what those cultural values are in the first place.*
>
> Bruce Hallas. Rethinking the Human Factor: A Philosophical Approach to Information Security Awareness Behaviour and Culture. *pp. 46-47.*

The challenge before you is to find ways for your security team (which is likely dwarfed by the size of your larger organization) to influence the entire organization—and to do so in an *effective* and *sustainable* manner.[8] This goes far beyond what you can hope to accomplish by simply rolling out a traditional information-based security awareness campaign and hoping for the best. This requires the thoughtful use of all the strategies I discussed in Chapters 3 and 4, combined with a few other bits of magic.

Getting Started

There has been a great deal of work done to try to understand the factors that shape culture within an organization. However, most of that work is focused around initiatives that a CEO or board of directors is driving, is related to issues around mergers and acquisitions, or is focused on large-scale organization-wide culture change initiatives to foster a new culture of innovation so that the organization doesn't lose significance or competitive edge in a rapidly evolving digital economy.

NOTE If you are struggling with executive buy-in, try explicitly mapping your security goals and values to the organization's goals and values.

While studies like those that I just mentioned do have some use, they address a slightly different situation than most security leaders are in; namely, they presuppose a top-down culture shaping initiative with full buy-in from the most important levels of leadership. The difference that most security leaders face is that the security team is seeking to influence the culture from the middle out. They need to get senior management buy-in for values and practices that may not immediately or easily be seen to map to other organizational goals. And they need to win the hearts and minds (and behaviors) of people at every level of the organization and across divisions, departments, and regions for which the security team may have little perceived authority or relevance.

While most books on organizational change management won't offer a ready-to-use road map for your security culture shaping journey, they still offer some interesting principles and considerations. One book I particularly like is *CULTURE RULES! The 10 Core Principles of Corporate Culture and How to Use Them to Create Greater Business Success* by management consultant John R. Childress. In the book, Childress outlines 10 core principles of corporate culture. They are as follows[9]:

Principle 1: Every organization has a culture.

Principle 2: Culture impacts performance.

Principle 3: Culture can be a significant business risk.

Principle 4: Culture works on human logic, not business logic.

Principle 5: Organizations are shadows of their leaders.

Principle 6: Cultural drift.

Principle 7: Policies drive culture (more than we realize).

Principle 8: You get the culture you ignore.

Principle 9: There is no perfect corporate culture.

Principle 10: Leaders and employees change cultures, not consultants.

You can probably already see the applicability of many of these principles to security culture. I don't want to get too far off the main topic of security culture, so I'm not going to do a deep-dive into each principle. But, if you are wanting more after seeing that list, then pick up a copy of his book. It will be worth your time.

Another book that I believe you may find relevant is Hilary Scarlett's, *Neuroscience of Organizational Change: An evidence-based practical guide to managing change.*[10] In this book, Scarlett outlines several facets that are relevant to organizational change that are also relevant to any type of large-scale organization-wide initiative. She discusses why we have mental resistance to change, the impact of social factors, how we are driven by emotion, cognitive biases, communication, storytelling, and how to plan organizational changes in ways that work with human nature rather than against. These are all core messages already contained within *Transformational Security Awareness*, but it is interesting to see the additional details that she teases out and applies.

Want to take a deeper-dive into the world of organizational culture? Use these resources as a jumping-off point:

- *Culture by Design: 8 simple steps to drive better individual and organizational performance* by David J. Friedman
- *CULTURE RULES! The 10 Core Principles of Corporate Culture and How to Use Them to Create Greater Business Success* by John R. Childress
- Netflix's original culture overview slide deck (`https://www.slideshare.net/reed2001/culture-1798664`)
- *Neuroscience of Organizational Change: An evidence-based practical guide to managing change* by Hilary Scarlett
- *A Perspective on Organizational Culture* (`https://www.strategyand.pwc.com/media/file/Strategyand-Perspective-on-Organizational-Culture.pdf`)
- *Six Components of a Great Corporate Culture* by John Colman (`https://hbr.org/2013/05/six-components-of-culture`)

Understanding Your Culture's Status Quo

The first part of influencing your security culture is assessing and understanding the culture as it currently exists. This can be accomplished via cultural surveys, focus groups, direct observation, behavioral metrics, face-to-face interviews, or any other format at your disposal.

CHOOSING YOUR DATA COLLECTION METHODS

Throughout this section, you'll notice that I use the term *survey* almost exclusively. I'm doing that mostly for clarity of writing. You should be using multiple methods to collect data whenever possible. Here are my quick thoughts on some of the different data collection methods you can use.

- **Computer-based surveys:** Computer-based surveys are prevalent because they are easy. They are generally easy to develop, easy to distribute, and allow for ease in analyzing the collected data. They can also allow for anonymous or nonanonymous completion. In short, computer-based surveys scale well. The only downsides to them are that they don't communicate empathy, you can't gauge body language and tone, and many people receive so many surveys that they can feel like added noise. In my opinion, these downsides don't overshadow the immense usefulness of computer-based surveys, but you do want to keep the downsides in mind and consider adding at least one other format whenever possible. Doing so will give you a more rounded and well-informed study.

- **Focus groups:** Group discussions are valuable because you can hear people speak about security in their own words and provide group feedback in a safe environment. You also get the advantage of seeing body language as people answer questions or discuss different topics. Questions should be open-ended, and your facilitator is there primarily as an observer, not to judge or argue with people! A focus group that turns into a judgment or correction session will only breed distrust, so choose your facilitator wisely.

- **Direct observation and metrics:** You take note of what you see physically and what behavioral data is available via the tools that your organization has deployed such as, security information and event management (SIEM), data leak prevention (DLP), endpoint protection platforms (EPP), web proxies, employee monitoring systems, and so on. These behavioral metrics are good because they show you *what* is happening, but keep in mind that they lack the ability to tell you *why* the behaviors occur.

- **Face-to-face interviews:** If possible, plan to conduct face-to-face interviews with members of the executive team. Ensure that the executive knows that both their time and opinions are valued; again, don't allow these sessions to turn into an argument. Use an objective, neutral facilitator to increase chances that the executive feels comfortable answering fully. Using a neutral facilitator also keeps you (or a member of your team) out of the awkward position of feeling defensive and potentially sabotaging your long-term relationship with the respondent.

The goal is to find reliable ways to measure the security-related aspects of your culture, such as knowledge, attitudes, perceptions, and more. But be aware that responses to your surveys will also likely be influenced by multiple factors, so it is important to build in controls to help you maximize the overall reliability of the results. For instance, because people behave differently when they know they are being watched (remember the honesty box example from Chapter 4?), surveys that are anonymous or observations when the subjects don't know that they are being observed may be more true to reality.

Because of this, survey participants who are not answering questions under the cover of anonymity may provide answers they believe the surveyors hope to hear; in the same way, employees who know they are being observed will generally behave in ways they believe are acceptable and expected. This means that an organization may value anonymous surveys in hopes that the subjects will provide more honest feedback. But they might also value nonanonymous surveys because they will likely be able to collect the answers that employees believe are correct to the given question or situation. Each of these inputs are valuable. And it is uber important for you to stress to your respondents that you value their open and honest feedback.[11]

MENTAL NOTE: THE PSYCHOLOGY OF ANONYMITY

While I personally believe that there is value in conducting both anonymous and nonanonymous surveys as outlined earlier, there is a growing amount of research[12,13,14] calling into question the validity of anonymous feedback. Specifically, anonymous surveys fail at fostering an individualized feedback loop. Additionally, participants who are completing a survey anonymously may see it as a checkbox type of activity and be lazy (such as just giving the same answer to all questions) in their responses, leading to inaccurate data. At the other end of the spectrum is the person who completes the anonymous survey in a way that allows them to vent strong emotions, again, potentially creating a skewed result.

A 2016 article in the *Harvard Business Review* by James R. Detert and Ethan R. Burris outlines three additional potential problems with anonymous surveys. Here's how they describe the issues:

The promise of anonymity is a common way to encourage frank input. Suggestion boxes, whistle-blowing hotlines, ombudspeople, 360-degree assessments, and satisfaction surveys all serve this purpose. Here's the logic: If no one knows who said what, no repercussions will follow, so people can be forthright about any topic.

This line of reasoning has three flaws.

First, allowing employees to remain unidentified actually underscores the risks of speaking up—and reinforces people's fears. The subtext is "It's not safe to share your views openly in this organization. So we've created other channels to get the information we need."

Second, anonymity can set off a witch hunt. That was a theme at one Fortune 500 company we studied. When employees provided negative feedback through hotlines, suggestion boxes, and such, some bosses demanded to know "Who said this?!" People in other organizations had similar experiences. Many told us that they go to libraries and coffee shops and use public computers to complete online employee surveys—because they worry they'll be tracked through their IP addresses otherwise. One man said he wouldn't even report a problem to an ombudsperson. When asked why, he countered, "Who pays his salary?"

Third and perhaps most important, it can be difficult to address issues while protecting the identity of the people who raised them. Reporting in a survey that a manager acts abusively, incompetently, or in racist or sexist ways won't do any good unless HR or an ombudsperson can assess the extent of the problem, explore the causes, and develop recommendations. That means interviews need to be conducted, stories corroborated, and additional data collected—all of which involve talking to the person who has accused the manager of wrongdoing. And if a complaint refers to a specific incident, it's often quite clear to the manager which person filed it.

"Can Your Employees Really Speak Freely?" by James R. Detert and Ethan R. Burris

Even with these potential issues, my personal feeling is that you should use a blend of anonymous and nonanonymous surveys. Why? The differences in how employees answer the questions between the two formats may be enlightening.

There are a few things to keep in mind as you develop your culture surveys. First, if permissible in your organization and region, be sure to collect sociographic/demographic data points (age range, gender, location, department, length of employment, etc.); this is so you can identify any culture strengths and gaps across multiple dimensions. For instance, it's one thing to know that 83 percent of the organization knows how to report a suspected security incident. But it's another thing entirely to be able to also say that only 12 percent of people in your customer service department know how to report a suspected incident. The first (organization-wide) metric might give you a false sense of comfort. But knowing that 88 percent of your people in customer service have no clue how to report an incident will immediately pinpoint that there is a disconnect between the culture in customer service and the broader organizational culture.

Now, think about taking it a step further: being able to compare departments against each other or having breakouts of multiple sociographic/demographic factors in a single department. For example, because you have granular sociographic/demographic data, you may uncover that people in IT who have been with your organization less than two years exhibit one attitude versus people in IT who have been with your organization longer than a year. Having the ability to slice and dice data based on sociographic/demographic dimensions is a recognition that your organizational culture is a collection of subcultures, each with different tendencies, needs, communication preferences, and pre-established value norms.

SOCIOGRAPHIC/DEMOGRAPHIC DATA IS A KEY TO TARGETED AND RELEVANT SEGMENTATION

If you remember back to Chapter 3, you may already be thinking about the concept of *segmentation*. That's absolutely where I am going with this. Having sociographic/demographic data enables you to create specific messages and campaign elements that you can direct to each segment. This is a key method for determining and ensuring that you are focusing your efforts smartly and in relevant ways.

Here are a few other points to consider:

■ Don't just try to collect data on what your people know; also seek to collect data on their attitudes, preferences, and opinions.

- Consider questions that evaluate which departments people within the organization believe exhibit the most and least secure behaviors, versus the group that the respondent represents.
- If you are asking people about threats, also assess if they know *why* it is a threat. In other words, can they associate the *threat* with a business or personal *risk/outcome*.
- Build your survey so that you have a chance to identify gaps in what your people say that they know and what they can truly demonstrate knowing.
- Pay careful attention to the survey results from each executive team member. Your findings will likely uncover that there are disconnects between how some of your executives view security-related risk, accomplishments, attitudes, and priorities. For instance, if your findings reveal that there is a critical disconnect between how your CISO and your CRO view risk, there is obviously a discussion to be had! Whenever you uncover disconnects, it is a chance to foster dialogue, evaluate the terminology used between departments, and have serious discussions that will help determine alignment and priorities.

RESOURCES FOR SECURITY CULTURE SURVEYS

Creating and administering a security culture survey can seem like a daunting task. Luckily, there are some great resources to help you get started. You may choose to fully adopt one of these or simply to use these as a model for something that you create specifically for your organization.

Here are a few to get you started:

- Lance Hayden's fantastic book, *People Centric Security: Transforming Your Enterprise Security Culture*, has two surveys that are available for use via Creative Commons licensing. You can review and download them from Lance's website at `http://lancehayden.net/culture/`.
- SurveyMonkey's security team used Lance Hayden's FORCE survey as the basis for an internal survey that they distributed in their organization. In the spirit of sharing, they've made the survey template available at `https://www.surveymonkey.com/curiosity/`

building-a-security-culture-starts-with-measuring/ and at https://www.surveymonkey.com/ create/?templateId=1613.

■ MIT's Sloan (CAMS) Research Consortium also created a study to measure elements of security culture. The survey was created to measure multiple organizations, but most questions would work extremely well for employees within a single organization. You'll have to walk through the study yourself to see the questions, but the survey is instructive. See https://community.isc2.org/t5/ISC-Updates/Building-a-Culture-of-Cybersecurity-Have-Your-Voice-Heard/ba-p/13148.

■ Kai Roar is a well-known expert in the world of security culture, and he publishes a yearly *Security Culture Report* that is worth your time. You can find it at https://get.clt.re. While the survey questions are not publicly available, you should take note of the dimensions that are used for reporting findings. They are as follows: attitudes, behaviors, cognition, communication, compliance, norms, and responsibilities. If you are designing your questions to fit into these categories, you'll be in good company.

■ The NorSIS *Norwegian Cybersecurity Culture Report* is an in-depth report on the prevailing cybersecurity attitudes and behaviors of Norwegian citizens. The report is compelling even if you aren't from Norway or interested in Norwegian cybersecurity culture. The data visualizations are beautiful, and the report authors included their full list of survey questions in Appendix B. See https://norsis.no/wp-content/uploads/2016/09/The-Norwegian-Cybersecurity-culture-web.pdf.

After your organization has a good idea of its current cultural norms,[15] you can begin planning your strategy for shaping and reinforcing behavior. This is where all of your messaging, campaign design, audience segmentation, and behavior management tactics come into play. And it is also important to put in social support structures; that involves making sure that people and groups of people distributed throughout the organization are all working in concert to influence behavior and culture.

Go Viral: Unleash the Power of Culture Carriers

I'd like to introduce a term that you may or may not already be familiar with: *enculturation*. Have a look at the following definitions.

> **enculturation:**
>
> 1: *the process whereby individuals learn their group's culture, through experience, observation, and instruction.*
>
> > Dictionary.com (*https://www.dictionary.com/browse/ enculturation*)

And I love the nuances that the Oxford dictionary adds to this idea:

> 1: *The gradual acquisition of the characteristics and norms of a culture or group by a person, another culture, etc.*
>
> > Oxford Dictionary (*https://en.oxforddictionaries.com/ definition/inculturation*)

Here's where I'm going with this. We have a few different cultural forces that we need to consider. We have an enculturating force from the larger organization that is influencing each person within the organization. And we have the enculturating force of your security program that is seeking to influence both the larger organization and the individuals within it. In other words, you have two targets: to influence the larger organizational culture and to influence the people within the culture. To do that effectively, you'll have to work *on* the culture and *in* the culture simultaneously: a top-down, middle-out, and bottom-up strategy all at the same time. You need to find ways to go viral.

I've mentioned the need to have a force multiplier a few times now; it's some way to better distribute and reinforce the security-related values and behaviors that you are hoping to build into your culture. For that, I'd like to introduce the concept of *culture carriers*. But first, let me give you a quick analogy that I'm sure you can relate to.

SURROUND SOUND: A CULTURE ANALOGY

Think about a stereo system. A stereo is relatively simple. It directs sound toward you from the front. There is separation in the left and right channels that can make things interesting and introduce distinction and clarity when needed. But it is all just coming from the front. A stereo is like working from the top-down in an organization.

With simple stereo, you can feel like sound (the message/content) is just coming *at* you. But, once you add additional components of a surround sound system, you get a richer experience. If you've ever listened to a great surround sound system, it doesn't just feel like the sound is coming at you; it can feel like you are immersed, like you are part of the environment.

Think of your culture carriers as surround sound speakers. When they are in place, your security messages aren't just emanating from the stereo speakers (from the security team or corporate leadership); your messages, values, and behaviors are now being reinforced from multiple points all around your people, creating an immersive experience that draws them in.

Traditional information-based security awareness programs are like a simple stereo blasting your audience from the front. A *transformational* security awareness program is more like a surround sound system. It is immersive by design.

What is your force multiplier? It's all the other people, groups, and social structures of your organization. They are your critical distribution network and the key to promoting the culture's overall sustainability. Here's the truth: your security team cannot actually control culture; rather, they can play a part in influencing the culture, helping to set the tone, and providing resources and support. But, because the core security team (your dedicated security FTEs) is only a fraction of the overall employee population, they need help in both carrying your message and amplifying your message.

One way of working to increase the influence of security values is by leveraging *culture carriers*. Within an organizational context, a culture carrier is "someone who has intimate knowledge of the company values and can have an intelligent discussion about why their company does what it does. They are ambassadors for their company and passionately work to promote the company values in their day to day dealings with clients and coworkers."[16]

Think for a moment about how the idea of a culture carrier might work within a security context. Imagine having groups of people across regions, across departments, and at all levels of your organization who have intimate knowledge of your security values and who model positive security behaviors; they can discuss why these values and behaviors are relevant and important. Imagine the power and influence that they would bring as they work to promote your values in their day-to-day work—as they interact with other people; as they initiate, comment on, and support projects; as they mentor new hires; and as they help other employees around them. This group of culture carriers becomes an enculturating force for other employees and the larger organization. Figure 5.3 illustrates how a network of culture carriers distributes your messages, values, and beliefs across the organization.

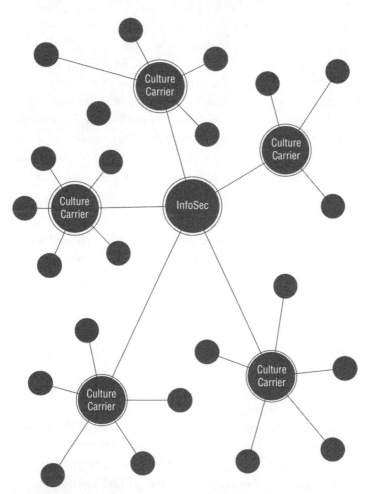

Figure 5.3: Visualization of how culture carriers are viral in nature

By distributing culture in this manner, your program is building a critical framework (or skeletal structure) for sustainability. The distributed nature of your culture carriers allows security content and values to reach various departments and regions of the company and with the ability to provide personal, local, and contextualized representation. How you engage your system of culture carriers, who you choose, and the methods used to acknowledge their value and support are all factors creating sustainability.

LANCE SPITZNER ON THE POWER OF CULTURE CARRIERS

Lance Spitzner, director of SANS Security Awareness, outlines the power of culture carriers as follows:

Hands down what I see working around the world is Security Ambassador Programs. These are programs where employees throughout your organization volunteer 2–4 hours a month to help communicate your program. They literally become ambassadors (also commonly called Champions, Advocates, or Sentinels). These programs are not as hard as you may think and have tremendous advantages.

- **Scale:** *Instead of just one person communicating a message you literally can have hundreds of "mini-me" awareness officers throughout the organization at a global level.*
- **Low Cost:** *Financial cost is minimal, the greatest cost is in time. Specifically you need someone to manage all the different ambassadors.*
- **Engagement:** *These ambassadors understand the challenges and cultures of the local groups they are responsible for. As a result, they are often far more effective at engaging and reaching their co-workers than you would ever be. This is especially true of organizations that are highly global, have numerous remote offices, or very diverse cultures or generations.*
- **Spies:** *In many ways, you have created your own communications network. Not only are they pushing out information that is critical to your mission, but they are collecting information and sending it back to you. Information such as what are the biggest risks they are seeing in their local office, what topics are the most popular, or metrics on the impact you are having.*

> *"The Power of a Security Ambassador Program"* by Lance Spitzner
> (https://www.sans.org/security-awareness-training/blog/
> power-security-ambassador-program)

A few of the labels commonly used for a formal network of security culture carriers include *security liaisons, security ambassadors, security champions,* and *security sentinels.* You can call them whatever you want; the phrase you use to describe this group in your organization isn't magic (just choose what fits best in your organization or make up a new name)—but the group's *impact* can feel like magic.

FINDING A STANDARD DESCRIPTOR

There are so many terms that security teams use for this function. For this book, I decided to go with *culture carriers*, the term that is used by organizational culture consultants. The phrase is very descriptive, and it is difficult for someone to wonder about any implied nuance as they may with *champion* versus *liaison* versus *sentinel* versus *ambassador,* and so on.

I'd love it if we, as an industry, standardized on the concept of *culture carrier* as a descriptor and then each organization created a *brand name* for their individual flavor and values of how they implement their culture carrier program.

Notice that I used the phrase "formal network of security culture carriers." This will be a group that you formally and intentionally create and support. They should come from multiple levels of the organization and across as many departments and regions as possible. Your team will work with your culture carriers to ensure that they are equipped and empowered to help represent the mind-set and behaviors that you need reflected. This group will also be a conduit back to you with stories, ideas, concerns, or issues that are surfacing from far-flung areas of the organization that you would otherwise have very little visibility into.

WHERE TO GET YOUR CULTURE CARRIERS

Who can you get, and how can you get them?

- People can apply.
- Managers can nominate.

- Other employees can nominate.
- Surveys can help reveal "influential people."

Ideally, your security culture carriers should already be respected and influential individuals within their departments and peer groups. In other words, it's best when they are the type of people who carry social influence. Your team will leverage their social currency and position. It is most effective if these people are "bought in" to and believe in the value of the program. It is also important to link incentives/rewards with the effectiveness that these culture carriers have.

MENTAL NOTE: USING SOCIAL STRUCTURES AND SOCIAL PRESSURES TO YOUR ADVANTAGE

As social creatures, we humans naturally exert social pressure and peer pressure in any social situation. So, the best possible thing is for these pressures to work in your favor. People want to feel a sense of belonging and to feel connected with something larger than themselves. You can use this to your advantage as you think about how to work with your culture carriers and other groups throughout your organization.

Consider the social structures and supports that can reinforce your messages, values, and behaviors. You may have heard of the concept of brand advocates and street teams before. Groups like these are created to build *social proof* for bands, TV networks, brands, or organizations. Such groups allow an entity's message to move far beyond the reach of the organization that they represent.

Jonah Berger, professor of marketing at the University of Pennsylvania's Wharton School, offers up an easy-to-understand and easy-to-remember framework for thinking through how ideas spread in his book *Contagious: Why Things Catch On*.[17] He provides six STEPPS (intentional repetition of the P) to a viral message.

- S: Social Currency. We share things that make us look good.
- T: Triggers. Top of mind, tip of tongue.
- E: Emotion. When we care, we share.
- P: Public. Built to show, built to grow.
- P: Practical. News you can use.
- S: Stories. Information travels under the guise of idle chatter.

When you review the STEPPS, I'm sure that you can immediately see that these are consistent with many of the communicative and behavioral levers that I outlined in Chapters 3 and 4. Do yourself a favor; pick up his book and use it to help think through how you might create messages and social structures that have resonance.

BE INTENTIONAL WITH MOTIVATION AND SUPPORT

Think about what you can do to make your culture carriers feel special and valued. What types of recognition and reward systems can you create? This doesn't necessarily have to translate into monetary rewards; it can be social status, swag, the feeling of having "insider" knowledge, peer recognition, and so on. The important thing is to recognize that your culture carriers are doing you a valuable service, and because of that, you should return some value to them.

MENTAL NOTE: REMEMBER YOUR BEHAVIOR DESIGN PRINCIPLES

Think back to the Fogg Behavior Model. Behavior happens when motivation, ability, and a prompt happen at the same moment. The great thing about using culture carriers is that you are creating the social dynamics associated with peer groups. This social pressure can help people attain the required motivation to perform a behavior.

And because we are social creatures, we help each other out. So, if someone is struggling with a concept, they have people to turn to who can help them (ability). Lastly, having a group of people around who espouse security values can help to serve as a prompting mechanism for employees.

Here are a few additional factors that can encourage virility and sustainability:

- Being seen as honest, transparent, and supportive.
- Ensuring that your content is relevant and useful to employee groups that you are targeting.
- Using multiple "channels" for distributing messaging (i.e., web, mobile, print, etc.).

■ Being proactive in finding ways to make employees' lives easier (for instance, streamlining interactions, finding products/processes that are easier to use, etc.).

■ Demonstrating that you are interested in ensuring your end users' success—for their sake, not yours.

■ Allowing your end users and culture carriers a seat at the table when creating policies, procedures, and (where possible) selecting technologies that they will interact with. Not only will this help you ensure that the policies, procedures, and technologies are usable by your end users, it will also create buy-in via the IKEA effect, as discussed in Chapter 4.

Related Books and Resources Carriage return
Books:

■ *Brand Advocates: Turning Enthusiastic Customers into a Powerful Marketing Force* by Rob Fuggetta

■ *Contagious: Why Things Catch On* by Jonah Burger

■ *People-Centric Security: Transforming Your Enterprise Security Culture* by Lance Hayden

■ *Pre-Suasion: A Revolutionary Way to Influence and Persuade* by Robert Cialdini

■ *Re-thinking The Human Factor: A Philosophical Approach to Information Security Awareness Behaviour and Culture* by Bruce Hallas

Web Resources:

■ How to Run a Focus Group (https://www.wikihow.com/Run-a-Focus-Group)

■ People-Centric Security Toolkit by Lance Hayden (http://lancehayden.net/culture/)

■ The Power of Social Currency by Erich Joachimsthaler (https://www.adweek.com/digital/erich-joachimsthaler-vivaldi-guest-post-social-currency/)

■ *Street Team 101* by Alan VanToai. (https://www.simplecrew.com/street-team-101-part-1-recruiting/)

■ *When Peer Pressure is a Good Thing* (https://www.sacap.edu.za/blog/psychology/positive-peer-pressure/)

- *What are the Components of a Corporate Culture?* by Dave Root (https://www.eaglesflight.com/blog/what-are-the-key-components-of-corporate-culture)
- *Who Are Your Culture Carriers?* by Digby Scott (https://www.linkedin.com/pulse/who-your-culture-carriers-digby-scott/)

Cultures in (Potential) Conflict: Remember Global and Social Dynamics

As you consider how to influence the culture of your organization, it's also important (vitally so) to be sensitive to the cultural contexts and pressures that are already influencing your people. If you are blind or insensitive to where your people currently are, then don't be surprised if they don't end up where you want them to be. Engagement models that do not account for global and social dynamics will have the effect of alienating your security department. Some of the traditional security awareness content and messaging that resonates in one culture may not translate well to another culture. For instance, you may find that a funny video that has your U.S. and UK audience in stitches will likely not be as effective in Asia. And, no, when it comes to creating messages for your other regions around the world, Google Translate is not your friend. Always ensure that your messaging and initiatives are reviewed by trusted in-country personnel and that you are open to modifications to account for cultural differences.

If you are building out a global program, you might find the annual Edelman Trust Barometer (https://www.edelman.com/trust-barometer) to be a useful resource. One facet of their study focuses on global differences in how much employees trust the companies that they work for (see http://www.statista.com/chart/4272/where-do-employees-trust-their-own-companies-the-most/). Understanding that these differences exist can help your organization better plan the content, tone, and methods that will most effectively engage employees across each region or—at the very least—may help you avoid a cultural snafu.

> **NOTE**   One of the biggest keys to shaping culture is cultural understanding and cultural sensitivity.

An often-overlooked factor in working through social dynamics is considering how messaging, content, processes, and other engagement methods should be delivered to employees with disabilities. Content accessibility for hearing or visually impaired employees, or employees with any accessibility need, should be something that is an integral part of your awareness program, rather than something bolted on at a later time. If you want your people to take your messaging and values seriously, then it's important to listen to them, understand their needs, and show them that they are valued as people.

Cultural Forces

The most important thing to keep in mind as you plan a culture-shaping initiative is that you are working with humans, not inanimate and unfeeling objects. You are working with, on, and for groups of social creatures that have needs, fears, desires, hopes, and a whole range of motivations.

I'm sure you've heard of Maslow's hierarchy of needs[18] before. What I like about Maslow's hierarchy of needs in a security culture context is that it provides us with an instant reminder of the basic needs and motivations that people have. Consider this: if people's basic needs aren't being met (physical and safety), then they will exist in a constant state of "fight or flight." They won't be able to mentally process information given, and they will struggle to think or act on anything that isn't going to potentially provide some relief from the distress that they feel.

Once those basic needs are fulfilled, then the person is primarily driven by social needs and things that may fill a longing for purpose. That's where your culture-shaping efforts will be applicable. How can you help people in your organization feel a sense of connection to a bigger purpose? How can you make them feel like they are part of a community? How can you build their esteem and self-worth? And how can you fuel their creativity and sense of purpose? Hmmmm, sounds like some great questions to answer in the way you structure your culture carriers program!

Here's how you can map your culture carriers program efforts to the hierarchy (see Figure 5.4):

- For people in the bottom third of the pyramid, find ways to **help**.
- For people in the middle third of the pyramid, find ways to **include**, **assimilate**, and **recognize**. These people will be key contributors to the efforts of your program.

■ For people at the top of the pyramid, offer ways to **encourage** and **support** their efforts. Give them additional freedom and additional responsibility to find ways to help the group.

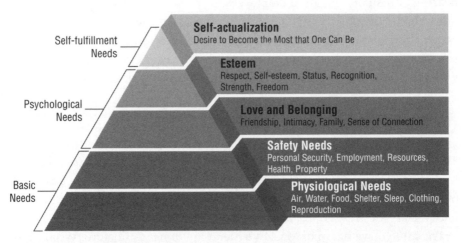

Figure 5.4: Considering Maslow's hierarchy of needs as it relates to security culture

MENTAL NOTE: THE CULTURAL POWER OF WORDS (SECURITY VS. SAFETY) OR SECURITY CULTURE AND THE ZOMBIE APOCALYPSE

Have you ever felt like your pleas for people to make better "security" decisions have fallen on deaf ears? Maybe it's because you are using a term that doesn't resonate well. Think about the term *security*. It sounds a bit sterile, a bit institutional, and maybe even a bit like a job role with duties to be carried- out only by official team members.

Now think about the word *safety*. I bet that feels a bit different. It feels more personal. It feels like something that everyone needs and should care about. The word *safety* is probably more comfortable for your end users, whereas *security* may come-across as scary because they feel like they are on the front lines of battle. The word *safety* can still imply a duty of care, but it is more nurturing rather than militaristic.

In every fight (like a zombie apocalypse movie), you have some people on the front lines with baseball bats and guns, and there are other people who are being protected, tending the wounded, or taking care of and comforting other people. Each role is important . . . and the important thing for us to note is that certain types of people will naturally gravitate toward each role (such as protector versus protected, or soldier versus medic). In fact, one of the reasons that different people groups cluster together is for the mutual *safety* and *protection* of their members.

So, here's a challenge. If you want your security-related messaging to be more personal and impactful, find words that feel deeper, more instinctual, and tribal. Remember, emotion is a Trojan Horse of the mind.

When I consider the things that influence culture, I think about four pillars: structures, pressures, rewards, and rituals. The following sections offer a quick rundown.

Structures

The people someone is around is one of the biggest determining factors in how that person will behave, what they will believe, and what they will value. Parents know this; that's why parents don't want their kids hanging around kids who are bad influences. Parents know that a kid's circle of friends can be either a positive or negative influence on their child, with repercussions that can last for decades. This is the power that a social structure can have on a person.

In your organization, there are lots of social structures to consider. We work with these in a few different ways:

- Your culture carriers are a social structure that has the explicit goal of influencing (and infiltrating) other social structures throughout the organization.
- Role-specific training to provide content and activities to people within identified groups (such as, executives, HR staff, IT staff, mobile workforce, etc.)
- The sociographic and demographic data collected in your culture assessments will give you a picture of the different groups within your organization and will provide some indications of the types of training and/or interventions needed.

Pressures

All cultures naturally establish a behavioral norm. People outside of the norm are treated differently. In the field of sociology, social control theory[19,20,21,22] provides an easy-to-grasp model of the social pressures that can help drive conformity to an acceptable behavioral norm. Here's a quick description:

> *In sociology, control theory is the view that people refrain from deviant behavior because diverse factors control their impulses to break social norms. Developed by thinkers such as Travis Hirschi and Walter Reckless in the late 1960s and early 1970s, control theory explains why people often do not act on deviant impulses. Some controls are internal, such as a person's conscience and motivation to succeed; others are external, such as one's parents, friends, and legal codes. For example, fear of potential embarrassment and store security might quell a person's desire to steal. Control theory links non-deviant behavior to socialization and social bonds: those who are more socialized as children and maintain stronger bonds with others are less likely to behave in deviant ways.*
>
> *Chegg.com*[23]

Social control theory posits four social bonds that help promote conformity to a standard and dissuade deviance from that standard. The four social bonds are as follows:

1. **Attachment:** The circle of close social ties connections that influence and provide feedback regarding both good and bad behavior (for example, management and peers).
2. **Commitment:** Has to do with how committed the person is to the group. This bond can be strengthened by recognition and reward systems, group activities that foster strong emotion, and simple habit.
3. **Involvement:** Continued involvement in social activities and messages that reinforce the desired behaviors and values.
4. **Belief:** Continual reinforcement of the shared beliefs, values, and vision. Understanding the stories behind why the social norm is best.

The four bonds are reinforced through social rewards and social sanctions. Rewards include peer recognition, acceptance, and inclusion ("one of us"). Sanctions include peer disapproval and exclusion ("You are *not* one of us"). A goal of your culture-shaping initiative will be that these social pressures help to support and reinforce your security-related values.

Rewards

People like to feel seen. They like to know that their efforts, intrinsic value, and good work is noticed and appreciated. You can implement a system of rewards to positively reinforce good security-related values and behaviors. Think about how you can reward people across the different social structures of your organization. For instance, your formal group of culture carriers should receive periodic incentives and rewards. These don't have to be monetary—but they do need to be meaningful! For ideas on ways to do this, see *Appreciate: Celebrating People, Inspiring Greatness* by David Sturt, Todd Nordstrom, Kevin Ames, and Gary Beckstrand.[24] This book, backed-up by detailed research, is full of ideas of how to celebrate your workforce.

> **NOTE** Remember from Chapter 4 that adding some unpredictability/variability in the reward frequency can increase engagement!

Your people will love the feeling of being appreciated and will crave that feeling again. Gamification, community competitions, real-time stats, and community encouragement can all be used to drive more engagement and to reward participation. Community-based apps and devices like Fitbit, MyFitnessPal, Peleton, running apps, and social media "liking" all show that these strategies work.

Rituals

We humans like ritual. Think about the process of making a morning tea or coffee, reading a book in your favorite chair, going for a morning run, and so on. Organizations also use ritual: morning meetings, team off-sites, awards ceremonies, and more. Rituals can be a key way to celebrate a value or practice a behavior.

What rituals exist in your organization? One way to begin to enculturate your security values is to find already existing organizational rituals and add a security component to them. For instance, if your organization has a meeting every morning, you can find a way to add a security update to the meeting or to formally thank/appreciate employees at the meeting who demonstrated a certain security behavior.

What rituals might you be able to create? Here's a great way to think about the process and opportunity:

Companies practice rituals of all kinds—celebration rituals, eating rituals, storytelling rituals, company cheers, 360-degree reviews, annual office parties, blood drives, community service events, and so on. Why are they important? Rituals engage people around the things that matter most to an organization, instilling a sense of shared purpose and experience. They spark behaviors that make the work and the company more successful.

Rituals can be powerful drivers of culture, so they should be thoughtfully designed and nurtured. This starts with setting an intention. What is the organization's unique purpose and set of values? What mindset and behaviors will help people deliver on those? A great ritual will reinforce that mindset and those behaviors in a way that feels authentic to the organization and its people. What works at one company, might feel totally foreign somewhere else.

It's also important to think about what will make a ritual stick. Why will people want to participate? Can it start organically and catch on, or will people look to certain leaders to model it first? Designing a ritual that will sustain over time requires tuning in to the organization's existing culture, beliefs, and behaviors.

Want to Strengthen Workplace Culture? Design a Ritual.
Huffington Post[25]

MENTAL NOTE: REMEMBER YOUR TROJAN HORSES!

When planning methods for using social influence, pressure, rewards, rituals, and more, don't forget about the four Trojan Horses for the mind that I introduced in Chapter 3.

Emotion, visuals, sound, and words and story have been useful in helping shape and reinforce the values of individuals and entire people groups since the beginning of recorded history. They will be powerful tools for you as well!

Tracking Results and Measuring Effectiveness

We've already spent quite a bit of time discussing culture surveys earlier in this chapter. So, rather than reiterating those points, I think we should discuss the importance of data integrity. You need to design your surveys to stand the test of time. You want a survey that you can repeat at regular intervals (quarterly, twice per year, or yearly) so that you can accurately measure change over time.

Additionally, I personally think that you need to commit to cultural goals. Don't just report where you currently are; report where you were initially and where you want to be in the next iteration of the survey. Doing so can create a powerful visual of your culture journey and shows that you are committed not just to reporting but to using the data to make informed decisions about how you will seek to further engage the organization.

Kai Roar, creator of the Security Culture Framework and author of the annual *Security Culture Report*, says this about the purpose of measuring culture:

> *One key reason to measure security culture is to understand how it changes and evolves over time. The end goal is to be able to control the change to such a degree that organizations can reduce risk and dramatically reduce the likelihood of a security incident originating from human factors. A measurement instrument that measures security culture must be able to measure the changes in the organization and report these changes in a meaningful way.*
>
> *Kai Roar*[26]

Key Takeaways

- A security culture lives and breathes within every organization. How strong, intentional, and sustainable is your security culture, and what do you need to do about it?
- *The power of culture lies in the fact that humans are social creatures.* People are shaped by the other people around them. Your people's thoughts, attitudes, beliefs, and behaviors are molded by their peer group. It's your job to enculturate the values and behaviors you want to become normative.

- *The first step of influencing your security culture is assessing and understanding the culture as it currently exists.* This can be accomplished via cultural surveys, focus groups, direct observation, behavioral metrics, face-to-face interviews, or any other format at your disposal.

- *Establish a system of culture carriers to make your security culture viral and sustainable.* Your team will work with your culture carriers to ensure that they are equipped and empowered to help represent the mind-set and behaviors that you need reflected. This group will also be a conduit back to you with stories, ideas, concerns, or issues that are surfacing from far-flung areas of the organization that you would otherwise have very little visibility into.

- *Design structures, pressures, rewards, and rituals.* Doing so will create a culture and support environment that is distributed, recognizes and addresses the unique differences between groups, implements social feedback, and is naturally encouraging and engaging. These pillars support sustainability.

Notes and References

1. *Introducing the Complete Guide to Building a Security Culture* by Dan Kaplan (https://www.trustwave.com/en-us/resources/blogs/trustwave-blog/introducing-the-complete-guide-to-building-a-security-culture/)
2. I've used this phrase in slide presentations in my time at Fidelity Information Systems and at Gartner. To my knowledge, this is the first time that the phrase is being used outside of a presentation.
3. *Re-thinking the Human Factor Podcast, Episode 13* (https://www.marmalade-box.com/podcast/episodes-review-louise-cockburn/)
4. This statement is almost universally agreed to be attributed to management consultant and author Peter Drucker. But there seems to be no original referenceable source for the quote.
5. *How Culture Works* (http://www1.humansynergistics.com/OurApproach/HowCultureWorks)
6. *2018 ISACA/CMMI Institute Cybersecurity Culture Report* (http://www.isaca.org/info/cybersecurity-culture-report/index.html)
7. *Re-thinking the Human Factor: A Philosophical Approach to Information Security Awareness Behaviour and Culture* by Bruce Hallas
8. Various studies have tried to estimate the needed number of information security personnel for an organization. While there is no definitive magic

number, it is safe to say that the number of dedicated security and risk management personnel is usually a small fraction of the overall employee count for a company (see http://www.infosecisland.com/blogview/8327-How-Many-Information-Security-Staff-Do-We-Need.html for more information). As such, the security organization needs to find effective ways to multiply its influence throughout the organization.

9. *CULTURE RULES! The 10 Core Principles of Corporate Culture and how to use them to create greater business success* by John R. Childress
10. *Neuroscience for Organizational Change: An Evidence-based Practical Guide to Managing Change* by Hilary Scarlett and Kogan Page
11. Please don't just fish for things that you are hoping that people will say. Avoid the temptation to conduct surveys whose goal is just to prove your point. Run culture surveys, focus groups, and interviews only if you are actually and honestly interested in your people. If not, your disingenuous effort will backfire, and you will end up widening the trust gap between your department and the rest of the organization.
12. *Anonymity may spoil the accuracy of data collected through questionnaires* (https://digest.bps.org.uk/2012/10/02/anonymity-may-spoil-the-accuracy-of-data-collected-through-questionnaires/)
13. *Is Your Anonymous Employee Survey Doing More Harm Than Good?* by Chris Cancialosi (https://www.forbes.com/sites/chriscancialosi/2015/01/12/is-your-anonymous-employee-survey-doing-more-harm-than-good/#7f8def5f44b7)
14. *Can Your Employees Really Speak Freely?* by James R. Detert and Ethan R. Burris (https://hbr.org/2016/01/can-your-employees-really-speak-freely)
15. I use plural here because you will likely notice some strong variances between the norms exhibited across different demographic groups in your organization.
16. *Why You Should Be a Culture Carrier* (https://medium.com/granify/why-you-should-be-a-culture-carrier-e8ed0dfba6ce)
17. *Contagious: Why Things Catch On* by Jonah Berger
18. *Maslow's Hierarchy of Needs* (https://en.wikipedia.org/wiki/Maslow%27s_hierarchy_of_needs)
19. *Control Theory* (https://en.wikipedia.org/wiki/Control_theory_(sociology))
20. *Social Control Theory*. Criminology Theories. iResearch.net (http://criminal-justice.iresearchnet.com/criminology/theories/social-control-theory/)
21. *Leverage Social Science to Improve IT Control* by Tom Scholtz

22. *The Social Bond: A Practical Way for Schools to Reduce Bullying* by Sameer Hindjua (https://cyberbullying.org/social-bond-practical-way-schools-reduce-bullying)

23. *Control Theory* (https://www.chegg.com/homework-help/definitions/control-theory-49)

24. *Appreciate: Celebrating People, Inspiring Greatness* by David Sturt, Todd Nordstrom, Kevin Ames, and Gary Beckstrand

25. *Want to Strengthen Workplace Culture? Design a Ritual* by Mollie West and Kate McCoubrey Judson (https://www.huffingtonpost.com/great-work-cultures/want-to-strengthen-workpl_b_11730914.html)

26. *2018 Security Culture Report* (https://get.clt.re/security-culture-report-2018/)

Additional Reading

Cyber Security Culture in Organisations. European Union Agency for Network and Information Security (ENISA). (2018), https://www.enisa.europa.eu/publications/cyber-security-culture-in-organisations.

David J. Friedman *Culture by Design: 8 simple steps to drive better individual and organizational performance*. (Infinity Publishing, 2018).

Erin Meyer *The Culture Map: Breaking Through the Invisible Boundaries of Global Business*. (PublicAffairs, 2014).

Hierarchy of Needs: Application in Urban Design and Community-Building. (2016), http://mallorybaches.com/discuss/2016/1/26/hierarchy-of-needs.

James A. (Sandy) Winnefeld Jr., Christopher Kirchhoff, David M. Upton. *Cybersecurity's Human Factor: Lessons from the Pentagon*. (2015), https://hbr.org/2015/09/cybersecuritys-human-factor-lessons-from-the-pentagon.

Kai Roar *Build a Security Culture*. (IT Governance Publishing, 2015).

Lance Hayden *People-Centric Security: Transforming Your Enterprise Security Culture*. (McGraw-Hill Education, 2015).

Paolo Guenzi *How Ritual Delivers Performance*. (Harvard Business Review, 2013), https://hbr.org/2013/02/how-ritual-delivers-performanc.

Robert Cialdini *Influence: The Psychology of Persuasion*. Revised Edition. (Harper Business, 2006).

Robert Cialdini *Pre-Suasion: A Revolutionary Way to Influence and Persuade*. (Simon & Schuster, 2016).

Susan Weinschenk *100 Things Every Designer Needs to Know About People (Voices That Matter)*. (New Riders, 2011).

6

What's in a Modern Security Awareness Leader's Toolbox?

We tend to formulate our problems in such a way as to make it seem that the solutions to those problems demand precisely what we already happen to have at hand. With respect to the conduct of inquiry, and especially in behavioral science, I label this effect "the law of the instrument." The simplest formulation I know of the law of the instrument runs this way: give a small boy a hammer and it will turn out that everything he encounters needs pounding.

Abraham Kaplan[1]

Well, here we are. We've spent the last three chapters together walking through multiple disciplines related to how humans think, understand, make decisions, and influence each other in groups. You appreciate that working against human nature is a recipe for failure, and you know that information alone is of little help in forming beliefs, shaping values, or driving desired behaviors.

Now that we have established a base-level understanding of the disciplines outlined in Chapters 3 through 5, and how they intersect with our goal of driving secure behaviors, let's take a look at some of the tools and methods that you have in your toolbox. I'm sure that you'll recognize most (if not all) of the tools that I mention here. Many of them are tools already used in traditional, ineffective security awareness campaigns. But, as the saying goes, "It's not about the tools. It's about how you use them." And our goal is to use our tools as precision instruments, smartly choosing the right tool, for the right job, at the right time.

You might find it interesting to know that I added this chapter at the last minute, and the opening quote that I chose is a perfect illustration of my reasoning for adding it. Kaplan's statement speaks to the fact that we are all susceptible to cognitive biases, and these biases skew the way that we see and approach the situations we enter.

All too often, our security awareness programs are crippled because the awareness program leader or the program sponsor is subject to Kaplan's "law of the instrument." They've been exposed to one method of trying to raise awareness or deliver training, and so that's the method that they immediately see as applicable and valuable.

My goal for this chapter is to help immunize your awareness program from the all-too-common disease of being a one-trick pony that can easily feel stale, repetitive, tired, and irrelevant. The cure for Kaplan's "law of the instrument" is to expand the number of instruments that you have readily available and front of mind.

NOTE Think about your awareness program outreach in three areas: content, experiences, and relationships.

Content Is King: Videos, Learning Modules, and More

Now we come full circle back to messaging and communication. Messaging and communication will always play a critical part in a security awareness program. The problem is that most organizations fall into the trap of believing that flinging a video or learning module at their employee-base is the way to "do" security awareness. But, doing so won't bring transformational results. In fact, if you get the communication and content part of your program wrong, your employees may just feel that the security team is irrelevant and out of touch. Not what you are hoping for!

First, let me start by saying that there is no one-size-fits-all awareness program or content strategy. What is appealing and culturally appropriate for one organization might not be the same for the next. And content that is interesting or useful to one person might feel totally boring and irrelevant to the person sitting one cubical over. Our awareness program and associated campaigns need to account for these factors.

When you start thinking about content selection and delivery in this way, some interesting things happen. I've always seen security awareness training as a multidisciplinary art that draws from the fields of marketing, design, journalism, entertainment, cognitive science, behavioral economics, and more.

It's important to understand how people naturally think, behave, express preferences, make choices, and adopt new beliefs if you ever want to be effective in shaping their security-related thoughts and actions.

> **NOTE**   It's important to understand how people naturally think, behave, express preferences, make choices, and adopt new beliefs if you ever want to be effective in shaping their security-related thoughts and actions.

The biggest problem with the security industry is that we always think we are unique, so we tend to try to create things without first learning from how other industries have approached similar issues.

I've been a big fan of Malcolm Gladwell's writing and speaking ever since I read his book *The Tipping Point*, and I remember back sometime in the 2004–2006 timeframe watching his TED Talk titled "Choice, Happiness, and Spaghetti Sauce,"[2] where he told the story of Howard Moskowitz, a food consultant and psychophysicist who has worked with Pepsi and Campbells Soup, among others. Moskowitz pioneered the practice of *intermarket variability*— creating many different types of a product to appeal to as many different tastes as possible.

I encourage you to watch the TED Talk and read an interview or two where Gladwell describes Moskowitz's approach. Here's a snippet from an interview with ABC that was focusing on Gladwell's thoughts related to education:

> *"People who were in the spaghetti business thought there was such a thing as the perfect spaghetti sauce. He was the one who disabused them of that."*
>
> *Moskowitz, Gladwell says, believed a company producing spaghetti sauce should be trying to understand all the different dimensions of human taste and catering to them.*
>
> *"How many people out there like there spaghetti sauce thick and chunky? How many like it spicy? How many like it heavy on the meat? How many like it thin, like classic Italian spaghetti sauce, which is very finely grained?" he asked.*
>
> *"He educated that world about the width and depth of human difference."*
>
> Author Malcolm Gladwell on what tomato sauce can teach us about educating our kids[3]

As you look at the success of Moskowitz's clients after taking his advice, it is clear that he was right. One of his mantras with any company he was working with was, "There is no perfect <u>(fill in the blank)</u>, only perfect <u>(fill in the blank)</u>s." For instance:

- "There is no perfect *Pepsi*, only perfect *Pepsis*."
- "There is no perfect *Prego*, only perfect *Pregos*."
- "There is no perfect *pickle*, only perfect *pickles*."
- "There is no perfect *mustard*, there are only *mustards that suit different kinds of people*."

Media companies know this well. Netflix has a ton of variety, but it knows that you are interested in only a subset of that. YouTube has a ton of variety, but you self-select the content that you like. The Internet has hundreds of millions of websites, but you self-select the websites that you need based on your preferences and the contexts of life that you are in.

Shouldn't security awareness content be the same way? Of course. That same diversity of thought and preference exists within each of your end users, and your strategy should account for that reality. Sometimes making the simple adjustment in the type and variety of content you deliver to your end users can become a tipping point for the good of your program.

THINK ABOUT CONTENT IN FLAVORS AND VARIETIES

It's best to have a variety of content on tap that you can use. Consider having content that varies in length (long-form versus short-form versus micro), tone (serious versus humorous), format (video versus animation versus traditional learning module), and so on. Variety is important: the security *facts* delivered will be the same, but the *format* and *flavor* will change.

Big Box Shopping: A Content Analogy

Here's an analogy that I use when thinking about content. I'm sure that you've shopped in a "big-box" retail store before (for instance, Wal-Mart, Target, etc.). In many ways, choosing your content will mimic that experience. For example, there may be five different brands of paper towels, but one will be right for you. It could be that you choose a luxury brand, a budget brand, the brand that your parents used while you were growing up, the brand with the most eye-catching package, the brand that claims to be the most absorbent, and so on. And you might choose a small pack, a normal-sized pack, or a mega pack. All of these are essentially the same thing, paper towels, but shoppers naturally self-select the brand and package size they want based on their needs and preferences.

Now let's expand that analogy and consider the entirety of the store. As you can see in Figure 6.1, there are several ways in which different content formats and styles naturally map to the types of departments in a big-box store.

Big-box retail stores strive to serve the diverse needs of a community. They realize that there are basic needs that everyone has, such as food, drinks, paper products, and other staple goods. And there are other more targeted needs, such as men's 32×30 dark-wash jeans. But, across all the types of items sold, there is variety. People have different tastes, budgets, expectations, and family sizes. So, there are different brands, price points, and packaging options galore—something for everyone. And that works.

Security awareness content is like that as well. Across most organizations, there is a body of universal, basic security facts (basic needs and staple items) that organizations need to train their employees on. But, because every organization/person is different and has different tastes, it's great to have a multiplicity of choices and flavors on hand. In other words, you can target one set of employees with brussels sprouts and another set with peanut-butter cups. But each option still has the same nutritional value.[4] Yum!

Big-box retail stores may also sell high-end and designer goods. These may not appeal to everyone, but they have a place. They emanate quality and have a distinct audience. Even people who would not consider purchasing items from this area can sense and appreciate the quality. But there is also an immediate attraction that some customers have to this section. They bask in the glow of the electronics or the designer goods and feel at home. In the same way, there will be some pieces of content that can feel ultra-high-end and curated. They will appeal to a segment of your employee population. And, even if an employee doesn't like the content itself, there will be an appreciation that what you've presented is of high quality and value.

In addition, big-box stores often have a pet supplies department. This is analogous to any favorite topics or "pet projects" that your organization (or a specific group of people in your organization) has.

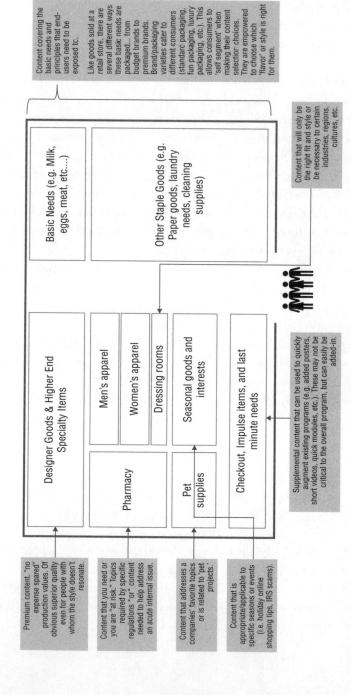

Figure 6.1: Content variety: big-box shopping example

And, like the pharmacy in a big-box retail store, you will need some content that helps to address emergency situations, deal with regulatory issues, or handle internal departmental issues. Sometimes you just need something to help with that mystery rash.

Then there are seasonal goods. In a big-box store, this is where they would put items related to each season and/or holiday. The products in these aisles are generally relevant only for certain time periods each year. When it comes to content, this would be like having content available to send to employees about things such as the types of scams and risks that are associated with holiday shopping, tax season scams, post tragedy phishing scams, and more. This content is good to use at the right time but outside of those specific times will feel irrelevant and will be ignored or quickly forgotten.

Lastly, there is the checkout aisle. This is where you find your impulse items. There are often fun little items like toys or candy located here. As we think about the content analogy, items in this category are generally additive to the program. They can be fun "quick hit" pieces of content. Or they can be posters, leave behind swag, etc. They help fill up the cart and can meet an immediate real or felt security-related need (for instance, reminders, tips and tricks, interesting tidbits, and so on).

REMEMBER TO THINK LIKE A MARKETER AND A STORYTELLER

It's important not to get caught up in all the content and forget the larger purpose. The purpose of content isn't just to have lots of content and options. The purpose is to use the content as a tool to meet a specific need, for a specific group of people, at a specific time, and in a specific place. Used well, your content will be powerful.

NOTE   Use wisely. Content is not an end in itself!

Types of Content

Now that you have a framework for thinking about how content may fit a variety of needs in your organization, let's briefly outline many of the different types of content that you might leverage.[5]

Videos

Videos are fast becoming one of the most sought-after content types. The reason why is simple. Television, Netflix, YouTube, Instagram, Snapchat, and video chat platforms like Skype and Facetime have made the humble video the communication method of choice for the current generation. So much of the information we consume each day is video-based. Our minds are conditioned to accept, and even hunger for, this format.

Video is a fantastic format for virtually any type of information delivery, from dry "talking head"–style teaching, to slapstick viral comedy, to suspenseful human drama, to world-class animation. Content creators can use video to simultaneously weave together all the *Trojan Horses for the Mind* (emotion, visuals, sound, words, and story). And that's powerful!

MENTAL NOTE: VIDEO CAN SIMULTANEOUSLY ENGAGE ALL THE
TROJAN HORSES FOR THE MIND

One of the great things about the time in which we live is that video is becoming increasingly easy to make. This gives organizations more options than ever before. Your organization might find multiple sets of preproduced videos that work well for audience segments that you want to reach, each produced in a different style and with lengths that suit differing attention spans. But you can also easily supplement those videos with homegrown video content like vlogs from your executive team, short YouTube-like videos created by different departments, and so on. And, because it is likely that everyone in your organization carries around their own video production kit (their smartphone) in their pocket, you can encourage employees to submit short videos with security questions, tips, funny skits, or anything else you (or they) can think of. If you are going for *viral* content, then video should be your "go to" format.

NOTE   Video is your "go to" format for content that you want to go viral.

Learning Modules

The phrase *learning module* usually refers to a formal computer-based training (CBT) module often delivered via a dedicated learning management system (LMS). Participants page through the module. Drawing from adult learning principles, these modules often incorporate multiple checkpoints for the learner to answer questions or practice a skill. Learning modules usually end with a learning assessment (quiz), and the learner's score is saved for reporting. This is the format that most people associate with corporate online learning.

Learning modules are popular with content designers because they easily allow for use of mixed media, utilizing the Web's ability to engage learners through multimedia and interactivity. For instance, an ambitious designer can combine slides, animation, live action video, voiceover narration, interspersed interactive "practice" sessions, and learning assessments. Because of the interactive practice checkpoints and the ability to assess a learner's knowledge and record the results for reporting, you can see why this format has become the default standard for corporate training, especially when there is a need to demonstrate completion and to enforce a minimum passing score (typically for regulatory/compliance/audit purposes).

A NOTE ABOUT CONTENT PACKAGING

Learning modules are delivered ("packaged") in specific formats. The most commonly used packaging formats for learning modules are Sharable Content Object Reference Model (SCORM), HTML5 (the language behind modern web content), and Experience API (xAPI). SCORM has been the de facto standard for several years but is now being supplanted by HTML5 and xAPI. If you intend to deliver training to mobile devices or in offline modes, then HTML5 and xAPI will be the most appealing option for you and your audience.

But, even more important, you need to ensure that any content you buy or create can be deployed to your users. If you can't use the LMS offered by your security awareness vendor, then you will need to ensure that the content you procure can be packaged in a format that is supported by your organization's LMS.

Microlearning

Your people juggle several responsibilities each day. Their attention is fractured by all they have to do, and *distraction is the rule rather than the exception.* Because of this, many organizations are adopting a strategy that utilizes microlearning. Rather than mammoth learning modules or videos that can last 30 minutes, 60 minutes, or longer, they are embracing shorter content delivered on a more frequent basis. Each microlearning module is ideally implemented in the path of a naturally occurring behavior and focuses on a single idea or skill. The concept here is that condensed messaging combined with high frequency will gain better engagement and retention.

> **NOTE** Place short learning videos or modules at the point of behavior. For example, embed a microlearning video on password management on your password change page. Short, just-in-time, single-topic, contextually relevant with your learner immediately able to apply their new skill.

Ancillary Support Materials (Posters, Newsletters, Digital Signage, and Swag Items)

Let's think about the marketing world again. Assume that you are a TV executive and planning to launch a new show. You are super excited about the show's concept, script, acting, timeslot, and even early reviews. It all seems like a winning recipe. But, being the savvy TV executive that you are, you also know that having the winning recipe doesn't guarantee success. You need a multi-layered plan to drive the audience to your show. And after they've watched, you'll want to find ways to keep up the engagement so that your viewership doesn't slip. What do you do? You use every marketing tool you have at your disposal. You advertise using commercials, social media, posters, billboard signs, web banners, celebrity talk show appearances, merchandising (T-shirts, coffee mugs, lunch boxes), and more. Anything and everything because, even with the winning recipe, you know that people get distracted.

Your security awareness efforts are much like that of the TV executive trying to grab and keep viewership. Even with an important message, you are in a war for attention. And even when you've won attention, you know that people tend to get distracted. That's where ancillary support materials come in. All of your security awareness posters, digital signs (like screens in lobbies and breakrooms), newsletters, and leave-behind swag come together to support your message. In other words, security awareness posters, signs, newsletters, coffee mugs, stickers, and plushies aren't the end goal; they are used to drive people toward the larger deliverables of your program, and they can be used as reminders about program elements.

NOTE   Your ancillary support materials should create the feel of a unified campaign; be consistent with your overall themes, brand identity, messaging elements, and tone.

MENTAL NOTE: THE BEHAVIOR SCIENCE OF SWAG

Think about how your swag items might function as context cues. For instance, if one of your core messages is that employees shouldn't write down passwords on sticky notes, then a fun swag item can be a sticky-note pad that says "Don't write your password here!" on each note.

In everything, think about how your program elements might be *prompting* a behavior, aiding with the *ability* factor of a behavior, or impacting the *motivation* to perform a behavior. Some swag items may just be for fun, but the *best* items are 1) useful to your audience and 2) follow behavior design principles.

Even things like T-shirts and coffee mugs can be useful in this way because they are subtle social cues. For instance, someone wearing your T-shirt is (at least outwardly) identifying as a member of your *tribe.*

PUTTING CONTENT INTO CONTEXT

Remember what we've discussed in the previous chapters. Find your "why" for each audience type and then develop your strategy for your segments. Combine great communication techniques (see Chapter 3) with behavior design principles (see Chapter 4) and leverage culture carriers (see Chapter 5) to reinforce your security-related messaging, values, and behaviors throughout the organization.

Your content can be targeted to the right segment, at the right time, and in the right context to help create behavior change. Used in this way, the content transcends traditional messaging; it becomes something that can increase *motivation* or *ability* for a desired security-related behavior. And of course, sending content at the right time also becomes a *prompt.*

In the same way, your content can be targeted to the right segment, at the right time, and in the right context to help *dissuade* undesirable security-behaviors. In this case, it can become a "demotivator" for the behavior that you are hoping to dissuade. Or it could become a distraction (and anti-prompt) to pull someone off-course.

Experiences: Events, Meetings, and Simulations

Experiences and events, the way that I define them, are segments of time in which a learner is more actively engaging in an element of your program. At their best, "experiences" should be well, *experiential*, requiring active participation rather than passively watching or paging through a CBT module. But, that's not necessary to be considered an experience. I generally consider anything like a meeting, a webinar, a lunch-and-learn, a team activity, or even an everyday interaction with a piece of technology, as an event-based experience. The key is that these are situations that people step into and out of. And, each of these can be leveraged to create a learning opportunity.

There can also be the idea of creating an experience or series of experiences out of a calendar-based opportunity. National Cybersecurity Awareness Month (NCSAM) is an example of this. The date range is declared and timebound. So, you can choose to use that time to do something special (an "event" or series of "events") or not.

KEEPING THINGS IN PERSPECTIVE

Here's something worth noting: an "event" cannot and should not be the entirety of your yearly security awareness effort. If you are doing the bare minimum for security training at onboarding and then doing only a series of events for NCSAM, you are still selling yourself and your people short. That's not how a marketing company would do it. The reason why is simple. That strategy just doesn't work. People remember less and care less the further they get from the event. So, if you are in an "either/or" situation, you are better off killing off all your NCSAM efforts and doing one mini-event each month, or sending out an interesting training campaign element every few weeks, than doing one big event per year.

Way back in 1998, B. Joseph Pine II and James H. Gilmore coined the phrase *experience economy* in an article for the *Harvard Business Review*. The article, titled "Welcome to the Experience Economy,"[6] described society's craving for engaging experiences. They broke down *experiences* into four quadrants. The horizontal axis ranges from passive participation to active participation, and the vertical axis ranges from immersion at the bottom to absorption at the top.

That results in the following four quadrants, and the goal (as much as possible) is to find the sweet spot in the middle, pulling in elements of all four quadrants:

The Four Realms of an Experience

- Passive Participation + Absorption = Entertainment Experience
- Active Participation + Absorption = Educational Experience
- Passive Participation + Immersion = Esthetic Experience
- Active Participation + Immersion = Escapist Experience

Pine and Gilmore then go on to describe five key principles for designing memorable experiences; they are as follows:

- Theme the experience
- Harmonize impressions with positive cues
- Eliminate negative cues
- Mix in memorabilia
- Engage all five senses

These principles are worth considering each and every time you begin planning an event or as you are brainstorming new ways to engage your people.

Meetings, Presentations, and Lunch-and-Learns

The best thing about each of these is that they are personal. There is generally not a screen separating the presenter from the participants. The formats are more open and interactive, allowing a greater sense of emotion and shared empathy to exist within the event room.

Yes, you can share great content, but you also have the benefit of directly interacting with your audience. This can help foster a bond of trust between your organization's employees and the security team. These are great forums for storytelling, "ask me anything" sessions, sharing about seasonal/topical issues, and more.

Special meetings with compelling speakers are always good, but not always necessary. An executive from your organization can also share how security is critical to the organization's success. You can conduct briefings about security incidents that succeeded or were thwarted. The most important thing is to *engage* your people. Don't set up these meetings to talk *at* them. Talk *with* them.

You can (and should) also find ways to integrate security messaging and values into regularly occurring meetings throughout the organization that you may not actually be able to participate in. For instance, there is great benefit in sending security talking points to all managers to cover in their team meetings. One benefit of doing this is that the employees hear security messaging from their primary point of motivation (their manager).

Tabletop Exercises

I'm a big fan of tabletop exercises (TTXs). What I like about them is that they are extremely flexible. You can easily create tabletop exercises that last anywhere from a couple minutes (so you can slip them into a team meeting) up to a full day or more. In essence, these are thought exercises structured around a "what if" scenario.

> **NOTE** One of the best benefits of a TTX is that it allows your people to mentally rehearse their reactions to scenarios at a time when the stakes aren't high. Their reactions and answers can be studied, and you can decide how best to augment your training, messaging, and playbooks based on what you are seeing and hearing.

With just a few minutes on Google, you'll see that there are a lot of good resources out there on how to create tabletop exercises. And, what you'll notice is that many of them come from the emergency preparedness field because that field is always having to develop plans and processes for how to deal with the next big "what if?" Everything from hurricanes, to pandemics, to bombings, and more. You can use these resources as a model for creating your own cybersecurity and physical security scenarios.

If your interest is piqued, check out this article on nine steps to creating a TTX: "Nine Steps to Design a Powerful Tabletop Exercise (TTX)" from Nexight Group (http://nexightgroup.com/nine-steps-to-design-a-powerful-tabletop-exercise-ttx/). FEMA, as you can imagine, also has extensive guidance on how to create and administer tabletop exercises; their guidance is codified in the Homeland Security Exercise and Evaluation Program (HSEEP), which is extensive, nuanced, and worth your time to review if you plan to create any type of TTX. See https://preptoolkit.fema.gov/web/hseep-resources.

IT DOESN'T HAVE TO BE OVERLY COMPLICATED

The great thing about a TTX is that it doesn't have to be complicated. It can be as simple as having managers toss out a question like, "What would you do if someone tried to piggyback behind you as you enter the building?" And then, they can just listen. . . .

Think about all the different perspectives that can come up. One person might say that if they know the person who is piggybacking, then it really isn't a security risk. And another person might say that they would try to gauge the trustworthiness of the person. A third person might admit that they'd be too afraid to speak up. And a fourth person might admit that they wouldn't even know who to report the incident to if they felt concerned.

That simple question can provide great insight into the thinking of your organization's workforce. And it can provide a great opportunity for any corrective or encouraging talking points that you want to distribute.

Here's an interesting tidbit: Matt Stamper, my technical editor on this project and a co-author of the *CISO Desk Reference Guide: A Practical Guide for CISOs*, mentioned a great recommendation that he gives. Here's his comment in full:

> *I take a similar approach relative to incident response training. I tell the CISOs that I work with to consider dropping verbal queues to their staff. I call it "water cooler" training. If I worked for you and you were my CISO, you may ask a simple question while we run into each other at the water cooler and ask, "Matt, what would we do if our domain were compromised?" The "asking" of the question starts the framing/prompting process for the recipient. The expectation is to keep incident response top of mind.*

NOTE You can also do these as role-play activities and put the participants' minds and emotions even more "in the moment."

Rituals

I briefly discussed organizational rituals in the previous chapter. Since rituals exist to embody and sustain the organization's cultures, it can be beneficial for you to see if you can incorporate some of your security-related messaging or activities into preestablished company rituals. If you have an "all-hands" meeting each morning, then see if you can incorporate security updates.

Rituals also serve the purpose of codifying organizational values, such as service. Can you incorporate security messaging into service rituals that already exist? Or perhaps even create new rituals that are modeled after popular rituals within your organization?

Webinars

Webinars are inexpensive and easy to do. While they are less personal than a physical meeting, when done well and with intentionality, they can still feel more timely, relevant, and interactive than generic canned content. Since webinars are usually scheduled for a specific date and time, you can have the benefit of your participant actively scheduling time to participate.

The reach that you have with webinars can be very broad. And your topic, format, number of speakers, amount of interactivity, etc., is really limited only by your imagination.

> **NOTE**   In addition to being a good method for communicating to the entire organization, "special topic" webinars can be a core support and communication channel for your culture carriers.

Games

Security-themed games are good for helping your people consider security topics through a different lens. The fun, challenge, and variable rewards associated with games make them effective Trojan Horses for embedding messages and habits. Games can be computer-based or physical games like Jeopardy, puzzle solving, card decks with scenarios, carnival-type games, and so on. Above all else, make your games fun, out of the ordinary, and rewarding.

> **GAMES AND GAMIFICATION ARE NOT THE SAME!**
>
> *Games* and *game-based learning* are what you would typically think about when someone mentions the word *game*. *Gamification*, on the other hand, uses game mechanics in nongame contexts to offer intrinsic and extrinsic rewards based on real-life achievements. Think badging, leaderboards, departmental competitions, etc.

You see examples of this when your utility company sends you a report that shows your energy consumption versus that of your neighbors versus customers who are the most efficient. It's all about engaging motivations related to challenge and reward.

Simulated Phishing and Social Engineering

The simulated phishing and social engineering market is relatively new, having arisen in the 2007–2008 timeframe. This methodology is now hugely popular because it provides organizations with a real understanding of how employees react to phishing emails or similar social engineering attempts (voice phishing, text-message based phishing, and so on). If you know where your gaps are, you can train (and condition) to help close the gaps.

Organizations recognize the value in simulated phishing exercises because the vast majority of successful cyberattacks are attributed to phishing. So, getting a baseline of your employees' susceptibility to phishing, and being able to offer just-in-time remediation and training, was groundbreaking for our industry. It was the first true example of implementing just-in-time training at the point of behavior.

NOTE Organizations that augment their traditional security awareness campaigns by adding at least one phishing simulation per month will see drastic results in their employees' resilience to phishing.[7]

WHAT'S THE FREQUENCY, KENNETH?[8]

In my time at Gartner, I spoke to a *lot* of people who were running phishing simulations. Sometimes they told me that the simulations were not changing behavior. Without fail, if I dug into the reasons why, it was because the organization wasn't phishing frequently enough. The typical pattern for these organizations that weren't seeing change was that they were doing phishing testing annually, twice annually, or quarterly.

Here's the thing: doing annual, twice annually, or quarterly testing is a baselining exercise; it's not training or conditioning. It shows you where your people are. But you can't change behavior at that frequency. *Remember, information and relevance fades with time.*

Think about anytime you are trying to build a new habit or learn something new. You practice *frequently*. You are seeking to build muscle memory and to avoid atrophy.

Phish frequently. Reinforce with training. And you'll see your failure rates fall and employee resiliency rise.

Other Simulations and Embodied Learning

Throughout this book, I've mentioned several times that our goals are to make things as immersive as possible, to help people feel like they are experiencing the situations we are describing, and to become storytellers and to leverage all of the Trojan Horses for the Mind.

Gaming, design, medicine, training, and a host of other fields are all about to experience a new wave of innovation that helps to create more immersive experiences. We are already seeing some of that emerge with the popularity of virtual reality (VR) headsets for gaming, augmented reality (AR) headsets for design and manufacturing, and more.

In 2016, Niantic released *Pokémon Go*, an augmented reality game for mobile platforms.[9] All of a sudden, kids and adults around the world were experiencing augmented reality, and they were *hooked*. They walked long distances, forsook sleep, and paid little attention to the real-world beyond the bezels of their screens. *Pokémon Go's* game mechanics, combined with the ability to explore environments, discover prizes, participate in a community, and compare stats among players was intoxicating. It created a craze.

We should expect to see more mainstream examples like this. And we should expect to see innovative vendors and end-user organizations adapting these platforms and principles to deliver new forms of immersive and engaging training.

My *current* thought here is that the main usefulness for VR and AR experiences are as a feature within the context of a large gathering of employees, such as a security awareness roadshow or as an attraction at a security awareness event. This drives interest and leverages the fun, social aspects associated with these gatherings.

But you don't have to go all the way to the bleeding-edge of technology to create engaging and immersive learning experiences. You can build or deploy games, tabletop exercises, or role-playing scenarios that put the player in the role of an attacker or defender. In doing so, your participants will learn to see the world through the eyes associated with those roles. Sending an employee a phishing test is one thing, but having your employees create their own phishing emails puts them directly into the mind of the cybercriminal. After that, they won't engage with their email the same way again.

You can also create an engaging experience by doing something as simple as setting up a few cubicles in your lobby. These would have the features of a standard office setup, complete with computer, file cabinet, whiteboard, phone, trash can, and so on. Throughout the cubicle(s), you stage a number of security-related violations for people to find (such as a password written on a sticky note, confidential papers in the trash can, or sensitive information written on the whiteboard). Then you have employees try to track down the security issues they see. If you have multiple security cubicles, set them up with different pieces of data exposed. Then the participant can put all the clues together to successfully breach the organization or gain a piece of coveted data.

Interactions with Other Technologies

Once you adopt the mind-set of a behavior scientist, you start actively seeking ways to influence decisions and actions as close to the point of behavior as possible. When you think this way, you may find several opportunities to inject messaging, prompts, or some little nudge to encourage or discourage a security-related behavior.

Here are three examples to get you started:

- If you are using a data loss prevention (DLP) product, add security awareness messaging to any user prompts. Perhaps include a URL that will direct the employee to a video, quick learning module, article, or anything else that will give them critical information, provide encouragement, or give them greater context to the decision they are making.
- Do you use a web proxy? If so, don't just block a user from going to an unwanted site. You've already got their attention. Leverage that moment. Embed a video, learning module, or something that will give them context to why that site may be harmful to the organization. Additionally, because some people in your organization may have a legitimate business need to visit some sites that are off-limits to a certain population, you can help facilitate the access request process by embedding a link to a form that allows the user to request access if they believe they need it for business reasons.

- Configure your secure email gateway (SEG) to indicate internal versus external senders on each email your users receive. Many mail filtering products can tag emails in this way. Additionally, you may be able to configure your SEG to add a banner to the top of the email content. The only caveat here is that you are always fighting prompt fatigue. So, over time, these messages and visual indicators will effectively become invisible to your users. You can fight this by changing them up randomly. Make them interesting, funny, alarming, encouraging; play with fonts, colors, images, etc., to fight prompt fatigue and to increase your signal-to-noise ratio.

NOTE Find natural interaction points by thinking through "a day in the life" of your target employee group(s). I'll cover this in more detail when we get to Chapter 8.

Relationships: Bringing Context to Content and Experiences

When it comes to security awareness, you should never downplay or underestimate the power of relationships. Humans are social creatures. We are influenced by what those around us say and do. We innately understand social structures and hierarchies. So, each individual person or social group's "voice" carries with it a unique and differentiated level of weight. Keep this at the forefront of your mind as you develop the strategies behind how you integrate into and support meetings, presentations, events, social media posts, and more.

Many times, the "who" behind who is delivering your message is just as important (potentially more so) than the message itself. After all, if no one hears or pays attention to your messaging because it doesn't come from a source they value, then you effectively don't have a message. Executives and other people in your organization who are already influential are your ultimate culture carriers. Use them well for helping with Q&A sessions, social media posts, on-the-job-training, and evangelizing your messages and values.

Humans are also naturally competitive and comparative creatures.[10,11] We compare ourselves to each other and want to feel the sense of achievement that comes from rising above the rest. This is where the power of gamification, leaderboards, and friendly challenges comes into play. They simultaneously leverage the powers of community, social pressure, and competition.

When people are put into a position where they can compare themselves to others, they want to see themselves or the group they represent do well. You see this in the manufacturing space all the time where defect rates from one facility are compared against another and in retail stores, hospitals, and warehouses where you see bulletin boards reporting the number of days since the last accident or other incident (no one wants to be the employee responsible for resetting that number back to zero). Boards of directors also love comparing their organization to others in the field or industry.

Be Intentional and Opportunistic, Always

As a security awareness leader, you should continually be on the lookout for good ways to communicate and influence. The key to being relevant is the effective use of stories, analogies, current events, cultural trends, seasonality, as well as bridging context to show how security issues reach beyond the work environment and into the most personal parts of your people's lives.

Stories and Analogies

Be a collector of stories and analogies and find different ways to convey impactful stories across multiple mediums. You may find some great stories and anecdotes that work well as part of a stage presentation, others that you want to give to managers to share in team meetings, others to be put into short videos, some to be put in newsletters, and maybe even some that could be turned into tabletop exercises.

NOTE   Having a difficult time finding stories? Bruce Hallas' "The Analogies Project" is a great resource to help get you started. See https://the-analogiesproject.org/.

Tapping into Cultural Trends

Have you ever noticed that society is fickle? The *must-see* TV show, *must-play* game, *hot* celebrity couple, new and *en vogue* fitness revolution, or *have-to-have-it* new gadget seems to be in a constant state of flux. For a moment, these trends capture the attention of the masses, and then the masses move to the next big thing. But, *here's* the thing: you can and should leverage these cultural trends to your advantage. One of the keys to capturing people's attention is to understand what *currently has* their attention. What are your people already captivated by?

> **NOTE**   One of the keys to capturing people's attention is to understand what *currently has* their attention.

For any cultural trend or obsession, ask yourself these two questions:

- Can you use the subject or content as a bridge/analogy?
- What is the deeper connection that people feel with this trend?

For example, if lots of people in your organization are obsessed with a series like *Stranger Things* or *Game of Thrones*, then leverage those cultural references as jumping-off points for a newsletter, poster, video, presentation, etc. Think about the imagery, characters, catch phrases, music, and storylines. Can these be used as analogies? Can you do parody videos that have a security theme? Can you use a clip to illustrate a point?

What deeper connections might exist that you can leverage? Sometimes you can look at a trend, see the inner workings of it, and really understand why people are captivated by whatever it is. For example, "escape rooms" have been popular for the past few years. And, in the same way that the popularity of a TV show or fashion trend will eventually fade, the "escape room" trend will someday pass. But there is good news. There is a set of underlying psychological and sociological factors[12] (the addictive adrenaline rush of solving a mystery or puzzle with a group of friends under time pressure) that you can understand and leverage as part of your awareness and training programs even when the term *escape room* doesn't generate as much immediate enthusiasm as it once did.

Opportunistic Campaigns Based on New Organizational Initiatives and Current Events

In the same way that you should always be on the lookout for stories and analogies, and looking for cultural trends, you should be looking for opportunities to leverage organizational initiatives and current events. Like cultural trends, organizational initiatives and current events have already captured the attention of your people.

Think about how to associate with and complement organizational initiatives. What security angles can you find? Is there a potential behavioral risk that you need to design for? Is there a bigger positive story that you can tell? A way that you can show how good security behaviors will help make the initiative a success? Linking to organizational initiatives reinforces the idea that security is relevant in "the grand scheme of things." It also gives you the benefits of *importance by association*. In other words, because you are associated with this initiative, which everyone agrees is important, your part must also be important.

Current events can serve as a good reason for you to provide timely security advice, like "Don't fall for scammers trying to get you to contribute to phony disaster relief funds." Current events can also give you great "ripped from the headlines" fodder to use for stories. So, in everything, look at what is going on around you and find ways to use those situations to further your program goals. Be a professional opportunist.[13]

The Critical "At Home" Connection

Nothing makes someone sit up and care about a topic as much as understanding how the topic impacts their personal lives and the lives of their loved ones. Whenever possible, you should provide relevant, timely information and guidance about the security considerations that impact people in the broad scope of their lives. Doing so is not only helpful to your employees but also breeds trust and can aid in building a security and risk lens that your employees will begin to see the world through.

> **NOTE** The upside of this for your organization is that employees who adopt a more secure mind-set at home will immediately begin making better security decisions at work and exhibiting more secure behaviors. They become natural culture carriers.

Use Your Metrics and Anecdotes to Help Tell and Reinforce Your Story

So, you may have realized that you are now a professional collector of stories. Use your story archivist and storyteller mind-set as you review your security metrics, your training metrics, and any program feedback that you are getting.

All these stories contribute to *the* story: the larger story of how your program is making a difference in the lives of your employees and to the overall risk posture and resilience of your organization.

When you report your metrics to the executive team, to your board of directors, or to the larger employee group, resist the urge to just show the numbers. Tell them what the numbers mean and why the numbers matter in the first place. And, since most people that you are communicating to aren't security professionals, use analogies and other references to help make the meaning concrete. In all things, and at all times, be a storyteller.

Key Takeaways

- *Think about your awareness program outreach in three areas: content, experiences, and relationship*: Leverage tactics from each of these three pillars to reinforce each other as you deploy meaningful and relevant content to target employee segments, create intentional engaging experiences, and exploit the power of social dynamics.
- *Content is not an end in itself*: Resist the urge to simply send content to your people and hope for the best. Your content is part of a larger strategy. The content, by itself, is not the strategy.
- *Think like a marketer, storyteller, and experience designer*: Think in terms of ongoing campaigns with frequent, relevant messages, experience-based learning, behavioral-intervention opportunities (like phishing tests), and meaningful social interactions.
- *Connect to cultural trends, organizational initiatives, and current events*: Find the things that your people currently like and care about and then leverage those things to bridge contexts from what your people already cherish over to the world of security. Use stories and analogies wherever possible. Seek to understand the "why" behind your people's fascination with cultural trends and then use that "why" as a model for new engagement opportunities.
- *Be a professional opportunist*: At all times, look at what is going on around you and find ways to use those situations to further your program goals.

Notes and References

1. *If Your Only Tool Is a Hammer Then Every Problem Looks Like a Nail* (https://quoteinvestigator.com/2014/05/08/hammer-nail/)

2. *Choice, Happiness and Spaghetti Sauce* by Malcolm Gladwell (https://www
.ted.com/talks/malcolm_gladwell_on_spaghetti_sauce)

3. *Author Malcolm Gladwell on what tomato sauce can teach us about educating
our kids* (https://www.abc.net.au/news/2017-09-01/gladwell-
what-tomato-sauce-can-teach-us-about-educating-our-kids/
8863468)

4. I speak metaphorically about security facts . . . not that actual nutritional
value differences between brussels sprouts and candy. No letters, please!

5. This obviously will not be a comprehensive list. I'm more listing these to
show a mind-set rather than for this to be a compendium of engagement types.

6. *Welcome to the Experience Economy* by Joseph Pine II and James H. Gilmore
(https://hbr.org/1998/07/welcome-to-the-experience-economy
#comment-section)

7. *KnowBe4 Unveils New Phishing Benchmark Data and Showcases Most At-Risk
Industries* (https://www.knowbe4.com/press/knowbe4-unveils-new-
phishing-benchmark-data-and-showcases-most-at-risk-industries)
"The study, drawn from a data set of more than six million users across
nearly 11,000 organizations, benchmarks real-world phishing results.
Results show a radical drop of careless clicking to just 13 percent 90 days
after initial training and simulated phishing and a steeper drop to two
percent after 12 months of combined phishing and computer based
training (CBT).
"The study anonymously tracks users by company size and industry at
three points: 1) a baseline phishing security test, 2) results after 90 days
of combined CBT and simulated phishing, and 3) the result after one year
of combined CBT and phishing."

8. REM song reference (https://en.wikipedia.org/wiki/What%27s_the_
Frequency,_Kenneth%3F). This is not relevant here, except that I like the
title for this topic.

9. *Pokémon Go* (https://en.wikipedia.org/wiki/Pok%C3%A9mon_Go)

10. *The Power of Competition: Effects of social motivation on attention, sustained
physical effort, and learning* by Brynne C. DiMenichi and Elizabeth Tricomi
(https://www.ncbi.nlm.nih.gov/pmc/articles/PMC4554955/)

11. *Why We Compete: A scientific look at people's obsessions with besting their
peers* by Matthew Hutson (https://www.theatlantic.com/magazine/
archive/2015/10/why-we-compete/403201/)

12. *Why Do People Love Escape Rooms?* (https://www.huffingtonpost.com/entry/why-do-people-love-escape-rooms_us_598b523be4b030f0e267c958)

13. I stole this phrase from UK-based magician and pickpocket James Brown (https://professional-opportunist.com/). James uses the phrase *professional opportunist* to describe his style because he is always finding subtle ways to take advantage of whatever unknown twist and turn might arise during his performances. As security awareness leaders, we should do the same.

7 Voices of Transformation: Interviews with Security Awareness Vendors

You have to have a big vision and take very small steps to get there. You have to be humble as you execute but visionary and gigantic in terms of your aspiration. In the Internet industry it's not about grand innovation; it's about a lot of little innovations: every day, every week, every month, making something a little bit better.[1]

Jason Calacanis, American Entrepreneur

One of the best parts of my job at Gartner, and in my current role at KnowBe4, is that I've had the chance to meet so many people who are passionate about their roles in helping employees to make better security decisions. In this first collection of "Voices of Transformation," I'm going to let you hear directly from a number of transformational people who currently work within the vendor community, developing tools and content to serve the broad security awareness market.

I hope you are inspired by the passion and professionalism that these individuals, and their companies, bring to the table. They aren't out to make a quick buck; they are working to make a difference in the world, one person, and one organization at a time. I'd also like to thank each of the individuals who allowed me to collect their perspectives and words for this project. I'm honored to share this market space with you!

Anna Collard, Popcorn Training

- Name: Anna Collard
- Title: Managing Director and Founder
- Company: Popcorn Training, a KnowBe4 company

What drew you to security awareness? In short, what's your story?

I've been working as a security consultant in the enterprise space since 2003 and felt that the security awareness programs run by the organizations I dealt with at the time were lacking creativity and didn't result in the desired behavior change.

As a kid I always used to draw a lot of cartoons and came up with different characters. Around 2011, I had the idea of creating cartoon animations that describe aspects of information security in a simple yet memorable manner. During my honeymoon, I sketched the first cartoon storyboards on the beach. Back at work I shared the concept with one of my clients, South Africa's largest insurance provider, Old Mutual. They loved the idea and asked me to create not just one but six of these stories into animated videos. As luck would have it, in exactly that moment a local animation firm producing content for Disney went bankrupt, and I had access to two really talented animators from Day 1.

The awesome part of the journey was how our customers guided us with regard to content, user friendly learning systems, and change management requirements, as well as the fun on the backend bringing the characters to life both in animated and live action form. Through the contacts I've had in the industry we were able to quickly sell to many other local corporates. What began as a little side project soon became a full-time business with many South African household brands as our customers and some international clients as well.

What makes your company/product/program unique? Why did you start your company? What problem are you helping with?

We believe strongly in creating content that is engaging and that people actually enjoy. Our human brains are built to memorize stories, and we find it easier to remember learning points when these are delivered via a story rather than as plain facts. For example, memory techniques such as memorizing the sequence of a deck of cards include spinning a story or context around the cards displayed to help the brain remember. Stories also motivate voluntary cooperation. By applying humor and visually appealing elements, as well as gamification techniques, we trigger people's emotions. This assists in improving engagement as well as retention. We also try to make content personally relevant, where possible. During the content creation phase, we always ask ourselves "Would I be interested in this? Would I watch this?" and if we feel it's too boring, too lame, or not good enough, we go back to the drawing board. This results in our content being quite authentic and sometimes a bit out there as it reflects our personal taste and sense of humor.

What's your elevator pitch on how/why security awareness can actually make a difference?

Bad guys find it much easier to hack a human than trying to break through sophisticated technology. We specialize in cyber and security awareness to help your users become more cyber savvy using engaging and fun campaigns that people actually enjoy participating in and that they will remember and find personally relevant.

What do you love about your role or mission?

I love taking complex topics and distilling them to their core essentials. I also really love helping people become more cyber savvy. And constantly thinking about how we can make the experience more enjoyable for the audience makes you focus on joy, design, and quality. We have fun coming up with cheesy characters and names, and the playfulness during the process is very rewarding.

Is there a favorite story that you'd like to share?

We had a large oil company client whose IT department bought all our cartoon animations. Their head of brand, however, stepped in to put a hold on to the whole program and said, "We hire a lot of highly intelligent engineers who will not want to watch cartoon clips."

The gentleman's decision to stop the project was initially a blow, but it pushed us into producing the same content just in live action format, resulting in a great and necessary expansion of our product offering to include live action as well as slightly more serious motion-graphic type content. This allows us to satisfy different audience and cultural needs.

Name a book, resource (e.g., TED Talk), or something else that really influenced the way that you think about awareness. Or it could be a book or resource that you always find yourself recommending to others.

Why Your Brain Loves Good Storytelling by Paul J. Zak (`https://hbr.org/2014/10/why-your-brain-loves-good-storytelling`)

Last thoughts?

Run your campaign like a marketing campaign, not an IT project. It's all about communicating. A security awareness campaign is a wonderful opportunity to represent the IT security team to the rest of the business. The more engaging, personally interesting, and joyful the experience for the end user, the better their attitude toward cyber security as well as toward the security team.

Chris Hadnagy, Social Engineer ━━━━━━━

- Name: Chris Hadnagy
- Title: CEO, Founder and Chief Human Hacker
- Company: Social-Engineer

What drew you to security awareness? In short, what's your story?

So, I've always been into tech and things like that. I started off in the "security" business as a vulnerability assessor; basically, that boils down to doing compliance-only testing. And then I took the Offensive Security course, at the time called *Penetration Testing with Backtrack*, and that literally changed my whole existence. It opened my eyes to a whole new field, a new way of thinking, a new way of solving problems. And in that course, I had cracked a couple of the servers they had in their labs that no one had cracked yet, and that led me to get a job offer from Offensive Security. I became their operations manager and their chief social engineer during pen tests. And that really launched everything. My passion and my desire to learn and to continue to grow this part of the security industry came from that beginning.

I just kind of had a knack for doing the social side of the pen test. So, after like a year or so of being successful at it, I suggested to Maddie like, "Hey, we should write a course on social engineering. I mean, we have some of the best courses on actual hacking, so why not?" And he's like, "Well, you're the SE, you do it." So, I sat down and started doing research online and found out there was nothing; I mean back then social engineering was, you know, Kevin Mitnick followed by a bunch of stuff like how to get free burgers from McDonalds, how to pick up chicks, and so on. There just wasn't much about it. So, I went back to him and said, "Man, there's no info out there." And he's like, "Yeah, you have to write the framework, man. You've got to actually make it."

That took about 10 months of a lot of research, reading a lot of books, writing a lot of things. When the Social Engineering Framework came out, I got my first book offer, which was *Social Engineering: The Art of Human Hacking*. Even today, shockingly that book still sells so good, but it's not really the best extensively written book. It has a few errors and some things like that, but that grew my company. It grew me from just being a guy working in Offensive Security to having a whole company that focused solely on social engineering.

Then I started hiring people and realized something. I had the situation where I had a framework, I had a book, I had a company, I was still working on my course, and I'm hiring people. And I need to teach those people how to do the very things that I'm doing. You can't just say, "Well, hey, go out and smile and people will give you answers." That didn't work; you have to create processes. So, for me, it became a scientific exercise to understand the process of social engineering and then to distill it to the science so I can then educate others on how to do the very things that I was doing. So, the focus for the human side came really from a need to grow the industry and my company and then to help people learn how to do what I was doing. From that, the more I understood, the more I fell in love with it, the more I fell in love with it, the more I wanted to do more with it. It was like a wheel that just kept turning in on itself.

What makes your company/product/program unique? Why did you start your company? What problem are you helping with?

When I started doing this, there was no social engineering industry; I feel like I had a large part in actually creating it. In addition, there were very few people doing this sort of thing. You look back 12 years, we had some red teamers, people like Chris Nickerson who has been doing this forever, but there wasn't anyone who was solely focusing on SE. And many professional social engineers could do it and do it really well, but they didn't understand why it worked. So, my motive came down to realizing that I wasn't just a guy who could be satisfied doing the SE stuff and just saying, "Wow, look at how easy it is to break in these places or get people to click on phish." I was driven to study the sciences behind it and to figure out the "why."

For example, let's say I send *this specific* phishing email and *this specific* guy clicks it. Let's figure out *why* he clicked it. Let's figure out what was the motivator. What was the reasoning behind it? What was the reason that that guy decided to take the action he should not have taken?

That still my motivator for being in this industry: trying to understand that "why" so that we can help fix the problem even if it's just a little bit. There's no real, huge fix. We can't make broad statements like, "Hey, you do this and you're never going to be hacked again by social engineers." But being able to understand the "why" gives us some ability to fix the problem, to build better education, and to understand how we can be better at fighting this.

What's your elevator pitch on how/why security awareness can actually make a difference?

So, an elevator pitch is usually 60 seconds, but let's put in a caveat. My caveat with the elevator pitch is that I can't blanket all security awareness together because I think we do that too often in this industry. We say "security awareness," and then we give an elevator pitch. And then people go, OK, I'm doing security awareness. No, you're not; because giving someone a 20-minute CBT on phishing once a year, that's not security awareness, right? So, my definition of security awareness is an active approach to educating people on the threats and how to mitigate in defense.

When we look at security awareness that way, then my elevator pitch is that security awareness must be a hands-on performance-based experience that teaches your population how it feels to actually be under attack and then reward them for handling that attack properly.

What do you love about your role or mission?

Oh, there's a couple things that I really love. First, I love the fact that I'm learning about humans and how we make decisions and being able to use that knowledge in helping people make better decisions. And what I have found through my career in the last decade is that when I do it right, I don't just affect someone from a security posture, but I've had students and clients say that the work we do with them has affected them in their life.

This is a really extreme example: I had a guy who, after taking my five-day course, told me that it fixed his marriage. I was like, "That was not the intent of the course, man." And he's like, "Yeah, but I took all the things you taught us about communication profiling, and about our communication profiles, and rapport and influence, and I went home, and I applied them. And my wife and I actually started communicating more like adults." And it fixed his marriage, you know? So, the right type of education in security can actually make such an effective change in people that it can adjust how they live their lives, not just how secure they are. And that's pretty powerful!

Is there a favorite story that you'd like to share?

I have an interesting story that I tell sometimes when I'm talking about the topic and someone says, "It's only stupid humans who fall for these things." We were working with a company where we were doing all of their phishing, and they had a large number of people in their organizations. We're talking in the hundreds of thousands. And we would do these groups of phishing tests where we would phish folks and then analyze what kind of phish they clicked. And we would increase the level of difficulty of the phish as time went on to be more and more realistic.

This one group, it just seemed like no matter what we did, they clicked everything. And at one point, as a joke, I said, to my point of contact, we should just send a phish to them that says, "This is a phish; don't click it!" So, I did;

I wrote a phish. And it came from the HR department. And it said, "This is a phish. Don't click here!" And then I put the "here" as a link. We got an unbelievable number of clicks. So, at this point, I'm thinking, OK, we've got to figure out what the heck is going on because this is a serious matter. And these people are clicking everything. And this may be a danger to the company. Being a security guy, I'm getting all up in arms, thinking, "These people, they need to learn their lesson; we need to figure out what's going on!" And the point of contact went and had a meeting with the manager of that group to find out why that phish had gotten clicked.

It came out in the end that this department was recently reduced from 370 people to 150, and they had the same amount of work. They were so busy— they were so inundated with work—that when they saw an email that came in from HR, they just clicked it. They didn't read; they didn't look; and then when they saw it was a test phish, they just deleted and moved on with their day. They didn't care. And instead of viewing those people as a giant group of the dumbest people on earth who were insecure, I had to change my perception and say these men and women were so overworked that they didn't have the time to think about security.

What we had to do was to step out of a security role for a second and try to determine if there's anything we can do to work with our client on helping this organization's workflow. Can we analyze how emails are coming in and out of their box and maybe reduce the spam and phish that come to them so that we can reduce their workload? Is there anything else that can be done to help lessen the load on them so they're not so inundated and feeling so stressed that they just don't care?

And I had to adjust my viewpoint at looking at this group of people like stupid people who didn't care about security, to wow, these people need some empathy. They're overworked, they're inundated, and they're probably at their cracking point. And that viewpoint for me, changed. Then working with the company, we were able to make an effective change for them and their work life. And for me, that was one of those things that's happened a few times in my career to where I think I'm just a little hacker, and then I do something that actually changes a life, and it feels good. And you're like, wow, that we could do so much more with this kind of field and this career than just securing people or just hacking people.

Name a book, resource (e.g., TED Talk), or something else that really influenced the way that you think about awareness. Or it could be a book or resource that you always find yourself recommending to others.

Well, there are a few! Dr. Paul Zack's book called *The Moral Molecule*. It's all about his research into the brain chemical called oxytocin, which is directly related to trust and rapport building, and it has so many applications. In his book and his research, he talks about the powerful effect of influencing people and winning people over by doing things that release oxytocin, which, again, is the link to trust and rapport. I've applied that in my field to how we conduct pen testing, how we conduct audits, and how we conduct security awareness. If you can create a situation where oxytocin gets released, if you get people to trust you, to feel good about you, they will be more inclined to listen to your training as opposed to if you're shaming them using guilt and fear. That's one.

Another one, Amy Cuddy's book *Presence* talks about the way that we can alter our own perception by helping our bodies release positive chemicals, using our own body language. That to me is a real big one that I use all the time, too.

And, anyone that knows me knows I'm a huge fan of Dr. Paul Ekman; so I recommend all of his work, but *Emotions Revealed* is probably my favorite book from him. It's not really security awareness related per se, but I use it every day in my practice.

Last thoughts?

About a year and a half ago, I started a nonprofit foundation called the Innocent Lives Foundation (https://www.innocentlivesfoundation.org/). It uses the white-hat community to help uncover and unmask people who trade, sell, and produce child pornography and exploit children on the Dark Web. And that came about because of the client work that I was doing. I was doing a security awareness exercise, a phishing, and pen testing exercise with the client. And we had noticed some log files from one of the nodes that we were able to access that were really, really strange, a lot of TOR, a lot of Dark Web stuff; we couldn't really figure it out. We were just trying to figure out what the heck was going on. And, long story short, we ended up finding that this guy was on the Dark Web, and he had produced his own child abuse material and then was trading it with other perverts online.

And our work helped with law enforcement, helping him get apprehended, arrested, and sent to prison, where he still is today. And that had a profound effect on me because it's one of these things like where, again, I thought I was just a security guy who is into hacking. I didn't really think I'd ever do anything with those skills that would be this life-altering. And now here we are, we saved some kids from being hurt because of it. So, you never know. If you apply these skills properly, you never know what path it can lead you to. And it can be something completely surprising that you never expected.

Drew Rose, Living Security ▬▬▬▬▬▬

- ■ Name: Drew Rose
- ■ Title: Founder and Chief Security Officer
- ■ Company: Living Security

What drew you to security awareness? In short, what's your story?

My background is in the military, where I spent nine years building the foundation for my career as a cybersecurity engineer. You might think this would be right at the cutting edge, but in reality we took the same training every year. The training never kept up with the pace of technology, which has been advancing at light speed.

I continued to build upon my knowledge and skill set through external training and certifications, and it wasn't long into my career that I realized machines and technology aren't the most important aspect of a secure environment at all. Humans are the key. From that day, my mission has been to make sure the people I work with know that they are, and will always be, the most crucial part of my team.

Human interactions are what make my day, not the high-tech security that protects us from the millions of attacks we see each day. Because even though these tools have the incredible ability to do things that humans can't, it's often the single right decision from one person that prevents the next incident from affecting us.

This need for a human-led, user-focused security awareness training platform is what drove me to work in cybersecurity and led me to found Living Security.

What makes your company/product/program unique? Why did you start your company? What problem are you helping with?

When it comes to cybersecurity, companies usually have two main objectives: making their staff care about it and being better placed to make smarter security decisions. So, we started Living Security to help them achieve both.

It's human nature that people are more engaged when they're having fun, so we're the first company to bring a security awareness–themed escape room to the market. This totally engaging and immersive concept makes every user absorb information that might have otherwise fallen on deaf ears.

We followed that up with the first fully gamified security awareness training platform, with some of the deepest metric insights in the industry. This gives clients complete control of their program so they can see what's working and where improvements need to be made.

What's your elevator pitch on how/why security awareness can actually make a difference?

Back to human nature again, people naturally want to make the right decisions. Mistakes only usually happen when there's a lack of understanding or when emotions get in the way of rational thought.

Training that's fun and engaging makes people understand the principles being taught and think about them in a more relatable way than with traditional manuals or guidebooks. The memorable material becomes ingrained in their decision-making process, reducing risks to them and their company.

What do you love about your role or mission?

My mission is to make people care about security on a personal level and motivate them to change their thinking, so our training goes beyond a box-ticking compliance-driven exercise.

Other security awareness training programs tend to deliver the information without much context, whereas ours gives managers an insight into their security culture, with detailed metrics that put them in the driving seat to reduce their risk.

And since we interact with the end user, I get to show people with little to no security experience how to reduce the risk to their organization. That level of personal contact makes it a win-win situation. I'm genuinely excited to come to work each day.

Name a book, resource (e.g., TED Talk), or something else that really influenced the way that you think about awareness. Or it could be a book or resource that you always find yourself recommending to others.

I love the book *Blink: The Power of Thinking Without Thinking* by Malcolm Gladwell because it mirrors my views on the cybersecurity industry and helps undermine the idea that security professionals have tossed around as fact for over 20 years: that users are the weakest links and nothing can be done to change it.

The truth is, yearly compliance-driven training won't result in a reduction of risk, just a poor attitude toward security decisions. His book makes it clear it's understanding that drives change rather than knowledge. It's a great starting point to learn about the importance of ongoing training that engages and empowers people.

Last thoughts?

Despite everything I've said, human error is still the number-one cybersecurity risk. But being well-informed is the greatest tool to safeguarding that risk to ourselves and our organizations.

As with my time in the military, technology is advancing at an incredible rate, so people need to be open to changing behaviors. That's exactly what I specialize in.

Gary Berman, The CyberHero Adventures: Defenders of the Digital Universe

- Name: Gary Berman
- Title: CEO
- Company: Cyberman Security, LLC, DBA *The CyberHero Adventures: Defenders of the Digital Universe*

What drew you to security awareness? In short, what's your story?

Beginning in 1988, I was the CEO of a successful marketing research and consulting company, and during the following 10 years, my better-half and a group of trusted employees built the company by servicing major corporate clients such as AT&T, Best Buy, Ford, General Motors, P&G, etc. We sold 49 percent of the company to the largest global marketing company, and we were on top of the world. Revenues were increasing rapidly, and we were in discussions to take over a small part of a sister company's operation, due to our outstanding work and reputation.

I had a near-death experience and was not involved in daily operations for an extended period of time, during which our revenues dropped precipitously. I anticipated a slight decline in revenue due to my absence, but the phones literally stopped ringing, we received zero traffic to our once-popular website, and our landlord threatened to evict us out of the blue. I was completely unaware of what was happening right under my nose, until one day . . .

My giant Motorola cell phone rang, and it was the CEO of one of my joint-venture sister companies (also our biggest, new client) who said, "What the #@!% is going on at your company?" I was in shock. The CEO went on to say that she had gotten a call from one of my employees who said that "there was rampant fraud within my operation, that we simply made up research results, and that I was under investigation by law enforcement." The person went on to say, "The best thing to do is to stop all communications with Gary Berman."

I was momentarily shocked and then went into action and found zero fraud. Time went by, and our clients continued to disappear, and the phones were silent until one day when I walked into an executive's office and found him downloading our customer data into an external hard drive. I asked what he was doing and he got incredibly nervous. I asked him to leave immediately and he said, "You have no idea what hacking is." And he laughed out loud.

We struggled mightily to keep the company open, but after several years, my wife and I lost everything . . . even our home. We painfully had to let go of our entire staff. During the following 10+ years, I worked on veteran's causes and cofounded the Anthem Project, a real-estate vision to help returning warriors re-integrate into civil society. Then, my wife and I founded Grasp Learning, an after-school tutoring program for children.

Beginning in 2016, in our continuing effort to provide for our family, I decided to test the waters by returning to the marketing industry again. After a speech at an industry event, I was overwhelmed by the positive response and the associated business development opportunities. That night, after returning home with the good news, I noticed that my LinkedIn account had been hacked, and upon further examination, two of my former employees had viewed my profile . . . after silence for 10+ years! The following day, the hacks *really* began, and I eventually documented 19 attack vectors including routers, cell phones, and even my car. I knew that mine was an improbable story, so I started to listen and learn about cyber security via podcasts, attending industry conferences and books.

My big pivot from victim to advocate was sparked after attempting to read *Cyber Security for Dummies* and finding myself lost after only 10 pages. I located the author and told him about how difficult the book was, and he broke out laughing! I asked why he was laughing and he said, "Well, the book is *not* really for beginners." I replied, then why do you call it *Cyber Security for Dummies*? That's when I realized that there had to be a better way to raise awareness about cybersecurity. *The CyberHero Adventures: Defenders of the Digital Universe* comic platform was born!

What makes your company/product/program unique? Why did you start your company? What problem are you helping with?

Given that the overwhelming majority of hacks are caused by simple, human error and that only 3 percent of the Cyber Venture 500 firms are listed as offering "training and/or education," I began connecting with the cyber security ecosystem via LinkedIn to listen and learn about using a superhero comic modality would be accepted as a viable alternative to "death by PowerPoint." I created a mock-up of the cover in my LinkedIn profile and asked CISOs, CSOs, CTOs, CDOs, and others to send me blinded, real-life stories of cybercrime and answering three questions: What happened? What were the consequences? What were the lessons learned? The last time that I checked, I had 21,000 connections!

I've learned that the *only* time that people hear about hacking or cyber security is when the black hats win! We have dedicated the comic to all of the unsung heroes who toil in anonymity to keep us safe while online. All of our comic characters are based upon *real-life* cyber heroes.

Our program is unique because we are *advocates* and not a vendor or end user. We donate all of the digital and printed comics by partnering with industry groups such as ISC², and our eventual goal is to have major corporate and industry sponsors that will customize the comic to align with their internal *and* external communications, and they will distribute the comic to their various stakeholders. We will produce eight editions of the comic focusing on critical infrastructure including financial services, healthcare, transportation, energy, etc. Our program is unique because it is engaging, empowering, and FUN!

What's your elevator pitch on how/why security awareness can actually make a difference?

Given that BYOD is becoming the norm at the office, practicing basic cyber hygiene will keep you and your family safe at work, home, and school.

What do you love about your role or mission?

I begin every day at 4 a.m. because I am so excited and blessed to listen and learn from the cyber security ecosystem. I have calls and meetings with thought leaders from large enterprises, small businesses, law enforcement, department of defense, vendors, academics, and many others. I love the creative process of distilling complex cyber security and tech information into digestible and entertaining stories. I especially love giving speeches and webinars to share my most improbable journey as the Forrest Gump of cyber security.

Is there a favorite story that you'd like to share?

I was invited as a guest speaker by Gartner to present at their Cyber Security and Risk Management Conference. I was eager to share my story in general but to solicit the audience feedback regarding the detailed evidence that I showed including pictures, videos, and forensics. After the speech, a group of attendees followed me as I went to return my microphone. Their kind words and thoughts were overwhelming, and they confirmed that I was on the right track. I received the audience feedback from Gartner, and I scored 4.5 out of a possible 5! Sometime later, I was asked during a podcast, "Did you find closure regarding what happened to you?" I replied, yes, at the Gartner conference, I found my new home.

Name a book, resource (e.g., TED Talk), or something else that really influenced the way that you think about awareness. Or it could be a book or resource that you always find yourself recommending to others.

The Marvel Way by Stan Lee.

Last thoughts?

Einstein was asked by a reporter how he reconciled physics and science with the possible existence of God. He replied, "Coincidence is God's way of remaining anonymous."

Jason Hoenich, Habitu8

- Name: Jason Hoenich
- Title: Founder, Chief Product Officer
- Company: Habitu8

What drew you to security awareness? In short, what's your story?

I love helping people understand complicated ideas. While I was working as a network administrator for a real estate company (years ago), I found myself spending more time at my co-workers' desks explaining to them why they had a virus and how that weird email they got was the culprit. Back then it wasn't called security awareness. It wasn't a thing yet. It wasn't until years later, while working as an infosec analyst for a large bank, that I realized what I had been doing all along was indeed that, security awareness. What I enjoyed most about those conversations was the challenge of getting each person I was speaking with on their unique path to the "ah ha!" moment. Once I got them there, they understood almost immediately what the risks were and what they could do to avoid them. I was hooked. When I finally landed my jobs at companies like Disney, Sony Pictures, and Activision Blizzard was when I started to see the nuance of programs and potential impact on a company's culture from well-designed programs and strategies.

What makes your company/product/program unique? Why did you start your company? What problem are you helping with?

Well, for starters, we're one of the only companies based on real-world security awareness experience. I've personally built the security awareness program for Disney. In 2014 Sony Pictures Entertainment experienced the most devastating cyber attack and probably one of the most notorious for its impact. They could have hired anyone in the world to come in after that and build their program, and I am very humbled to have been selected for that monstrous task. That was a really great experience. Prior to both of those I was working in the gaming industry at Activision Blizzard . . . talk about working with technology elitists!

So, I've made lots of mistakes and had lots of success, and I know what actually works in the day-to-day operations as a security awareness professional. All of this carries over into the product and approach of Habitu8. We're uniquely positioned to deliver experiential value to the industry that others just can't.

What's your elevator pitch on how/why security awareness can actually make a difference?

I started Habitu8 because I was frustrated. As an awareness practitioner, I was seeing the guidance in the space that was being provided by the existing vendors. It wasn't good, quite frankly. A lot of the suggestions and research that was being toted was done in theory and did not take into consideration mental models or the simple fact that when people are at work on their computers, they make different decisions than in a lab. People just aren't rational. So, I wanted to bring a product to the industry that I wanted while I was creating these programs myself. I wanted high-quality content, funny videos, with conversational dialogue. I wanted to be entertained while I learned, and the majority (if not all) at the time was very compliance-driven, "corporatey" training. I can't tell you how many calls we have where people are just openly complaining about their existing training content.

What do you love about your role or mission?

Habitu8 is helping with engaging employees with sharp, high-quality content specifically for training modules. Our videos are the highest-quality product on the market. We invest heavily in the production process. We hire Screen Actors Guild (SAG) talent and union crew members. Our writers have worked in Hollywood for over 10 years. So, we deliver an experience that feels like what you would watch on Netflix, Amazon, or Hulu. That's a big win. If your content looks and feels like what your co-workers are used to seeing in their daily lives, you win. What we're focused on helping with is bridging that communication gap between security teams and end users. We want to provide the right content at the right moment versus all the training all at once and hope our co-workers can remember a few months later when they need to recall it.

What's your elevator pitch on how/why security awareness can actually make a difference?

Security awareness hasn't made a difference up to this point because it hasn't been done correctly. Now, with behavioral science and studies, marketing concepts, and focusing on user experience, security awareness can be a game-changer for most companies. Imagine being able to provide a single valuable piece of information at the right moment for someone, when they need that information. Then you're focusing on the right behaviors and moving from check-the-box compliance initiatives that don't work. When you can give someone something of value in a moment when they need it, you change their behavior. That is security awareness.

What do you love about your role or mission?

I have been extremely fortunate in my career working in security awareness. I've worked for literally the biggest names in the world. What I love about my role is I get to share that experience and knowledge with my peers to help them be better with their own programs. It's why I offer a mentoring program through Habitu8. Why should only I benefit from my experience? You need to share what you know to make the world better. I get to positively change an industry I am deeply passionate about. That's just awesome.

Is there a favorite story that you'd like to share?

I was working as the security awareness manager for the Walt Disney Company. My very first project was to update the annual/required security awareness training for the company. This included all corporate employees, but also included Marvel, ESPN, ABC, Parks & Resorts, Imagineering, and Disney Stores, Disney Animation Studio, with potential for Pixar and Lucasfilm's, the whole works. I looked at the vendor options available at the time and decided that I couldn't put any of the training videos in front of the folks who literally just released Disney's *Frozen* and were about to release *Guardians of the Galaxy*. I somehow persuaded management to let me build custom training internally using all of the available resources (we were, after all, a big movie and feature animation studio). They agreed.

As I worked diligently to write the scripts for live-action videos and the animation videos that would comprise the new training (and would ultimately become the blueprint for Habitu8), I was dumped into a new world I was unfamiliar with: Hollywood production. We had our live-action production team locked down and were beginning shooting on-location at places like Disneyland. Part of the animation process required finding voice-over talent to narrate the training modules.

I was doing my best to seek voice-over artists, looking for a specific "vibe." One day my studio counterpart who co-owned the project, Haley, said she had an option for us that was offered up.

A few weeks later, we had signed Mark Hamill on to narrate the training. Mark Hamill, aka Luke Skywalker, would be reading words that I wrote, over animation and storyboards that I created.

People are still tweeting about that training today, years later (as they are still using it). It was such an amazing experience to be able to deliver a training experience that excited users and engaged them in a way I had not seen before. That's the power of security awareness training that is designed with the user in mind. Sure, Mark brought a unique twist to the training, but that showed that if you build it with design and experience in mind, people will pay attention.

Name a book, resource (e.g., TED Talk), or something else that really influenced the way that you think about awareness. Or it could a book or resource that you always find yourself recommending to others.

Start with Why by Simon Sinek is a foundational table-stakes resource for anyone doing security awareness. The concept of really knowing your "why" of what you're doing is incredibly powerful.

Last thoughts?

My number-one, easily quickest way to success has been and always will be strong and transparent communication. Tell people what you are doing and what you expect them to do to help you. Have a clear and strong plan and strategy. And laugh.

Jim Shields, Twist and Shout

- Name: Jim Shields
- Title: Creative Director
- Company: Twist and Shout Communications/Twist and Shout Media

What drew you to security awareness? In short, what's your story?

Back in 2010 we were creating marketing videos and internal communications videos for corporations. Mostly tech sector, mostly comedy. Within that same year we were asked by two of our blue-chip clients to create information security campaigns aimed at employees. It was weird—we'd never really come across this before in any of our briefs. And now twice in one year? The campaign we did for Barclays Bank won some international awards, and they started to show clips of the film to audiences during the thought leadership presentations they'd give to security audiences at events around the world. Thanks to that publicity, within two years we'd made over 30 films about cybersecurity.

What makes your company/product/program unique? Why did you start your company? What problem are you helping with?

Seven years ago, it was deemed risky to make light of such a serious subject as cybersecurity. We realized that much of the training that was out there was pretty dull, and companies were asking employees to take on this extra responsibility of keeping their sensitive company data safe. It was a big ask. So we knew it needed to be framed as a marketing problem, and not just a training issue. We had recently specialized as comedy creators for business, so the next step was obvious. A comedy series that anyone could license. I mean, post 2008 was tough for the creative industry, and we needed a way to generate another, more stable revenue stream. That was when "restricted intelligence" was born: the world's first sitcom about cybersecurity for employees.

Now companies could get a TV-quality "training by entertainment" resource for a fraction of the cost of making their own. It proved popular and has been our flagship product for five years now. For many companies, this was the solution for the fact that compliance training was really dull, and everyone treated it like a chore. Now people would watch our episodes while they ate their lunch, and it wouldn't even feel like training. They would even share the clips with their colleagues, adding a viral element to the campaign.

What's your elevator pitch on how/why security awareness can actually make a difference?

Your employees are almost always present when there is the first contact of a breach situation. They might click that link or use that free USB stick—and it's downhill from there. It all starts with a person. If you can educate people as to their responsibilities, they are effectively able to act as your network of sensors throughout the company. Technology can help, but it's people who will really protect your information.

What do you love about your role or mission?

Honestly, I really love getting feedback from the employees who watch the series. They love it. It gives us a buzz when, say, someone wants the title music as their ring tone. When that happens you really know you've got them on board. You've created a fan base!

Is there a favorite story that you'd like to share?

My favorite story came from a really odd request from a client. They asked us for some 15-second clips from the series. That was very short, so we asked why. They told us they'd worked out how to replace the "Your coffee is being prepared" animation on the screen of their company coffee machines. By swapping out the video file for our clip, it would show a promo for the series every time someone was waiting for a coffee. We loved that ingenuity. It just shows that you can get to employees in the least obvious of places with a bit of tech savvy.

Name a book, resource (e.g., TED Talk), or something else that really influenced the way that you think about awareness. Or it could be a book or resource that you always find yourself recommending to others.

John Cleese, of *Monty Python* fame, used to make and license comedies to train employees in areas such as salesmanship, staff assessments, meetings and customer service. They were hilarious. I know because I saw every one of them. Working as an in-house AV tech (as well as a camera assistant), I was responsible for showing the 16mm projected films to potential clients on his behalf. It was the best business training, and I had all of it for free. I met John a couple of times when there were big client meetings. He taught me that potentially dull subjects could be hilarious when done properly.

Last thoughts?

My favorite TED talk is by Sir Ken Robinson, "Do schools kill creativity." See `https://www.ted.com/talks/ken_robinson_says_schools_kill_creativity`.

Kai Roar, CLTRe

- Name: Kai Roer
- Title: Cofounder and CEO, creator of the Security Culture Framework, author
- Company: CLTRe, the yardstick of security culture

What drew you to security awareness? In short, what's your story?

Being in the industry since the mid-1990s, I have worked on technology, communication, and leadership most of my career. When I chose to focus on security after the dot-com period, I realized that a major challenge in security is to deal with human behaviors. The realization led me to go back to university to learn about people. I asked questions like: What makes us unique? What traits are similar? What triggers are there? Which triggers are learned, and which are not? What can we do to change behaviors? Social engineering had demonstrated *that we* are vulnerable. I wanted to understand the science behind human factors. I wanted to understand how we can change behaviors, not just point at the bad behaviors. It's about fixing the problem, rather than just recognizing it.

This interest brought me to create the Security Culture Framework, a free and open framework to build and maintain security culture. This work spurred a global group of people, the Security Culture Community, who run meetups sharing their experiences, improving the framework, and so forth. My work was also picked up by ENISA and used as the foundation for their cybersecurity culture framework.

What makes your company/product/program unique? Why did you start your company? What problem are you helping with?

CLTRe (pronounced "culture") is a security culture measurement company. Over the past three years, we have created a scientific measurement instrument to measure security culture. We have packaged the instrument in a product that automates the analysis of security culture at our customers' organizations. Our customers use our tool to create a baseline of their current security culture and measure how they improve over time. Using the actionable data, they create security culture programs and can source the security awareness content they actually need. Further, they measure the effectiveness of the program.

I started this company as a direct result of requests from organizations using the Security Culture Framework. They requested a tool to accurately help them measure security culture—instead of counting completion rates, they wanted something they could use to learn where they had their strong points, their weak spots, and who in their organization would need attention. A benefit of using our vendor-neutral measurement instrument is that we are not trying to make something we sell look extra nice. We only measure culture; we do not provide awareness training content.

What's your elevator pitch on how/why security awareness can actually make a difference?

Research has shown again and again that awareness is not changing behaviors. Knowledge and skills, on the other hand, do. Tuning security training programs toward bridging the skills gap of employees when it comes to using and applying security controls is important. The critical part is training employees on what to do when they happen to click something. Research into the human factors leaves only one conclusion: people *will* click that link and open that attachment. It is how we are built. What we can train both our colleagues and our organizations on is how to handle those events when they occur.

What do you love about your role or mission?

I am changing the current discourse in security awareness. I drive knowledge of the issues at hand, based on research and scientific evidence. I provide, for free, methodologies and templates to build and improve security culture, used by organizations worldwide. Most importantly, I provide data to our customers so that they can make fact-based decisions on where and how to improve their security culture. I love to debunk myths with facts, I love challenging the anecdotal proof presented by the current discourse in our industry. I fight back against the echo chamber.

Name a book, resource (e.g., TED Talk), or something else that really influenced the way that you think about awareness. Or it could be a book or resource that you always find yourself recommending to others.

Build a Security Culture, by yours truly.

Last thoughts?

It is possible to change culture. It may not even have to be as hard as many consultants will want you to believe. Applying a structured approach, like the Security Culture Framework, will help you create change and document that change so that you can demonstrate it to your stakeholders as well as learn which parts are working great and where you need to improve.

Lisa Plaggemier, InfoSec Institute

- Name: Lisa Plaggemier
- Title: Chief Evangelist
- Company: InfoSec Institute

What drew you to security awareness? In short, what's your story?

I started my career in sales and marketing for Ford Motor Company. Automotive is a fiercely competitive business with very thin margins. If you don't have a great product with a strong brand, it can be deadly to your bottom line. I was surrounded by a lot of very smart people at Ford that were intensely driven, but the market kept us humble in the '90s. We knew that every sale, every relationship with every customer was valuable. People have lots of choices when it comes to buying a vehicle, and so I was taught early in my career the value of every customer interaction with your brand—from making it into their consideration set all the way through to repeat purchase intention and loyalty, we worked hard to be a respected, trusted brand.

I learned marketing before the Internet, before digital marketing. We didn't have click-throughs and page views as metrics. We had Nielsen ratings and circulation figures from print, and of course, sales. Marketing was more art than science. You had to really understand the market and have good intuition of what would work and what wouldn't. You got that by spending time with customers and salespeople, not sitting in meetings.

Later I worked in marketing for a B2B technology company in the automotive space. That job taught me how to translate between the technologists and our customers, making sure we were really tuned into solving clients' pain points. If we didn't understand them and their businesses, our marketing and our products would fall flat. Some of our applications had security attributes, so I worked with the CSO to hone the marketing message around security. Security is a very nuanced product feature to communicate—you can't pound your chest and say you're "completely secure" because there's no such thing.

That's when I learned to translate between the security team and our customers. That company was a division of ADP, the payroll and human capital management company. It was spun off from ADP in 2014, so there was an opportunity then to join the new security organization as the training and awareness lead. I jumped on it. I found the subject matter fascinating, and the opportunity to help people and protect the company was really compelling to me. I would read Krebs and a few other journalists, and I was intrigued but at the same time frustrated that most people—businesspeople, consumers—didn't know this stuff. There was a clear communication gap between the security professionals and literally everyone else. I saw a new way to use my marketing and sales skills that felt more purposeful and altruistic than the marketing work I had been doing previously.

There are a few things that my early experience taught me that served me well in security training and awareness.

- Understanding the power of a brand
- Producing high-quality creative work
- Valuing every interaction you get with your "consumer"
- Having a deep understanding of your audience and their pain points

What makes your company/product/program unique? Why did you start your company? What problem are you helping with?

InfoSec Institute's mission is pretty simple: We're making cybercrime less profitable through education. We've been frustrating cybercriminals since 2004. We have classes for security professionals (think boot camps, certifications, etc.); we also offer training and awareness for all employees of an organization and a phishing simulation tool. We're relentlessly client focused, and that makes it a really fun place to work, too. We were a latecomer to the phishing simulation business, but that has been an advantage. Our application is incredibly easy to use and feature rich. I've only been with InfoSec Institute for a few months. When I first saw our application, my impression was "this is the tool I wish I had" as a practitioner. We're doing some really neat things around automation and customization—trying to solve customers' pain points so they can get more done in less time.

What's your elevator pitch on how/why security awareness can actually make a difference?

I can't think of any other industry that sees people as the problem quite as much as ours. That's actually pretty sad when you think about it. I see technology as enabling humanity, not humans as ruining technology.

One of the ways we often describe a good application is "ease of use" . . . by humans. We conduct UX and UI tests with . . . humans. Somehow in security, that gets turned around, and humans are the problem and get all the blame. We should be blaming the criminals. Humans are their victims, not "the problem." Victim shaming is not a sustainable way to positively influence someone's behavior. Sure, there will always be malicious and downright reckless folks, but for the most part, most people don't want to create a security incident. As an industry, we need to change the way to talk to people.

What do you love about your role or mission?

Exercising my creative muscle. This is an industry that needs more creativity—more creative ways to engage, to tell stories, to influence behavior. If you look at the training and awareness material out there, whether from a vendor or developed in-house by the security organization, the vast majority of it is awful. You wouldn't choose to engage with it. People are consuming some really good creative content in their lives—Netflix, YouTube, podcasts that are really well done, but our industry by and large is still producing boring stuff that talks down to people. There's a lot of opportunity for people and companies doing high quality creative work. I'm starting to see more and more of it, and it's exciting to be a part of it.

Is there a favorite story that you'd like to share?

When I was Culture of Security Director, I was known for my humorous video campaigns. I remember briefing the rest of the security department on a new campaign I was launching. The cast of characters we created, and the scripts were really funny, and you learned something, too, of course. One of the technical members of the team said, only half under his breath, "I don't know why we're using humor to communicate about security. This stuff isn't funny!" In other words, we should all be very, very afraid and serious in our company communications to effectively express the gravity of the situation. After he said that, you could hear a pin drop in the meeting.

Basically, it's attitudes like his that keep people from engaging with the security team. This is also why I advocate for recruiting from marketing or communications for training and awareness managers. In the end, what that engineer wanted from our awareness program was more engagement with his team (demand for their services) and for people to report more incidents. That campaign increased incident and phish reporting 250 percent, so it worked. Come to think of it, he never did thank me for that . . . .

Name a book, resource (e.g., TED Talk), or something else that really influenced the way that you think about awareness. Or it could a book or resource that you always find yourself recommending to others.

Brian Krebs. I heard him speak at a really small conference in Washington, DC my first month working in security. He is a fantastic storyteller. He's a journalist by trade, not a techie. That was inspiring to me—that a writer and journalist could take the deep dive into this world and do such great work and tell the story so that even a marketing bozo like me could understand it.

Last thoughts?

If you're responsible for running a training and awareness program and you're blessed with technical skills more so than creative ones, find creative talent to help you with your program. Whether it's a vendor with really great creative content that gets people's attention, stimulates behavior change, and makes them want to learn more, or maybe someone in your marketing or communications department, seek out the talent to help you. And if you're a creative who's new to security, dive in, find people that will explain things to you, take some courses, but then when it comes to running a successful program that resonates and changes culture and behavior, follow your creative instincts and rely on your campaign experience.

Masha Sedova, Elevate Security

- Name: Masha Sedova
- Title: Cofounder, Chief Product Officer
- Company: Elevate Security

What drew you to security awareness? In short, what's your story?

I've been in the security world for 17 years starting from my university days. What drew me to the field initially was the idea of defending the good guys against the bad guys. I was motivated by the fact that my work could help thousands of people protect themselves against cyberattacks. I initially started my career as a cyber analyst in the defense industry.

Having seen the ability of state-sponsored attackers, I knew that compliance-mandated training did little to help employees and businesses defend against these threats. I believed that as long as security is perceived as burden and chore, the "bad guys" would always win. In 2012, I started a team at Salesforce that focused on creating a security-first culture. I couldn't get the question out of my head, "How do we get people in organizations to want to do security instead of having to?"

That question led me to study the fields of behavioral science, positive psychology, and game design, which I used to create a new approach to creating people-powered security across Salesforce's employees, developers, and customers. In 2017, I cofounded a cybersecurity company, Elevate Security, based in Berkeley that combines security education with behavioral science into an innovative security behavior change platform.

What makes your company/product/program unique? Why did you start your company? What problem are you helping with?

At Elevate, we are building and delivering a security behavior platform. We believe that trust security readiness is not about what employees know; it's what they do. Our platform leverages the latest advances in behavioral and data science to deliver a suite of products that help employees create better security habits.

Our first product, Hacker's Mind, is designed to motivate people to understand why security matters to them. Without this, security training is pushed down to employees as a mandate, without the understanding of why the information is essential to each employee.

Our second product, Snapshot, focuses on providing security teams visibility and insight into the status and improvement of the organization's employee-centered security state. This allows them to understand better what areas to focus on, where they are excelling, and what security campaigns are working at their best (and worst).

What's your elevator pitch on how/why security awareness can actually make a difference?

For decades, we've tried to solve the human-element security problem with technology solutions, and it remains unsolved. This isn't solely a technology problem but also a social, behavioral, and cultural one. Unless we look at it holistically, we are doomed to keep making the same mistakes. A complete security program involves robust people, process, and technology, and if we don't address the human component, we are fighting with only two-thirds of what we have.

What do you love about your role or mission?

I always wanted to work in a field that had an impact and improved people's lives. Security awareness work does just that. When a person knows how to be secure online, it empowers them to use the Internet and technology at its maximum as an incredibly powerful tool in their lives. Without this knowledge, their actions can jeopardize their information and that of the people and organizations around them, an outcome no one wants (other than hackers). Security education, when done with the recipient's time, intelligence, skill set, and role in mind, can and should benefit an individual at a personal and professional level and make a positive impact in their lives.

Name a book, resource (e.g., TED Talk), or something else that really influenced the way that you think about awareness. Or it could be a book or resource that you always find yourself recommending to others.

Drive by Daniel Pink, because it talks about what motivates us and why.

Last thoughts?

One of the reasons I love this field is that it's still quite new. There are so many unsolved problems that need all the bright and creative thinkers we can get! A security practitioner doesn't have to look a specific way or specialize in any one area. Every individual has a unique set of experience and can connect dots between ideas that no one else can. We need as many creative minds as it can get if we ever want to stand a chance against the evolving threat landscape and its hackers.

Stu Sjouwerman, KnowBe4

- Name: Stu Sjouwerman
- Title: CEO and Founder
- Company: KnowBe4, Inc.

What drew you to security awareness? In short, what's your story?

This is my fifth startup. In the last one we built an endpoint security platform from scratch, including antivirus, antispyware, sandbox technology, a firewall, and intrusion detection and prevention. We had a few million endpoints out there and a floor full of tech support people who continued to get trouble tickets from end users having their machine infected with malware, despite our state-of-the-art technology.

It turned out that the bad guys were using social engineering to get around all the software defenses and simply hacked the human in front of the machine. We had no reply for that, and I started looking at effective ways to create an additional security layer that would address that particular attack vector.

What makes your company/product/program unique? Why did you start your company? What problem are you helping with?

Our platform was created for IT pros who have 16 fires to put out. That means extremely user-friendly, intuitive, short ramp, and fast deployment. Other platforms were built for InfoSec professionals that do that job all day long and have more time. It turns out that large enterprises also highly appreciate our platform as it allows them to focus on higher-priority security tasks.

What's your elevator pitch on how/why security awareness can actually make a difference?

Old-school awareness training had a bad rep, because herding your users in the break room and keeping them awake with coffee and donuts while they suffer through death-by-PowerPoint is not very effective. New-school awareness training as we are now delivering it to tens of thousands of organizations worldwide is extremely effective in creating a security culture that gets both employees and IT on the same page, keeping the bad guys out of the network.

What do you love about your role or mission?

It's fantastic fun to build a company and see it take off like this. Getting feedback from hundreds of "happy camper" customers is also great and keeps you going to provide even better service.

Is there a favorite story that you'd like to share?

People always ask how I met Kevin Mitnick, my business partner. Well, my wife Rebecca and I one night went for dinner with Karen and Nico, new friends we had made on the block next to us. As you usually do when you meet new people, we asked what they did for a living. Nico answered his was in oil contracting, and when I explained what I was doing (keeping hackers out of networks), Karen commented, "Oh, my cousin Kevin went to jail for that!" My mouth fell open, and I asked . . . "Not Kevin MITNICK, right?" And she innocently answered, "Yeah, do you know him?"

So, two weeks later I sent Kevin an email and asked him if he was willing to partner. And told him he could check me out with his cousin Karen, which he did because he gets a lot of crank emails! She must have given him the green light . . . .

Name a book, resource (e.g., TED Talk), or something else that really influenced the way that you think about awareness. Or it could be a book or resource that you always find yourself recommending to others.

Well, the book I mostly recommend is Kevin's *Ghost in the Wires: My Adventures as the World's Most Wanted Hacker* because it explains social engineering from the perspective of the hacker, and it's an exciting read at the same time.

Last thoughts?

Creating a security culture takes time and air cover from your C-levels. It gets easier over the years, though, and when you set your plan up right, your users react very positively and become your best allies in fighting the bad guys.

Tom Pendergast, MediaPRO

- Name: Tom Pendergast
- Title: Chief Learning Officer
- Company: MediaPRO

What drew you to security awareness? In short, what's your story?

I'm not sure that it was security awareness that drew me to this field so much as the opportunity to help people function effectively in a complicated environment—this world of sometimes-bewildering technology and always-on information access. When I started college back in 1982, I strongly resisted giving up my IBM typewriter for a computer because I thought I didn't need it. Boy, was I wrong! Today, we all "need" an unbelievable array of electronic gadgets, and we've all opted in to sharing our personal data with an information processing ecosystem of unprecedented reach and power. I'm fascinated by what that means for us as a culture and what it means for individuals. And to be present and to participate in just one part of that—the part that helps educate employees about data protection risks—is just pretty darned fascinating to me.

I've always been fascinated by complicated puzzles, and this phenomenon where we strive to adapt to "surveillance capitalism," or whatever you want to call it, is a pretty complicated puzzle. A big part of what drives me is the desire to make complicated things like this simple (this, by the way, is the closest I get to a mission in life: to make complicated things simple). It's that mission that took me through completing my PhD and writing my dissertation (later published as "Creating the Modern Man," where I examined what the transformation to consumer capitalism did to notions of masculine identity in the United States); that led to my wife and I founding and running a book packaging company for a number of years (check out my name on Amazon; you'll see what I mean); and finally that led me to lead the cyber security and privacy training and reinforcement solution at MediaPRO. This work at MediaPRO brings together my personal interests in a really powerful way, and I think also that we in the "awareness business" have a real opportunity to do good for companies and for people, as we help them adjust to a changing world.

What makes your company/product/program unique? Why did you start your company? What problem are you helping with?

There are a couple of things that make MediaPRO unique in our industry. I'd say the first is that we've been in this business longer than most, and we've got a really long track record in terms of creating quality training experiences. Back in 1992, our founder Steve Conrad started a business that created custom elearning training for big companies like Boeing, Microsoft, Oracle, and many others. They started off selling this training on floppy discs, then CDs, but very quickly moved over to web-based training delivery. Over the years, they got really good at developing interactive learning experiences that asked employees to really dig in deeper to the learning, where most web-based training was kind of flat and dull. One of the keys to understanding MediaPRO is to know that many of our professionals are trained in instructional design, so they are applying the best research in terms of what helps people retain and apply the knowledge they are gaining.

It was while the company was doing this work back in the late 1990s and early 2000s that we (it was really Steve and Scott, then, I hadn't joined) starting doing more and more information security and privacy awareness training, and this ultimately led to some of our clients saying, "You ought to make a 'product' out of this—more and more companies are seeing the need." And that's what led MediaPRO to release the first Privacy Directions product in 2003 (I believe), followed shortly thereafter by a Security Directions course. There were more sales and utilization of these courses, but they were a little difficult and complicated to "customize," which means to modify terminology and images and message to fit the company brand. So, a few years after I came to the company in 2007, me and a couple others (Jen Castillo, Scott Urstad) decided that what we needed to do was to blow up the underlying architecture of the curriculum to make it really, really easy for our clients to choose which content they wanted to cover and then customize. We released our first training built in the "Adaptive Architecture" in 2011, and we've been adding to it and modernizing ever since, with coverage of all the key risk areas in the modern security and privacy domains.

What's interesting about our approach to our clients is that all of our content is aligned with risks, and if you know your risks and your regulatory environment, you can pretty much use our CourseBuilder technology to hone right in on the content coverage you want. And you can use role selection or even testing out to make sure that you're not wasting people's time with training they don't need. We just offer a huge amount of flexibility to our clients in the ways that they can configure their training. And of course we've added to that with a growing "reinforcement" library of videos, posters, articles, and games. We call it reinforcement because it reinforces and expands on the content in the training, often in humorous or unexpected ways, which we believe enhances the learning experience.

What's your elevator pitch on how/why security awareness can actually make a difference?

Every single person in this world (unless they are totally off the grid) can benefit from expanding their knowledge and aptitude around cyber security and privacy. So we're offering people a set of skills that will make them better employees but will also make them better consumers and citizens and parents. I truly believe that everybody can care about cyber security and privacy, once they reach the tipping point and recognize that it really is critical to their well-being.

What do you love about your role or mission?

Whenever I hear from our clients that something we created helped make a difference in their company or helped someone understand how to do their job better or see how their work fit into the big picture, that's pretty joyful to me. Creating content is really rewarding, and when you make something good, that feels pretty damn awesome. I also really like seeing what others create and understanding how others solve the same problems.

Is there a favorite story that you'd like to share?

We had a client who worked for a big financial services company, and they were initially really skeptical about taking any "chances" with their security awareness training and reinforcement. They were worried about keeping the training very "corporate" and safe, but they were also drawn to shaking things up a bit, so they liked some of our goofier animated videos. One day, they finally decided to release what we call our "Lucky Jane" video about protecting data while traveling, and they got such a positive result—such great feedback from employees and managers—that they decided to go with more humorous, edgy treatments on all their subject matter. And they just got great results, with much higher levels of engagement and enjoyment from their employees.

Ultimately, I'm convinced that security awareness doesn't have to be this deadly serious matter, so I'm really gratified to see companies shaking it up a bit.

Name a book, resource (e.g., TED Talk), or something else that really influenced the way that you think about awareness. Or it could be a book or resource that you always find yourself recommending to others.

I'll just stick with one, and it's Malcolm Gladwell's *The Tipping Point*, where he talks about what it takes for people and societies to transform. I've always been a big believer that everybody has their cyber security tipping point (or privacy tipping point), the point that they reach when they really do start to care about this stuff. And I guess I just want everybody to reach that tipping point.

Last thoughts?

Take the chance that when you show people what you are passionate about—even if it's security awareness—that your passion will matter and they will engage with you. I just hate it when I hear people complain about how "users are stupid" or "security awareness is boring." Neither one is true, and it's up to us to prove it to the world.

Winn Schwartau, The Security Awareness Company (SAC)

- Name: Winn Schwartau
- Title: Founder and Chief Visionary Officer
- Company: The Security Awareness Company, LLC

What drew you to security awareness? In short, what's your story?

It began on a dark and stormy night.

My 1991 congressional testimony and first books, *Terminal Compromise* (*Pearl Harbor Dot Com/Die Hard IV*) and *Information Warfare*, were causing a political stink. Apparently, I talked too much about classified stuff that I didn't know was classified; I thought I had made it all up on my own. That made me an expert in their eyes. Go figure.

Invitations from spook, spies, and goblins around the world poured in, asking me to teach their military, government, and intelligence groups about cyberterrorism, electronic Pearl Harbor, and how the Internet would become a war zone.

Phase II of SAC arrived unexpectedly. In 1995, a quasi-government organization asked us to build an online learning center and develop training materials; this was years before real "standards" like SCORM existed, but we built a first-generation "LMS" anyway. Then word got around, largely through our coordinated efforts with the nascent FS-ISAC, and we began working with financial firms and creating the basis of security awareness programs, their management and metrics, multimedia multiple-vector content creation, and deployment.

I, along with my wife, Sherra, and a few others were having a ball pioneering a small but important industry segment. Family businesses provide huge flexibility! We could try lots of cool ideas, see how they worked, modify, redeploy. We applied an OODA-loop for awareness 20-plus years ago (https://en .wikipedia.org/wiki/OODA_loop). We permitted ourselves to fail occasionally; we saw that as part of the inventing and pioneering spirit and actually encouraged it with our small, but brilliant, staff. Unless we tried new, innovative ideas—unless we pushed the edge—we couldn't lead. So, we pushed.

As a father, I became acutely aware of the security and privacy issues with kids. Watching my daughter online was a huge eye-opener. Sherra and I became heavily involved in the school system, trying to point out what the education world could really use and take a leadership position with. I wrote and Sherra edited *Internet & Computer Security for Kids, Parents and Teachers* in early 2001, to evangelize security, privacy, and good behavior to the K-12 market, which helped us evolve the company quickly. We and our business partners believed that security awareness was a results-oriented marketing and advertising campaign, targeted at specific audiences, with specific goals and measurable results. I guess I would call that the beginning of Phase III: getting the kids and families and folks at home into the equation.

The Security Awareness Company (SAC) got very personal. We created awareness programs, content, and messaging so enterprise users could involve family and friends. We gave them a reason to care about security by touching their soft inner core: their love for their family and friends. The approach worked immediately, and the industry has come to agree with us. My daughter, Ashley, now the COO of SAC, joined and brought new visions, approaches, and techniques to enhance our security awareness programs. We were a small, growing family business that was garnering a formidable reputation for awesome content, customer relations, and the ability to tailor programs for multiple specific use cases.

To make learning more accessible, we used a century of advertising history as a guideline for what made people pay attention and remember messages. We stole the lessons of history and applied them. One of my favorites is the rule of three (https://en.wikipedia.org/wiki/Rule_of_three_(writing)).

People resonate with threes. Jokes, acts in a play, and numbers! So, based upon the traditional CIA security triad, we expanded and created more security triads.

- **The 3three-lives triad:** "Home, work, and mobile."
- **Domains:** "Physical, cyber, and human."
- **Population:** "Users, techs, and execs" and other triads are core learning tools for all SAC-based training and awareness.

It took quite a while for awareness to become mainstream. For 25 years, we continued to push, creating and trying new ideas and enjoying the heck out of ourselves! No one other than SAC was developing comprehensive innovative security awareness content and programs in those days. So, we made it up as we went along, in partnership with our clients.

For two years running, SAC was honored to be recognized as a Leader in the Gartner Magic Quadrant. This led us to become KnowBe4 Inc.'s first acquisition, back in 2016. Our operationally independent subsidiary status has allowed us to hyper-focus on developing exceptional content, delivery, and interactivity methods for myriad audiences. After our acquisition by KnowBe4, the rest of the awareness industry followed by example, going crazy with lots of mergers and acquisitions. We saw a lot of awareness industry hyper-consolidation. But SAC still dominates in creative content and delivery. That's all we do and have ever done: hyper-focus.

I am so proud of our team for being the first and best for so many years. And, thanks to them all, our creative future is even brighter!

What makes your company/product/program unique? Why did you start your company? What problem are you helping with?

We've been doing awareness since 1991, longer than anyone. From governments, financial, commercial, and educational markets, we have seen and done it all. That depth of experience is priceless. Beyond that? Take a look and make your own decision.

What problem are we helping with? Let's make that three problems; it's a triad after all.

- Corporate security culture and user behavior needed improvement. We influence, alter, and improve the behavior of users with top-down management participation.
- Humans natively sense their environment to make rapid decisions. That's how we survive. SAC exploits humans' highly developed internal

detection mechanisms to be more situationally aware of their security environs in all three domains.

■ Since we began some 28 years ago, incident response policy and procedures were clearly not functioning well. Users rarely knew how to report or whom to report a potential incident to. SAC's approach to security awareness first focuses on developing a user population's automatic senses of urgency to react to potential security events in as short a time period as possible.

What's your elevator pitch on how/why security awareness can actually make a difference?

Three (big surprise) quotes I made up. They seem to stick, and they symbiotically reinforce each other.

■ "We don't want to turn your users into security experts. We want your users to know when, how, and why to contact the security experts!"

■ "It's all about time. Your number-one responsibility is to report any suspected physical, cyber, or human security incident—immediately. Do not pause. Do not pass Go!"

■ "Do it right. Listen to your audience. Change it up. Then do it all over again, differently. Then start all over. Security awareness is an Observe-Orient-Decide-Act (OODA) loop and one-size does not fit all."

What do you love about your role or mission?

Good word choice: love. I love security and awareness. SAC loves security awareness. We have thrived on it for almost 30 years, in all of its evolving facets.

Awareness is an addictive passion that every member of our remarkable creative team has succumbed to. Personally, my job is to think about new stuff: new approaches using different lenses; tech integration; anthro-cyber-kinetic systems behavior; neural science and optimization methodologies to maximize positive engagement with users—no matter the audience.

I have the incredible fortune of having a healthy addiction to learning and teaching the human-machine behavioral interface.

Is there a favorite story that you'd like to share?

A long, long time ago; in a city far, far away; before the cloud . . . .

Company A had a great security profile. Their IT and security departments were generously supported by the board. Their awareness program that we developed was second to none and received awards because it was so far ahead of its time. Their controls were spotlessly enforced. Their audits were a breeze.

And then the IT hit the fan.

A partial blackout caused by a nearby substation failure. No problem, right? Switch over to batteries. Perfect. It worked. Certainly, the power company would restore power within four hours. Right? They didn't, but no problem, right? The batteries will switch over to the generators and they could keep their bits and bytes moving. Right . . . ?

Well, in theory. Except. Somehow. Someone. Somewhere. They forgot to include exercising their business continuity and disaster recovery and BC/DR policy all the way down to the generators. The oil had not been changed since . . . well, long since their policy was written.

Prrrf! Snigggkkk! Smoke. Dead generators. They waited for the power to be restored like the rest of the neighborhood. They went to the generator store the very next day.

The point is stay aware of exercising all failsafe and BC/DR mechanisms regularly. Backing up is easy. Restoring is what you really care about. How will your cloud instance fail? Are its BC/DR/etc. tested regularly? Exercise your users. They may pass a "security quiz," but that is not the same as knowing how they will behave in a real or simulated security situation. Security awareness is for techs and execs, too.

Awareness is not just about not "clicking on s***." More importantly, it's about what to do when the IT hits the fan.

Name a book, resource (e.g., TED Talk), or something else that really influenced the way that you think about awareness. Or it could be a book or resource that you always find yourself recommending to others.

One? Three? LOL. I'd rather categorize them because there are so many. Create your own learning and growth path.

I think the *Milgram Experiment* on obedience to authority figures offers a view of one extreme of what a security culture could become under certain leadership models. Negative leadership creates negative reactions. Expand reading from there. See https://en.wikipedia.org/wiki/Milgram_experiment.

Neuroscience, and now AI, are at the heart of learning, individuality, influence—and all things human sensory. You will get your mind blown with some history while "grokking" basics of what science has learned and not learned about the brain and how it relates to AI. *The Deep Learning Revolution* is an enthralling first step.

My audio-triggered synesthesia (https://en.wikipedia.org/wiki/Synesthesia) created vast visual displays of dynamic streams of color; essentially, I was seeing audio, which was good for my first career. Then I heard about tetrachromacy (https://en.wikipedia.org/wiki/Tetrachromacy) through an artist friend. The art of the first tetrachromatic artist (https://concettaantico.com/) just shows us, especially in a world of endless multimedia onslaughts, that we must cater to the perceptual capabilities of all audiences, regardless of content. We all see and hear and sense the world differently. The bottom line is that one size does not fit all. (That's a crass pitch for SAC since that's what we specialize in.)

Last thoughts?

Be different. Show off. Your users have the attention span of a goldfish. (Seriously!) You only have a few seconds to capture their attention. You have to shake it up. And then do it again. And again. Awareness is an OODA loop of grabbing their attention and never letting go.

Reference

1. *Calacanis calls time on the internet "me-toos"* by Zoe Margolis (https://www.theguardian.com/technology/2008/oct/16/internet-startups)

The Process of Transformation

8

Living Your Awareness Program Through the Eyes and Lives of Your Audience

> "If you can learn a simple trick, Scout, you'll get along a lot better with all kinds of folks. You never really understand a person until you consider things from his point of view, until you climb inside of his skin and walk around in it."
> Atticus Finch in *To Kill A Mockingbird* by Harper Lee

Back in the 60s, 70s, and 80s, there was a well-known public service announcement that asked: "It's 10 p.m. Do you know where your kids are?"[1,2] That's an important question. And it's simple enough to answer: a simple yes or no. An answer of yes implies that your kids are safe and that they are good kids. But, a no response had two implications: if you don't know where your kids are, then 1) they are likely in danger or 2) they may be participating in, well, unsavory activities.

I've got a similar question for you: It's 2 p.m. Do you know where your users are? Do you know what they are likely doing? That's an important question because the more you know and understand your users' behavior patterns, the better you will be at anticipating how you can best intersect with their lives in meaningful ways.

That's the concept of this chapter. In my original outline, this was a subtopic of a larger chapter. But I really felt that while the substance of what I am talking about won't take long, the *concept* itself deserves the full attention that a chapter title can give.

NOTE You need to understand the lives, actions, and interactions of your users so that you can intersect with their lives with relevant awareness, behavior, and culture strategies.

That's it. End of chapter.

OK, that was a joke. But notice how by simply doing something unexpected, I piqued your interest a bit? There is an awareness communications lesson in that. I intersected with a specific moment in your day and found a unique way to alter your attention. Now let's move on and brainstorm a bit on how to create a journey map of sorts to analyze the flow of your users' daily lives.

A Learner Journey Map: Awareness in the Context of Life

The concept of a *journey map* finds its roots in the worlds of marketing and product development. Marketers and product designers need to understand all the touchpoints that a customer or potential customer will have with the product or experience being designed. Here is how the Nielson Norman Group defines a journey map:

> *Definition: A journey map is a visualization of the process that a person goes through in order to accomplish a goal.*
>
> *In its most basic form, journey mapping starts by compiling a series of user actions into a timeline. Next, the timeline is fleshed out with user thoughts and emotions in order to create a narrative. This narrative is condensed and polished, ultimately leading to a visualization.*[3]

Sarah Gibbons, *Journey Mapping 101*, Nielson Norman Group

RESOURCES FOR A DEEPER DIVE INTO JOURNEY MAPPING

Journey mapping can be a rigorous process, and you may or may not want to take it as far as a marketing or product design team would. Most of the time, you'll be OK using the brainstorming worksheet from table 8.1 and simple thought experiments that I'll provide later in this chapter. But, if you are working through a full security experience as it relates to a system interaction, or other touchpoint, you may decide that a comprehensive journey map for that specific use-case is beneficial.

Here are a few good starting places if you want to dive into journey mapping to the fullest:

- *5 Essential Components of Effective Customer Journey Maps* by Phil Goddard and Kathleen Hoski (`https://www.tandemseven.com/journey-mapping/5-essentials-for-customer-journey-maps/`)
- *How to Create an Effective Customer Journey Map [Examples + Template]* by Aaron Agius (`https://blog.hubspot.com/service/customer-journey-map`)
- *Mapping Experiences: A Complete Guide to Creating Value through Journeys, Blueprints, and Diagrams* by James Kalbach
- *The User's Journey: Storymapping Products That People Love* by Donna Lichaw

For the purposes of this book, I'm using the concept of a journey map loosely. Here's the ultimate takeaway: I want you to intentionally step into the mind, shoes, and experiences of your target audience and spend some time there. Imagine life and events from their perspective. Have empathy. Think through their day as a story with tons of interesting touchpoints and subplots. Figure 8.1 captures that concept.

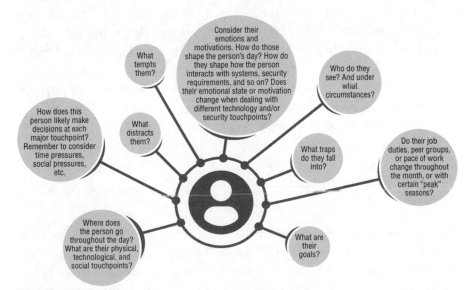

Figure 8.1: Live your awareness program through the eyes and lives of your people.

NOTE   Step into the mind, shoes, and experiences of your target audience and spend some time there.

Here is the mind-set you should adopt and some starter questions to think about as you create your journey maps:

- Be honest/realistic in your assessments.
- Do journey mapping at a persona/role level. Your employees each have different roles. And those roles impact the systems they interact with, the schedules they have, peer groups, social expectations, and more.
- Get a generic idea of what the person's day is like.
- Do their job duties, peer groups, or pace of work change throughout the month, or with certain "peak" seasons?
- Consider their emotions and motivations. How do those shape the person's day? How do they shape how the person interacts with systems, security requirements, and so on? Does their emotional state or motivation change when dealing with different technology and/or security touchpoints?
- What and who influences them? What is the social component? Are there times of day or seasons of the year that may cause a flux in behavior? For instance, busier times like holiday seasons? Times when the organization has an influx of temporary workers? Times of mass movement within the office (like lunch, morning meetings, etc.)?
- How does this person likely make decisions at each major touchpoint? Remember to consider time pressures, social pressures, etc.
- Where does the person go throughout the day? What are their physical, technological, and social touchpoints?
- Who do they see? And under what circumstances?
- What are their goals?
- What traps do they fall into?
- What distracts them?
- What tempts them?

In all of these, you are looking for discrete points of behavior or decision. You can, and should, also be on the lookout for opportunities to capture their attention. When you identify those opportunities, you can design for points of intersection using the Fogg Behavior Model, nudges, influence tactics, social interventions, just-in-time training, or context-based messaging, or by revising processes or configuring your technology-based systems differently (Figure 8.2). Where you can't find good points to alter the behavior at the point of context/intersection, then you may decide that you need to offer more practice in the form of training. In all things, remember your Behavior Design and behavior debugging techniques (see Chapter 4).

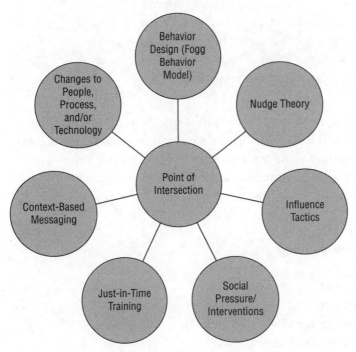

Figure 8.2: Example tactics to use at points of behavioral intersection

Your purpose for all of this is to better see how you can find points of time, locations, and contexts to design for within your awareness training program (for example, when a user clicks a URL in an email message, as they enter a secure area, and so on). Can you add a gentle nudge at the point of behavior? How about a timely reminder? Or maybe find a way to alter the social dynamic around a type of behavior. And, in these points of intersection, consider how you can reward and reinforce successes while also providing just-in-time, at the point of behavior (or as close as possible) interventions to help minimize failures.

A GENERAL NOTE ABOUT PRIVACY AND "CREEPINESS"

Of course, as you create your journey maps and awareness plans, you should be conscious of the privacy laws and social expectations of each user population. This method of interaction can be extremely personal and context-driven based on aggregated SIEM, DLP, training, demographic, and employee monitoring data, or you can simply be opportunistic with messaging and awareness-related artifacts in locations and contexts that employees will naturally encounter. The more personal and targeted your efforts become, the more you will need to ensure that you aren't unintentionally crossing legal or social boundaries.

Table 8.1 is a quick, down-and-dirty brainstorming worksheet template to get you started. You will have one worksheet per role or persona per location/behavior that you are designing for. This allows you to specifically and intentionally design your awareness and behavior intervention points for locations such as the following:

- In the parking lot
- Walking in the building
- In the lobby
- Near the elevator
- Inside the elevator
- Walking through the office environment
- Approaching their workstation
- At their workstation
- Logging in to their computer
- Navigating to, and interacting with, specific systems
- In the breakroom
- Near trash and paper shredding bins
- Approaching the restrooms
- Inside the restrooms (bathroom stall doors = captive audience)
- In the meal areas

You get the picture. Don't forget to address the diversity of each environment differently. For example, you will likely discover that you need distinct messaging in call centers, application development areas, finance offices, and so on. Why? The workflow, systems, and interactions with data often change from department to department. If you want to truly serve your people, then you will create messaging and experiences that are tailored to their individual needs.

NOTE If you want to truly serve your people, then you will create messaging and experiences that are tailored to their individual needs.

Table 8.1: Security Behavior Journey Map Brainstorming Sheet

Function	Answers	Additional Notes/ Comments/ Observations
Who are they?		
When is it? (time of day)		
Where are they? (location)		
What are they doing or about to do? (event/behavior)		
What is their goal?		
What are they feeling? (emotions)		
Who else is around? (social)		
Are there any other interesting or important aspects of the context they are in?		
How might they make mistakes or deliberately make insecure choices?		
Thoughts on Fogg Behavior Model (B=MAP) elements for encouraging secure behaviors?		
What program elements can we use to encourage and reinforce the behavior we want?		
How can we reward people who are doing the right thing or people who accept intervention?		

Table 8.2 is the same table with representative values filled in.

Table 8.2: Security Behavior Journey Map Brainstorming Sheet (Completed Example)

Function	Answers	Additional Notes/ Comments/ Observations
Who are they?	General employees/everyone.	This is for everyone, regardless of role.
When is it? (time of day)	Early morning, beginning of the workday.	
Where are they (location)?	Building entrance.	
What are they doing or about to do? (event/behavior)	Enter the building.	
What is their goal?	Get to work on time.	
What are they feeling? (emotions)	Hurried and potentially distracted thinking about home issues or distracted thinking about what they need to get done today.	
Who else is around? (social)	Others entering; more traffic than at other times during the day.	
Other notes about the context they are in	General business, lots of other conversations, people bringing breakfast, coffee, work bags, etc.	
How might they make mistakes or deliberately make insecure choices?	This is a prime time when someone might tailgate or allow someone to tailgate.	Business, hurriedness, distractedness, and social graces (holding the door for someone) conspire against an anti-tailgating policy.

Function	Answers	Additional Notes/ Comments/ Observations
Thoughts on Fogg Behavior Model (B=MAP) elements for encouraging secure behaviors?	The behavior we want is for everyone to badge in. How are we *prompting*? Do they have the *ability*? Do they have the *motivation*?	If we aren't prompting, then add a prompt (see the next row). If the employee doesn't have the ability, then problem solve for the ability. Are their hands full? Find a way to solve for that. Are they not motivated? Staff and culture carriers may give the added social push merely by their presence.
What program elements can we use to encourage and reinforce the behavior we want?	We can add a *prompt* in the form of a sign at the door. Something like: "For the safety of our associates, we require that everyone badge in. One badge = One entry."	We may also be able to station security staff and culture carriers at the doors to encourage the right behavior in a non-threatening way. For instance, if someone's hands are full, staff can offer to hold the associate's bag so that they can fish out their badge and enter properly.
How can we reward people who are doing the right thing or people who accept intervention?	A warm, genuine "thank you" from staff at the door. Randomly awarding gift cards for helping encourage a safe work environment.	Positive social feedback. Variability of reward.

A "DAY IN THE LIFE" VIEW HELPS TO FOCUS YOUR EFFORTS AND INCREASE EFFECTIVENESS

Once you begin to think about how your program elements intersect with discrete points in the lives of your people, you'll become more intentional about how and when you deliver those program elements. An example of that is when you send security messaging or training enrollment notifications via email.

There have been numerous studies on when the best time is to send emails that you hope will capture the attention of your people. For instance, research from Yesware[4] demonstrates that time of day isn't the only important factor in this equation. Why? Because people in different cities/locations have been shown to have different email habits.

As you design your program, review research conducted by relevant groups (e.g., marketing agencies), think through how that research may be accurate or may vary in your organization, and plan accordingly.

Key Takeaways

- *Understand the lives, actions, and interactions of your users.* By doing so, you'll be able to plan strategies for intersecting with their lives with relevant awareness, behavior, and culture strategies.
- *Use a journey map approach for thinking through the daily and seasonal routines of your people.* Step into the mind, shoes, and experiences of your target audience and spend some time there. Use the simple brainstorming worksheet and the list of starter questions to begin thinking through the lives and events of your people from their perspective.
- *Be sensitive to regulatory or social issues that may cause your interventions to be seen as illegal or creepy.* The more personal and targeted your efforts become, the more you will need to ensure that you aren't unintentionally crossing legal or social boundaries.
- *Think through each point of your user's routines where you might be able to intersect.* Nothing is off limits, including lunchrooms, boardrooms, and bathrooms.

Notes and References

1. *Do you know where your children are?* (https://en.wikipedia.org/wiki/Do_you_know_where_your_children_are%3F)
2. *The Origin of "It's 10 p.m. Do You Know Where Your Children Are?* by Jara Kovalchik (https://mentalfloss.com/article/30945/origin-its-10-pm-do-you-know-where-your-children-are)

3. *Journey Mapping 101* by Sarah Gibbons (`https://www.nngroup.com/articles/journey-mapping-101/`)
4. *Best Time to Send Email: A Matter of When and Where* by Richard Ng (`https://www.yesware.com/blog/best-time-to-send-email/`)

9

Putting It
All Together

Marketers have the empathy to know that those they seek to serve don't want what the marketer wants, don't believe what they believe, and don't care about what they care about.

Seth Godin, *This Is Marketing*

U p to now, I've primarily been discussing the components of a transformational security awareness program along with a bit of information on how those components complement each other and support the overarching goal of shaping behavior and culture. That's all well and good, but here's the thing: We can read and understand all of this and still not be successful. *Success comes in the doing, not the knowing.*

Let's suppose you are ready to implement several ideas in this book. You still may not be able to successfully *do* (pardon the bad grammar). Here are two reasons why:

- In the same way that your target audience faces the *knowledge-intention-behavior gap*, so do you—unless you methodically and intentionally set a plan to move forward and take the first step. Taking that first step is crucial.
- But there is also a second reason that you might not be able to successfully *do*. You very likely require buy-in and participation from others in your organization before you officially kick off your program, obtain budget, ask for people's time, communicate broadly across the organization, purchase any materials and tools that you want, plan events, and the list goes on. It's not *about* you, and it can't all be done *by* you.

NOTE Security awareness—it's not *about* you, and it can't all be done *by* you.

After that brutal introduction, let's get down to business. This chapter is about trying to fill in program-related gaps and help you head off some of the issues that I've seen security awareness leaders fail to plan for until those issues become pain points. While at Gartner, I took several hundred inquiry calls and one-on-one meetings each year from CISOs and awareness program leaders who were grappling with these topics and issues. This chapter is all about helping you learn from their pain and successes so that you can minimize the pain and maximize the success. I'm also going to give my perspective on how the pieces of your program fit together.

Before You Begin

Let's face it. Achieving anything worthwhile takes planning and goal-setting. That's where this section fits in. We can know a ton of cool facts about human behavior, communications skills, and culture management, but that knowledge won't translate into value unless you set yourself up for success. And the only way to do that is to approach your security awareness efforts as a structured program.

My goal here isn't to communicate the fundamentals of program management to you. Rather, I hope to provide you with a specific mind-set and some tips related to how you approach your program.

The Five Secrets of Security Awareness Success

Over the past couple years, I've been referring to what I call the "five secrets to security awareness success" (see Figure 9.1). As you read them, I'm sure you'll notice that I've already embedded each "secret" multiple times throughout this book. However, I want to briefly crystalize each secret and draw-out a bit of additional detail. If you use the information presented thus far in this book, and apply these five secrets, you will achieve a game changing level of security awareness and behavior transformation.

Secret 1: Have a Vision of What "Good" Looks Like for Your Organization

The key to this secret is implementing a framework to help ensure that you are approaching things in a structured manner, rather than simply making it up as you go. Especially in large global organizations, I recommend conducting

5 Secrets to Awareness Success

Have a clear vision of what "good" looks like for your organization

View awareness through the lens of organizational culture

Leverage behavior management principles to help shape good security hygiene

Focus on understanding the different personalities, drivers, and learning styles within your organization

Be realistic about what is achievable in the short-term, and optimistic about the long-term payoff

Figure 9.1: The five secrets to security awareness success

a series of interviews or quick surveys to understand how different divisions, divisional leaders, and other demographic groups view security, understand policy and best practices, and what they truly hold important.[1] It is always interesting to see the differences and similarities that this process can help uncover. The process of conducting these surveys and interviews will also help you understand if your key executives are in alignment and if there are some political or logistical hurdles that you need to work through.

With the knowledge gained from your surveys and interviews, you can begin to create your goals. For this, I like the SMARTER goal setting framework proposed by several productivity gurus. There are a few different versions of the SMARTER framework (see Figure 9.2); for our purposes here, I'm using the Michael Hyatt version.[2]

Figure 9.2: The SMARTER goal setting framework

SMARTER framework goals, in the context of a security awareness program, are comprised of the following:

- *Specific enough to focus and direct your efforts.* What exactly are you hoping to achieve in the next *n* weeks/months? Think about this both in terms of content delivery, behavior change, culture shaping, and any other goals that you can refine enough to be specific about.

- *Measurable so you can keep track of progress and identify gaps.* Identify beforehand what you are going to measure. I've included thoughts on metrics and measurement in each chapter. Some of the easier metrics to gather include number of campaigns; course completion percentages; average test scores by department; phishing test resiliency change over time; number of special on-site training events, such as tabletop exercises; number of self-reported suspected security issues; and number of reported suspected phishing emails versus the number of accurately reported phishing emails and known unreported phishing emails. These are just examples of some relatively easy metrics to gather. You can also gather metrics around password hygiene, physical security–related issues, engagement of your culture carriers, culture survey response change over time, and more. The point is to find measurable attributes/outcomes of your security awareness program that are relevant to your organization, the change you are trying to drive, *and the story that you want to tell.*

- *Actionable with a clear initiating verb that prompts specific activity.* Your security awareness program will likely have several goals attached to it. Each outcome should be clearly stated with an action verb. Here are a few examples:

- "*Reduce* our overall phish test failure percentage from 22 percent to 2 percent within the next 12 months."
- "*Establish* our security awareness dashboard and *deliver* agreed-upon metrics by the end of Q1."
- "*Increase* use of official shredding bins by 50 percent as determined by weekly volume (to be reported/validated by our shredding vendor)."
- "*Reduce* instances of tailgating by percent within the next two quarters. This will be validated by auditing CCTV camera footage over multiple randomly selected dates."

- **Risky enough to leverage our natural tendency to rise to challenges.** Ask yourself where you can afford to be risky here. For instance, what's your goal for reducing your organization's susceptibility to social engineering attacks, reporting suspected security incidents, training completions, and more? Go ahead, take a risk and be aggressive in your estimate! Doing so will force you (and any in the approval chain for your program) to be proactive and intentional in how you approach each goal area. You'll find yourself adopting multifaceted tactics across the people, process, and technologies related to each goal. Or maybe your risky goal is to take your program global for the first time. If so, stating your goal will force you to work with other areas of your organization to ensure that you have the best chance for success as you implement your program in each region.
- **Time-keyed so you're prompted exactly when to act.** This is self-explanatory. Unless you've committed to a specific time frame, you may be likely to just see your goal as vague. Once you have a date attached to it, you have much more incentive to work to meet the date. And that forces you to work backward from the target date and break down the goal into well-defined, manageable chunks.
- **Exciting enough to inspire and harness the power of your intrinsic motivation.** This is all about moving you from a "check the box" mentality and into a crusader mind-set. Think about why each aspect of your program is important. How does it improve the overall organization? Getting in touch with the underlying "why" behind each aspect will serve as a catalyst for your excitement and will keep you energized throughout the year as you ride the waves of both success and frustration.

- *Relevant within the overall context of your organization and people.* Don't make security an abstract concept. If you are training about things that aren't relevant to your organization or people, they will disregard and forget the content. Make it real, make it relatable, and make it relevant. Have a look at the concepts and tactics discussed in Chapters 3, 4, 5, 6, and 8 again. As I emphasized throughout those chapters, the real power of transformation will manifest when you use multiple messaging, behavioral, and cultural tactics and touchpoints across different departments, regions, roles, and other demographic groups. Go ahead and embrace it—it's worked in the marketing world for quite a while now, and it will work for you as well.

OBJECTIVES AND KEY RESULTS (OKRs)

Another great method for helping set goals and associated measurements comes from the book *Measure What Matters: How Google, Bono, and the Gates Foundation Rock the World with OKRs* by John Doerr. This strategy, used by many of the most successful organizations on the planet, offers a simple and easy-to-use method of deciding what is most important (the *objective*) and then breaking down ways of obtaining and demonstrating success (the *key results*). For each *objective*, you should have three to five *key results* that map out how you'll meet the objective.

Let's get specific by reusing one of our previous examples and structuring it as an OKR.

- **Objective (O):** Reduce our overall phish test failure percentage from 22 percent to 2 percent in the next 12 months.
- **Key Result (KR):** Conduct a baseline phishing test to assess the organization's current level of phishing resiliency.
- **Key Result (KR):** Work with relevant teams to approve and schedule multiple phishing testing scenarios each month.
- **Key Result (KR):** Ensure that phishing tests are paired with just-in-time training opportunities or are followed up quickly with learning/correction opportunities.
- **Key Result (KR):** Assess and positively engage employee segments who are consistently more susceptible to phishing.
- **Key Result (KR):** Develop gamification, reward, and recognition programs to create positive energy and positive social pressure.

You can see how phrasing your goals in this way will immediately provide clarity and help you build action plans to achieve your objectives. If you are interested, be sure to read *Measure What Matters* and/or review many of the online resources that provide example OKRs.

Secret 2: View Awareness Through the Lens of Organizational Culture

As discussed in Chapter 5, your security culture is a subcomponent of your larger organizational culture. In other words, your organizational culture will "win out" over your security awareness goals every time unless you are able to weave security-based thinking and values into the fabric of your overarching organizational culture.

NOTE Your organizational culture will "win out" over your security awareness goals every time unless you are able to weave security-based thinking and values into the fabric of your overarching organizational culture.

Remember the survey and interviews that I mentioned at the start of the first secret. This is where you'll really get an idea of any organizational culture gaps that you need to account for. When you find these gaps, you'll have a few choices: modify your awareness program's expectations and goals based on the identified gap, work with organizational leaders to see how you can help influence the larger culture, or use a hybrid approach where you modify some goals while also doing the work of trying to influence the larger culture.

Of these, the first option is clearly the easiest but has little reward associated with it; it's the "safe" route. The second and third options involve more work, politicking, and likely a bit of frustration, but they offer the greatest long term benefit for the organization and for you. This is also where you can leverage your security culture carriers to help infuse security-related values throughout the organization to create consistency and sustainability.

NOTE Taking the "safe" route with your program (e.g., doing what's always been done) will ultimately result in greater organizational risk because the "safe" route fails to account for the knowledge-intention-behavior gap.

Secret 3: Leverage Behavior Management Principles to Help Shape Good Security Hygiene

This is obviously a major focus of a transformational program. You know that your awareness program shouldn't focus only on information delivery. This comes back to the "three realities of security awareness" that I've outlined a few times now. As a quick refresher, they are as follows:

- Just because I'm *aware* doesn't mean that I *care*.
- If you try to work *against* human nature, you will *fail*.
- What your people *do* is way more important than what they *know*.

If the underlying motivation for your program is to reduce the overall risk of human-related security incidents in your organization, you need to incorporate behavior management practices. Review the Behavior Design models and principles from Chapter 4 including the Fogg Behavior Model, nudge theory, System 1 and System 2 thinking, reinforcement schedules, and segmentation.

Use these principles as you decide the who, what, when, where, why, and how of delivering both content and innovative behavioral interventions. And, as discussed in Chapter 6, these principles will help inform your decisions on which tools are most appropriate for each given context.

Secret 4: Focus on Understanding the Different Personalities, Drivers, and Learning Styles Within Your Organization

This is a callback to the *Specific* and *Relevant* attributes of the SMARTER framework. It is critically important to understand your overall organizational context, the different types of people within the organization, regional contexts, divisional and departmental contexts, and demographic contexts. This not only helps you tailor content, behavioral interventions, and culture-shaping elements that will best speak to each of the groups but can also help you avoid stepping on potential landmines.

Secret 5: Be Realistic About What Is Achievable in the Short Term and Optimistic About the Long-Term Payoff

So, here is where the rubber meets the road. You have all the planning out of the way, created SMARTER goals, understand the nuances of your organization, and are focusing on creating real, sustainable change. Now it's time to get started and to commit to perseverance. Your program isn't a single training event. It's an ongoing campaign. Many aspects of your program will be spaced throughout the year, so it is important to commit to being consistent with your efforts and understand how each contribute to the greater whole. The beginning is just that: the beginning. Transformation takes time.

NOTE Even when your program has produced transformational results, you are not done. You will never be done.

In the same way that your people and organization are always in a state of change, a transformational security awareness program must constantly adapt and commit to a process of continual improvement.

Tips for Gaining Buy-In

Here's a fun play on words that represents a harsh truth. One of the only things you can't buy for your security awareness program is "buy-in." Yeah, I know that's a cheesy line, but it's so true. It doesn't matter how much you know, how great your tools are, or how well you plan, your ultimate success will (in so many ways) hinge on obtaining buy-in from key people in your organization.

NOTE Keep in mind that "key" people exist at all levels of the organization from the CEO and other C-level executives setting the tone at the top to cultural carriers—staff—that espouse the right values and do the right things day in day out.

In my time as an analyst and as a CISO advisor, I helped countless security leaders and program managers work through the process of "selling" their initiative(s). The process is similar regardless of whether you are trying to get buy-in for an identity and access management (IAM) program, a third-party risk management program, obtaining support for a security awareness program, or trying to "sell" any large-scale organizational initiative. It's all about understanding your stakeholders.

Back in my early Gartner days, I wrote a short research note titled "How to Use 'Visioneering' Principles to Drive a Successful Identity and Access Management Program."[3] That paper turned out to be transformational for many IAM leaders—so much so that I created Gartner workshops and toolkits around it. And, the ideas I presented in that paper are still core to the way that I help security leaders define their visions, keep themselves motivated, gain broad support for their programs, and evaluate their success. One element of that paper was a simple brainstorming worksheet that I created for IAM leaders needing to gain buy-in.[4]

Here's why the worksheet is powerful: it was designed to tap in to the various "whys" that organizational leaders across all departments held dear. And that information was coupled with the ability to prethink through any objections or concerns that those organizational leaders may have. So, it was all about addressing the needs, concerns, and emotions of each stakeholder.

Here's how I've evolved that same worksheet concept for working with security awareness leaders. You'll likely complete this worksheet twice. Complete the worksheet once before you meet with any stakeholder to present your program and ask their thoughts. And then complete it again post-meeting to correct any inaccurate assumptions and capture additional thoughts. Table 9.1 is an example of the worksheet, precompleted with some sample data for you and questions that you can ask yourself to help complete a similar worksheet for your organization.

Once you've gone through the exercise of completing the worksheet, you'll be armed for any conversations that you have with stakeholders. You'll know what is important to them. And you'll be able to pitch your program to them in ways that speak to their needs, address their concerns, and greatly increase the chances that they will see value in your program.

Be on the lookout for ways to do the following as you work to evangelize your program:

- Align your program to the organization's strategy, mission, and initiatives.
- Tie your program to compliance requirements.
- Use current events and stories about organizations that are similar to yours in terms of industry, size, or other demographic characteristics. Note: Be careful not to do this in a way that will be perceived as alarmist or as fearmongering.
- Map your program to established industry best practices (such as the NIST Cybersecurity Framework, the National Association of Corporate Directors guidance on cybersecurity, and so on).

Table 9.1: Brainstorning worksheet for obtaining stakeholder support

Stakeholder Name	Title and Department	Stakeholder's Primary Business Drivers and Needs	Potential Stakeholder Concerns, Questions, etc.	Departmental Benefits If the Program Is Successful	Benefits to Stakeholder If the Program Is Successful	Other Notes and Comments
Jane Doe	Head of _____	What is Jane's core business?	How might elements of your program feel like they work against Jane's core mission and values?	How might elements of your program make Jane's department look good?	How might elements of your program increase Jane's social currency?	Additional pre- or post-meeting thoughts go here.
		How is Jane's success measured?	Might elements of your program feel like they take focus from areas that Jane is measured against?	How might elements of your program help Jane's program perform better?	How might elements of your program help Jane's career?	
				How might elements of your program help Jane's department link to a greater organizational mission or support a broader goal?	Can this help Jane feel connected with a greater cause?	

Stakeholder Name	Title and Department	Stakeholder's Primary Business Drivers and Needs	Potential Stakeholder Concerns, Questions, etc.	Departmental Benefits If the Program Is Successful	Benefits to Stakeholder If the Program Is Successful	Other Notes and Comments
Mary H.	Head of Application Development	Needs developers to create solid code. On budget. On time.	May fear that training initiatives will take focus and time away from production activities and timelines.	Application developers will be more aware of the ways that attackers find and exploit vulnerabilities. They will be more conscientious as they develop applications and peer review code. As a result, there may be fewer security-related issues flagged during the Q&A cycle. There will also be fewer issues found during vulnerability scans. Fewer exploitable bugs make it into production.	The stakeholder will ultimately run a department filled with security-conscious coders who are known for developing reliable, secure code. Coders also see the stakeholder as someone who is enabling them to learn new skills and enhance their careers.	During meetings with Mary, we noticed that she feels like this is the "right thing to do"; but has a number of production timeline commitments. She wants to wait until Q3. Can we potentially help evangelize this training and the benefits to the CIO so that she feels greater executive support?

Stakeholder Name	Title and Department	Stakeholder's Primary Business Drivers and Needs	Potential Stakeholder Concerns, Questions, etc.	Departmental Benefits If the Program Is Successful	Benefits to Stakeholder If the Program Is Successful	Other Notes and Comments
Aliana R.	EVP of Legal					
Mark J.	VP of Marketing					
Name	Title of Department					
Name	Title of Department					
Etc.						

MENTAL NOTE: FOR THE LOVE OF IKEA

At times, you can build a support base within other departments using the following sneaky tactic: just ask for help.

Remember the IKEA effect that I mentioned in Chapters 4 and 5? It's time to use that to your benefit. When you receive help from other departments and department leaders, they will feel invested in your success. So, don't be shy!

- Have your marketing department help create messaging.
- Ask your head of product development for ideas on how to successfully launch your program.
- Ask the head of your legal department what issues they want to ensure your program covers.
- Ask your public relations and internal communications teams for hints and tips on employee engagement.
- And remember to recognize and appreciate them for their efforts!

These people will buy in to your program because, in effect, they've already bought in by helping you. In fact, they didn't just buy in, they invested.

Leverage Cialdini's Principles of Persuasion

Fun fact: From the moment I decided to write this book, I've known that I was going to include Cialdini's principles of persuasion,[5] from his book *Influence: The Psychology of Persuasion* and the follow-up book, *Pre-Suasion: A Revolutionary Way to Influence and Persuade.*

At first, I was going to include the principles as communication techniques in Chapter 3, then as behavior shaping influencers in Chapter 4, and finally as ways of exerting social influence and pressure in Chapter 5. But, frankly, the Cialdini principles were slippery. They are and are not each of the things that were central to those chapters.

As it turns out, however, this is a great chapter to introduce the principles of persuasion because they prove useful in two different ways: as ways to influence your stakeholders for the purposes of gaining and sustaining support, and as pervasive principles that will permeate your overall program. As you read each one, I'm sure you'll see how they can be leveraged to achieve buy-in and build greater connectedness with your stakeholders as well as how they can be used within your end-user-facing program elements and strategy.

Reciprocity

People don't like to feel in debt to someone. So, doing a favor (even a small one) for someone will make them feel like the relationship is unbalanced until they pay back the favor.[6] How can you offer help and support to your critical stakeholders? To your culture carriers? To your end users? You can use the reciprocity principle as a pathway to greater rapport.

Scarcity

People don't like to feel like they are going to miss out. Pressure is felt in "limited time" and "limited resources" situations. There are a few great ways to use scarcity in your awareness program. When seeking support, be sure to mention that there is a short window for gathering input on your program. And, in your program, you can have limited time and limited availability swag, access to cool resources, and so on. And don't forget your culture carriers—they are naturally part of a "limited" group. Make them feel privileged by sharing things (information, materials, swag, etc.) that are *exclusively* available to official culture carriers or people who should be recognized for something special.

Authority

People will follow the lead of others who they perceive to be experts or people who they perceive as being "in charge." Determine who the influential voices (from executives to SMEs) are in your organization. Make it a priority to get them on your side and then leverage their power of authority to influence others. Additionally, find out who influences your influencers! It may be authors, industry leaders, or some other type of person; but once you know who or what influences your influencers, you can be on the lookout for ways to leverage those voices to shape their opinions.

Commitment and Consistency

The idea of *commitment and consistency* is that people don't want to be seen as fickle or wishy-washy. After all, one of the premiere insults for politicians to lob at each other is *flip-flopper*. In other words, as humans, we really want to see current words and actions line up with the things that we and other people have previously said and done. This is where you can revisit the information you collect in the Brainstorming Worksheet for Obtaining Stakeholder Support (Table 9.1). Once you know what each stakeholder values, position your program as something that aligns with, or provides, those values. And, if a stakeholder promises to support your program, they'll not want to go back on that promise—especially if the promise was made in front of other people.

Liking

The *liking* principle is expressed well in the following quote that is often cited in the sales and marketing world[7]:

> *People will do business with, and refer business to, those people they know, like and trust.*

> Bob Burg

Here's a great excerpt on the principle of liking from Robert Cialdini's website[8]:

> *But what causes one person to like another? Persuasion science tells us that there are three important factors. We like people who are similar to us, we like people who pay us compliments, and we like people who cooperate with us towards mutual goals.*

The same article goes on to quote a fascinating research study,

> *In a series of negotiation studies carried out between MBA students at two well-known business schools, some groups were told, "Time is money. Get straight down to business." In this group, around 55% were able to come to an agreement.*

> *A second group however, was told, "Before you begin negotiating, exchange some personal information with each other. Identify a similarity you share in common then begin negotiating." In this group, 90% of them were able to come to successful and agreeable outcomes that were typically worth 18% more to both parties.*

> *So to harness this powerful principle of liking, be sure to look for areas of similarity that you share with others and genuine compliments you can give before you get down to business.*

What's all this mean? Simple. People are more likely to say *yes* to you if they like you. So, this gets back to empathy. You need to be genuinely interested in your stakeholders. If you aren't interested in them and don't like them, they'll sense it. Take time to see things from their point of view. Take time to get to know them as people—not people who you need something from.

NOTE   Consider using the "Other Notes and Comments" column of the Brainstorming Worksheet for Obtaining Stakeholder Support (Table 9.1), or adding a new column, to capture shared interests that you have with each stakeholder, things that you genuinely admire about the stakeholder, and things that you want to be able to thank them for or complement them on in the future.

Here's another thing to keep in mind about the principle of liking: If the people speaking to your end users aren't "likeable," then the facts and values they communicate may be discounted. That means that the people doing in-person presentations need to be genuine. And the people represented in videos need to be likable. And even the voiceovers used in LMS modules, explainer videos, or narrated PowerPoints, all need to be genuine, respectful, and relatable.

Social Proof (Consensus)

The big idea with this principle is that people will tend to conform to what they see others around them doing and saying. I'm sure that you remember this theme from Chapter 5. This, again, is where the work you do early on with stakeholder engagement will pay off. If you are using the Brainstorming Worksheet for Obtaining Stakeholder Support (Table 9.1) and meeting individually with each stakeholder, then you'll be able to identify the group of stakeholders who will become your initial basis of support. And then you use their support as social proof to win additional stakeholders. It's like saying, "Hey. Can you lend your support to this? Bob, Mary, Jeffrey, and Sara are on board and excited!"

The same works as part of your end-user strategy. This, again, is where your culture carriers really help. They, in and of themselves, are a form of social proof. Their job is to advocate for (explicit social proof) and demonstrate (implicit social proof) the values, beliefs, and behaviors that you want to spread through the organization. And they create virality and sustainability by serving as a continual form of social proof.

Unity

Have you ever noticed how people seem to experience an immediate sense of comradery when they realize they are from the same hometown, from the same college, have worked for the same previous employer, or had the same terrible middle-school teacher? That's the unity principle in action. The unity principle is all about being members of the same *tribe*. When people feel the deep sense of connection that comes from having a shared core identity or shared unique experiences, they value your input. Members of the tribe will listen to other members of the tribe more readily than they listen to an "outsider."

How do you establish *unity* with your stakeholders? There are many common factors that you can use to demonstrate unity, and you can intentionally build frames (see Chapter 5) that allow unity to be seen and felt. Start by expressing shared values and common goals. You both want what's best for the organization and the people within the organization. Appreciate and learn the stakeholder's language. Each specialty within an organization has its own terminology and way of referring to things. Learn that language and speak it. Find non-work-related common interests, such as movies, music preferences, coffee, or even your shared disdain for morning traffic.

A sense of unity will help you gain the support of your stakeholders. And a sense of unity will make your communications resonate more deeply to your end users. And, again, this is where your culture carriers can be gold. Your culture carriers live in the very regions, departments, and demographic clusters that you hope to target; they speak the same language in both the literal and metaphorical senses of the phrase.

CRITICAL NOTE: OF CARROTS AND STICKS—THINKING ABOUT TONE

Here is an element of your program that you can't afford to leave to chance: *tone*. Your security awareness program is the face and voice of your security department to all the employees who you will never meet and personally interact with. So, in many ways—from the messages you send out, to the content you select, to the way that you respond to employees who fail phishing tests, to the way that you recognize and reward incident reporting, and more—your awareness program will either draw people in and create a sense of community and shared purpose, or it will reinforce an "us versus them" mind-set.

In everything you do, ask if you are conveying a tone and message that will help employees want to trust and confide in the security department or if you are pushing your employees away. If your messaging (or even your underlying thoughts as you deliver messages) implies that users are stupid, or childlike, or unworthy of the business systems they use, then you will create a culture of people who will not report security incidents, will hide when they've accidently clicked a real phishing email, not come to you for help when they've been infected with ransomware, and will always believe that security is *someone else's* responsibility.

Avoid adopting a tone that can feel like you are standing in front of them pointing your finger and lecturing. Instead, you want them to feel like you are coming alongside them, working with shared purpose. And, when you are offering suggestions and correction, it should feel like it is coming from a concerned friend or family member—a person working in the best interest of both the individual (the employee) and the family (the organization).

Making Adjustments

You've heard it said that the only constant in life is change. That's true of the world and is true within your organization. And that means your program needs to be ready to adapt with those changes. Static, repetitive programs become (or will be viewed as) increasingly irrelevant and out of touch. A transformational program has more in common with a conversation than it does a monologue.

Your ongoing surveys, work with your culture carriers, discussions with stakeholders and audience segments, and your monitoring of behavioral indicators (security behavior-related incident reporting as well as SIEM, DLP, and other employee monitoring technologies) all serve to help you put a finger on the pulse of your organization's security-related sentiments and actions.

Be ready to adapt. The heart of your program is one of service—service to your organization and to your people. That means that—at any given time, with any given person, and in any given season—you are proactively seeking out the most relevant ways to engage. A transformational security awareness program is adaptive and anticipatory, always seeking ways to meet your people where they are with the security-related information and interventions that they need.

NOTE A transformational program has more in common with a *conversation* than it does a *monologue*.

Thoughts About Crafting Campaigns ▬▬

We've already covered significant ground related to communications, behavior shaping, culture shaping, tools, and campaigns; but, one of the downsides of tackling each of those topics in separate chapters is that there may still be a few dots left to be connected. I don't want to overwhelm you with program or campaign management thoughts, but I would like to tie up a few loose ends and answer some of the most common questions that awareness program managers have.

A transformational program will transcend one-size-fits-all messaging and approaches. It will consider each core message or behavior, evaluate the support structures that are most relevant and beneficial, and then leverage those supports to specific target groups (segments) of your employee populations. It will seek to use the right method (communication strategy, behavior strategy, culture strategy, technology strategy), and target the right people, at the right time, in the right context (see Figure 9.3).

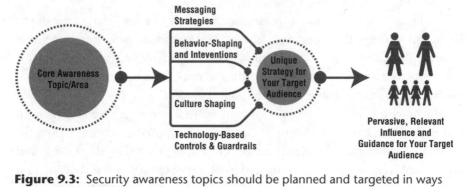

Figure 9.3: Security awareness topics should be planned and targeted in ways most relevant to each target segment.

OF FORESTS AND TREES: REMEMBERING YOUR JOURNEY

Don't worry if you are feeling overwhelmed with information at this point. It's like that old expression about not being able to see the forest for the trees. I've spent a lot of time showing you individual trees. Take a moment now and mentally try to step back a bit. One good way to do that is to flip all the way back to the beginning of this book. Don't worry about rereading everything, but look at the figures for each chapter. Let them retell the story for you.

Beginning with Chapter 1, Figure 1.1, you see four groups of people (audience segments) that you need to account for in your program, and you also see many of the behaviors that you need to account for in your messaging, training, and behavior shaping (Figure 1.2).

Moving on to Chapter 2, Figure 2.1, you can recall the need to understand your goals and corporate culture.

Chapter 3, Figure 3.1 shows you the process you should go through when crafting communications campaigns. Figure 3.2 reminds you to find your "why," and Figure 3.3 lists the *Trojan Horses for the Mind* that you can use to embed messaging.

Chapter 3 will naturally feel immediately applicable because security awareness inherently involves communication.

You'll notice that Chapters 4 and 5 feel much clearer this time because you now have the additional interpretive lenses of Chapter 6, "What's in a Modern Security Awareness Leader's Toolbox?" and Chapter 8, "Living Your Awareness Program Through the Eyes and Lives of Your Audience."

Now think again about the Fogg Behavior Model (Figure 4-3), the reminder that everything is interpreted through context (Figure 4-7), and the four behavior groups that we can target within the Fogg Behavior Model (Figure 4-10). And think again about the core message of Chapter 5 (Figure 5-3), which is that your program will create and depend on a network: social structures to create virality and sustainability for your program.

Continue that pattern for the remainder of the book and see what happens. That simple exercise of reacquainting yourself with the visuals of each chapter can be extremely valuable. You'll be surprised by the added perspective that you have.

You can recall concepts about marketing campaigns, such as the idea of segments, and now you see target audience segments with your people and behavior groups. You remember concepts related to behavior shaping, and you can see points within the user's journey where behavior shaping techniques might be used. You understand the power of social dynamics and how to gain support. And you have a better grasp on which tools to use at a given time, within a given context, to influence a given person.

Thinking Through Target Groups

Here's the main takeaway when thinking about target groups. You have specific topics that comprise the central themes of your awareness training program. The first thing you should do, if possible, is to understand what the current organizational baseline is with regard to that topic. If it is a behavior-related topic, then you want to see and understand those behavioral indicators to see where your praiseworthy groups are and where your problem groups are. One way of thinking about those groups was in Chapter 1 (Figure 1.1), represented again in Figure 9.4 for your convenience. You can now think of each of those four groups as a target segment.

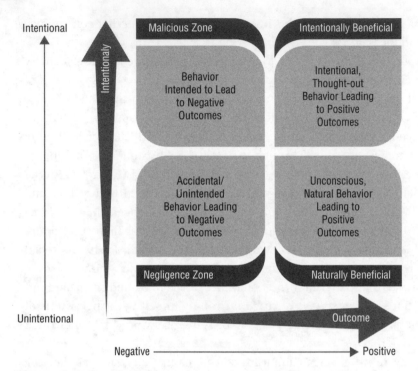

Figure 9.4: Security behavioral outcomes (reprise)

These four segments exist for any individual security-related behavior you can name. Regardless of whether the behavior relates to password management, incident reporting, safe web browsing, acceptable use, document handling, tailgating, clean desk expectations, or anything else, you will have people who range from just doing the right thing because they naturally do it without thinking, to people who do the right thing because they intentionally think about what they are doing and know the security-related costs and benefits associated with their behavior, to people who are just unaware and negligent, to people who know better but don't care.

I tend to be a pragmatist. So, my preference (unless a regulation or audit requirement states otherwise) is to only train people on topics and behaviors that they demonstrably need to be trained on. That means, if you have a group of people who are always doing the right thing related to a specific behavior, you don't need to train them, or you present them with a modified training. You can give them back some time or find new ways to make the training relevant for them.

Wherever possible you should provide people in each of the two *positive outcome* group some type of recognition and reward. People in the *intentionally beneficial* group across several target behaviors are likely great candidates for appointment as official culture carriers.

People in the *naturally beneficial* group are interesting. They tend to do the right thing but may not understand why; that's where your recognition and reward can really help. By recognizing them and rewarding them for doing the right thing, you are indirectly training them. You are saying, *here's why we appreciate you and why that behavior matters to the organization.* From then on, the "why" is encoded within that person's mind and—thanks to the reciprocity principle—they are likely to feel a bond with you.

Of course, you'll have more work to do with people on the negative side of the quadrant. People in the *negligence zone* will need more programmatic effort. You'll want to use your Behavior Design debugging principles here from Chapter 4. First analyze whether they are being prompted for the behavior that you want. If so, then analyze to see whether the prompt is effective (hint: it may be invisible to the person because of prompt fatigue). If the prompt is a potential issue, change the prompt. Add cues and prompts in different contexts. Is there an issue with their ability? You can add training to level up the relevant skill(s), or you can provide them tools to help make the behavior easier and more natural. If none of that works, then you may have a motivation issue. If the issue is motivation, then your levers are positive and negative motivation, positive and negative social pressures, or trying to find times and contexts where the person's motivation may naturally be higher.

Lastly, people in the *malicious zone* are the most difficult. They are aware but just don't care. These people know better and are either too busy to care or have a more nefarious reason for their behavior. You can go through the same Behavior Design debugging process to see whether anything improves. The most positive ways of working to change malicious behavior is by somehow reframing the behavior to something that they may care about, demonstrating that you are aware of the behavior so that the observation effect provides a psychological nudge, or providing a technical control/guardrail. However, if the motivation is truly malicious, then you'll have to resort to negative pressures and consequences.

Behavioral Testing and Training: Simulated Social Engineering

The phishing simulation and training market was born in the 2007–2008 timeframe and, since then, has created a resurgence of interest in security awareness. For the first time, security leaders were able to gather behavioral metrics that demonstrated security-related competencies and offer just-in-time training and remediation.

Now, auditors and regulators are beginning to expect organizations to implement this type of behavioral reporting and training. But there are differing opinions on how best to implement this strategy. Here's my take as bluntly as I can state it: Organizations that perform phishing testing less than one phishing simulation activity per month are not providing training—they are taking a metric.

If your organization conducts phishing simulations once per year, once every six months, once per quarter, or every six weeks, then you are not getting the full benefit that these tools can provide. Like any training, you face issues related to decay of knowledge and decay of relevance. And, like any exercise or skill, the only way to get stronger and to improve is constant training and practice. Your goal with simulated social engineering should be to build habits, muscle memory, and strength. At all times you are either creating strength or allowing atrophy.

> **NOTE** Organizations that perform phishing testing less than one phishing simulation activity per month are not providing training—they are taking a metric. *At all times you are either creating strength or allowing atrophy.*

A robust security awareness training program will include all the rich communication, culture, and behavioral strategies that we've discussed. And it will test resiliency to the very types of attacks and situations that your users will be subject to. Anything else will provide a false sense of security and leave your organization more vulnerable than you know. Your program should use a combination of marketing and attack simulation techniques and strategies to reach your users (see Figure 9.5). In other words, *plan like a marketer and think like an attacker!*

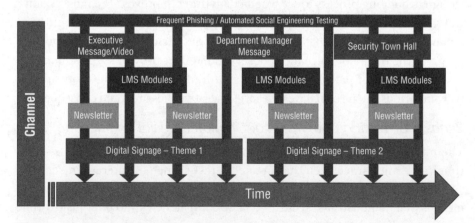

Figure 9.5: A robust security awareness program is a combination of multichannel marketing and attack simulation.

MORE SOCIAL ENGINEERING FOR AWARENESS

It is also becoming increasingly popular to expand on the success of phishing simulations by adding automated voice-based phishing (vishing), text message–based phishing (smishing), and a variety of nonautomated (real-world, in person or over the phone) social engineering activities to test an organization's users.

This is a positive trend because it allows organizations to adapt their training and technology-based controls based on these tests. When adding real-world, physical social engineering testing, it's important to keep in mind that the purpose of these tests is to benefit the organization and its people, not necessarily to win at all costs.

To this end, Chris Hadnagy's organization, Social-Engineer.org, developed a *Social Engineering Code of Ethics.*[9] This ethics statement provides a valuable mind-set and practical guidance.

The Social Engineering Code of Ethics accomplishes three important goals: 1) it promotes professionalism in the industry, 2) it establishes ethics and policies that dictate how to be a professional SE, and 3) it provides guidance on how to conduct a social engineering business. Chris Hadnagy, CEO of Social-Engineer LLC has a motto, "Leave them feeling better for having met you." This motto developed into a core company value that resonates throughout the code of ethics that Chris designed. The following 11 bulleted points comprise the Social Engineering Code of Ethics:

- Respect the public by accepting responsibility and ownership over your actions, and their effects on the welfare of those in, around, and involved with the engagement.
- Before undertaking any social engineering engagement, ensure you are fully aware of the scope and effects on others and their well-being.
- Avoid engaging in, or being a party to, unethical, unlawful, or illegal acts that negatively affect your professional reputation, the information security discipline, the practice of social engineering, others' well-being, or the parties and individuals in, around, and involved with the engagement.
- Reject any engagement, or aspect of an engagement, that may make a target feel vulnerable or discriminated against. This includes, but is not limited to, sexual harassment, offensive comments (verbal,

written, or otherwise) related to gender, sexual orientation, race, religion, or disability; stalking or following, deliberate intimidation, or harassing materials. Additionally, lewd or offensive behavior or language, which may be sexually explicit or offensive in nature, materials or conduct, language, behavior, or content that contains profanity, obscene gestures, or gendered, religious, ethnic, or racial, slurs are all to be avoided. Employing any of these tactics reduces the target's ability to learn and improve from the engagement.

- Do not negatively manipulate, threaten, or make others uncomfortable in any way, unless specified by a client due to unique needs and testing environment.

- Minimize risks to the confidentiality, integrity, or availability of information of your employer, clients, and individuals involved in engagements. After performing a social engineering engagement, ensure the security of obtained information is a priority. Never disclose information to outside parties as private and confidential information must remain private and confidential. Do not misuse any information or privileges you are afforded as part of your responsibilities.

- When training future social engineers, consider that training will leave a lasting impact on your students and the methodology with which you train will echo through all students' future engagements. Provide students with the knowledge and tools to create positive learning environments and productive scenarios for their future engagements and clients.

- Ensure the social engineering practices of yourself and your students include conscientious, thoughtful, and considerate ways to escalate engagements to eventually emulate real-world attack vectors. Recognize our clients are seeking ways to improve their security posture and work with them to increase the difficulty of realistic attack vectors.

- Respect that social engineering engagements involve human vulnerability and avoid publicizing vulnerabilities, whether through a blog, social media, or other medium, that result in harmful effects, emotions, or feelings for your client and the individuals and parties in, around, and involved with the engagement.

- Do not misrepresent your abilities or your work to the community, your employer, or your peers. Ensure you have the experience and knowledge promised to your clients and stakeholders.

- Leave others feeling better for having met you.

Be Intentional with Recognition and Reward

I've hit on this several times already. Bear with me as I add a few more thoughts. We know that recognition and reward are a psychological key to helping form bonds between people (or groups) and are a psychological trigger for creating habits. Use the power of variable reward systems so that people don't know when the next reward is coming, but they have full faith that it will come if they continue doing the right thing.

Consider implementing a system where employees can report each other for "doing the right thing." This can be a key element of your security culture-shaping program and will have an impact on the virality of your program and the shaping of behavior. You can, and should, also see whether your organization is already using an employee rewards system.

Many organizations are using systems like O.C. Tanner's Culture Cloud recognition suite (`https://www.octanner.com/products.html`), PerksWW (`https://perksww.com/employee/`), or Kudos (`https://www.kudosnow.com/`). If so, this is a great opportunity for your program to leverage an existing and deployed system to spread your culture and recognize exemplary employees.

Assembling Your Culture Carriers

Review the sections on culture carriers from Chapter 5. Assembling this group will be a great step in increasing your reach and influence. Look for influential people or employees who are highly motivated. Consider having them sign a term of commitment (12 to 18 months). This helps keep them engaged via the principle of commitment and consistency; and, if not, at least it gives you the leverage to gently and respectfully remind them what they committed to.

And, like I just mentioned in the previous section, recognition and rewards will be key motivations for this group. Treat them well. Appreciate them and they will continue to be great assets for your program. Also give them the ability to recognize other employees throughout the organization. This leverages the reciprocity principle and also just feels good to them!

So, you ask, what do these people actually do? Well, there's no set-in-stone answer for that. They can literally do anything that you and your organization believes will be valuable to the program and that you have the buy-in from senior management to task your culture carriers with. The program can be informal—similar to a "street team" group that exists to evangelize security values in their department and keep you informed of any concerns or issues they hear about. Or your culture carrier program can be extremely formal and task-oriented, responsible for finding and closing security vulnerabilities, implementing security policies, and so on. Or your program can be somewhere in between. That range of responsibilities is why I use the phrase "culture carrier" for this group; the responsibilities can range from evangelist to ambassador to deputy to officer. There is no right or wrong answer. There is only what works for your program and your organization.

Lastly, set up support structures for your culture carriers. Email groups, team wikis, forums, SharePoint sites, monthly calls and sharing sessions, in-person meetings, and exclusive information and swag will all help to form rewarding social bonds for the group. The result is that your culture carriers feel like they are part of a tribe, appreciated, empowered, and valued.

Measuring Your Success

I discussed measurement strategies and philosophies in each major section of this book. There is no one-size-fits-all measurement strategy. The main thing to consider is that you can, and should, find *something* that provides valuable insight about each large strategy item in your program.

> **NOTE** The main thing to consider is that you can, and should, find something that provides a valuable insight about each large strategy item in your program. Become a master storyteller about the value of security awareness in your organization.

Phishing and training stats are easy. Event attendance, web-based newsletter views, video views, reported security incidents, etc., are also all easy and are good at providing indicators of engagement. Other behavior stats can be found by giving thought to what actually happens at the point of behavior. If the point of behavior is on a computer or mobile device, chances are you can find a way to count it (SIEM, DLP, event logs, employee monitoring systems, web proxies, etc., are all your friends when used legally and ethically). For physical behaviors that you are hoping to shape, you can rely on surveys, employee reporting, physical audits, etc. Don't give up if the engagement or behavior change isn't as drastic as you hoped. This is an ongoing program. You are constantly learning and adjusting in a continuous improvement model.

And, in all of the talk about metrics, measurement, and ROI, don't discount the power of stories and anecdotes. At the end of the day, that's what good metrics do—they tell a story. So, why not collect some value statements from employees and stakeholders about what the program is accomplishing or can accomplish in the future? Be a master storyteller about the value of security awareness in your organization.

What Does the Future Hold?

Because security awareness is a fundamentally human-focused program, there will always be critical work that only a program manager and a group of engaged stakeholders and culture carriers can accomplish. That being said, there are several technology-driven advancements on the horizon for security awareness training. The most simple and concise way of phrasing the future of security awareness is this:

> **NOTE** The future of security awareness is context-based, learner-aware, organization-aware, risk-aware, and adaptive.

Advancements in data aggregation, artificial intelligence, and machine learning mean that awareness vendors will be able to leverage aggregated data from multiple systems such as security systems, HR systems, training systems, learner profiles, social media profiles, behavioral data, risk-related data, and more to form a well-rounded understanding of what a user's behavior patterns are, what their learning styles are, how they prefer to engage with content, what content types they like, what risks they are prone to, and more.

These systems will adapt to what's best for the user and the organization—all with minimal input from administrators other than setting parameters and permissions for what is wanted and allowed. In addition to providing all of those benefits within a traditional training context, the simulated social engineering side of things will also evolve. Imagine a continually learning and evolving automated red team that is working to evaluate user risk, test resiliency, and provide valuable insight to your security team. Just-in-time training, risk-based testing, messaging, behavioral interventions, technical controls, and more can all be continually adapting based on learner conditions, context, organizational needs, and hosts of other factors.

The right training, to the right person, and the right time, in the right context can be determined algorithmically. And that means a single organization can have an infinite number of security awareness programs—as many programs as employees. Awareness platforms will also be able to help facilitate the physical "last mile" components by proactively reminding awareness program managers and other parties of what they can and should do next.

This is automated, adaptive, learner-centric security awareness, which is a transformational idea.

Key Takeaways

- *A transformational program has more in common with a conversation than it does a monologue.* Be ready to adapt. The heart of your program is one of service—service to your organization and to your people. That means that—at any given time, with any given person, and in any given season—you are proactively seeking out the most relevant ways to engage. A transformational security awareness program is adaptive and anticipatory, always seeking ways to meet your people where they are with the security-related information and interventions that they need.

- *Even when your program has produced transformational results, you are not done. You will never be done.* In the same way that your people and organization are always in a state of change, a transformational security awareness program must constantly adapt and commit to a process of continual improvement.

- *Understand as much as you can about your stakeholders, what they value, and what their concerns are.* Use Table 9.1 (the Brainstorming Worksheet for Obtaining Stakeholder Support) as a guide for helping you develop relationships with your stakeholders and obtain real, lasting buy-in.

- *Plan like a marketer, think like an attacker.* A robust security awareness training program will include all the rich communication, culture, and behavioral strategies discussed throughout this book. And it will test resiliency to the very types of attacks and situations that your users will be subject to. Anything else will provide a false sense of security and leave your organization more vulnerable than you know. Your program should use a combination of marketing and attack simulation techniques and strategies to reach your users.

- *Be a master storyteller about the value of security awareness in your organization.* There is no one-size-fits-all measurement strategy. The main thing to consider is that you can, and should, find *something* that provides valuable insight about each large strategy item in your program. It's your job to tell (and sell) the narrative behind all of the metrics and anecdotes you collect.

Notes and References

1. Review the "Understanding Your Culture's Status Quo" section of Chapter 5 for more details.
2. *How to Use Activation Triggers™ to Reach Your Goals this Year* by Michael Hyatt (https://michaelhyatt.com/activation-triggers/)
3. *How to Use 'Visioneering' Principles to Drive a Successful Identity and Access Management Program* by Perry Carpenter
4. I believe the idea for that worksheet germinated from a book that I read several years earlier when I was a developer: Michael Howard and David LeBlanc's excellent *Writing Secure Code* from Microsoft Press. I remember being struck with how well they covered concepts related to selling ideas and projects internally. When I first read their book, I was a geeky coder. The fact that they covered the social and internal politics aspects of a program was eye-opening to me. In retrospect, it is Marketing 101; but, in many ways, that book set me on the path that I'm on today. Thanks, Michael and David!
5. See https://www.influenceatwork.com/principles-of-persuasion/ for a quick summary and breakdown.
6. And, the funny thing is, asking for a favor also tends to generate a feeling of connectedness by the person who is asked because humans like to be helpful. Remember the "bonding chemical," oxytocin, mentioned in Chapters 3 and 7? That comes into play when humans help each other. So, the simple act of giving or receiving help (even small acts) results in a feeling of connectedness.
7. https://www.azquotes.com/quote/1033891
8. *Principles of Persuasion* (https://www.influenceatwork.com/principles-of-persuasion/)
9. *Social Engineering Code of Ethics* (https://www.social-engineer.org/framework/general-discussion/code-of-ethics/)

10 Closing Thoughts

Let's think the unthinkable, let's do the undoable. Let us prepare to grapple with the ineffable itself, and see if we may not eff it after all.
Douglas Adams, Dirk Gently's Holistic Detective Agency

Well, here we are! Thank you for coming with me on this journey. It is my sincere hope that you learned a few things along the way and that you were simultaneously *fascinated* by the complexities of human nature, *inspired* by the insights provided by other fields we've surveyed, and *challenged* to never settle for anything less than a transformational program.

Wondering where to go from here? I have three next steps for you.

1. Leverage the power of community.
2. Be a lifelong learner.
3. Be a realistic optimist.

Let's take a minute to look at each of these recommendations.

Leverage the Power of Community

The power of community and collaboration can serve as a catalyst for your program. It becomes fuel for new ideas and continued encouragement. So, make it a priority to get involved in communities that will support and challenge you. As a companion to this book, I've created a LinkedIn group to help support discussion, idea sharing, and group problem-solving; just search *Transformational Security Awareness* on LinkedIn and you'll find it (or go to https://www.linkedin.com/groups/12207804/). Additionally, there are a few other fantastic communities to be a part of. Consider the following:

- **The International Association of Security Awareness Professionals (IASAP):** The IASAP is a members-only organization comprised of security awareness professionals interested in sharing best practices, challenging each other, and pushing the industry forward. They have monthly webinars, three in-person meetings annually, and a private online community for year-round connection with resources, member question-and-answer sessions, and event recordings. Go to https://iasapgroup.org/ for details.

- *Re-thinking the Human Factor* **LinkedIn group:** This is the companion group to Bruce Hallas' book and podcast of the same name. You can search for *Re-thinking the Human Factor* on LinkedIn or go to https://www.linkedin.com/groups/8658401/.

- **SANS Security Awareness Summits:** Each year, SANS holds security awareness summits in both North America and Europe. These are vendor-neutral, community-driven events with agendas focused on program management, metrics, user engagement, and more. You can find information at https://sans.org/SecAwareSummit.

- **KB4-CON:** KB4-CON is KnowBe4's annual user conference. There is content for everyone from CISOs to full-time security awareness program managers to IT admins with 15 other fires to put out. With keynotes, breakout sessions, and workshops, there is something for everyone. Keynotes sessions always include Kevin Mitnick with live hacking demonstrations, as well as other KnowBe4 executives (like yours truly), industry luminaries, and other speakers with interesting and insightful messages. The cost is free for KnowBe4 customers. Non-customers are welcome but are charged a nominal fee. Go to https://www.knowbe4.com/kb4-con for more information.

CONTINUE THE DISCUSSION: JOIN THE *TRANSFORMATIONAL SECURITY AWARENESS* GROUP ON LinkedIn

Search *Transformational Security Awareness* on LinkedIn or go directly to https://www.linkedin.com/groups/12207804/.

Be a Lifelong Learner

You never know when inspiration will strike, but you can up the frequency of the insights you have if you cultivate a lifestyle of continually digging in to new and different fields of study. To take advantage of how the book has woven in insights from different disciplines, find anything that you can that helps you understand what makes people tick, what people like, what they dislike, how to design engaging interfaces, how attention and distraction work, behavioral economics, negotiation and influence strategies, leadership principles, user experience principles . . . you get the picture. Think broadly and expansively as you develop your program.

> **NOTE** It's time to unleash a generation of liberal-arts, renaissance security awareness leaders and culture carriers across the world. That starts with each of us.

I've mentioned a *lot* of books and references over the past couple hundred or so pages. But let me give you my five all-time favorites for you to start with. For each book, I'll provide a quick quote from the book's marketing copy, and then I'll follow up with what I love about the book.

- *Predictably Irrational, Revised and Expanded Edition: The Hidden Forces That Shape Our Decisions* by **Dan Ariely**

  From the "back-of-book" description: *"Why do our headaches persist after we take a one-cent aspirin but disappear when we take a fifty-cent aspirin? Why do we splurge on a lavish meal but cut coupons to save twenty-five cents on a can of soup?*

  When it comes to making decisions in our lives, we think we're making smart, rational choices. But are we?

  In this newly revised and expanded edition of the groundbreaking New York Times bestseller, Dan Ariely refutes the common assumption that we behave in fundamentally rational ways. From drinking coffee to losing weight, from buying a car to choosing a romantic partner, we consistently overpay, underestimate, and procrastinate. Yet these misguided behaviors are neither random nor senseless. They're systematic and predictable— making us predictably irrational."

What I love about this book: If you ever feel the need to be convinced that simply giving people good information won't necessarily result in correct behavior, then this book is for you! This is an easy read packed with example after example of situations that demonstrate just how strange human behavior and decision-making really is. This book, along with Daniel Kahneman's *Thinking, Fast & Slow*, are both compelling. The only reason I don't have *Thinking, Fast & Slow* on this list is because it is slightly more information-dense.

■ *Pre-Suasion: A Revolutionary Way to Influence and Persuade* by Robert Cialdini

From the "back-of-book" description: *"The acclaimed New York Times and Wall Street Journal bestseller from Robert Cialdini—'the foremost expert on effective persuasion' (Harvard Business Review)—explains how it's not necessarily the message itself that changes minds, but the key moment before you deliver that message.*

What separates effective communicators from truly successful persuaders? With the same rigorous scientific research and accessibility that made his Influence an iconic bestseller, Robert Cialdini explains how to prepare people to be receptive to a message before they experience it. Optimal persuasion is achieved only through optimal pre-suasion. In other words, to change 'minds' a pre-suader must also change 'states of mind.'

Named a 'Best Business Books of 2016' by the Financial Times, and 'compelling' by The Wall Street Journal, Cialdini's Pre-Suasion draws on his extensive experience as the most cited social psychologist of our time and explains the techniques a person should implement to become a master persuader. Altering a listener's attitudes, beliefs, or experiences isn't necessary, says Cialdini—all that's required is for a communicator to redirect the audience's focus of attention before a relevant action."

What I love about this book: *Pre-Suasion* offers extremely insightful advice on how to craft the moments before you ask someone to take an action. In other words, it's all about framing. Cialdini's earlier book, *Influence: The Psychology of Persuasion*, is already a longstanding classic; and, in my opinion, his newest work is even more relevant and practical. *Pre-Suasion* will help you understand how to frame your messages and how to build and sustain relationships.

- *Contagious: Why Things Catch On* by Jonah Burger

  From the "back-of-book" description: *"Contagious provides a set of specific, actionable techniques for helping information spread—for designing messages, advertisements, and content that people will share. Whether you're a manager at a big company, a small business owner trying to boost awareness, a politician running for office, or a health official trying to get the word out, Contagious will show you how to make your product or idea catch on."*

  What I love about this book: Jonah Burger's *Contagious* is easy to read and packed full of practical insight into what makes messaging stick and how messages and ideas go viral. This book provides multiple profound insights for awareness communications professionals.

- *Language Intelligence: Lessons on persuasion from Jesus, Shakespeare, Lincoln, and Lady Gaga* by Joseph J Romm

  From the "back-of-book" description: *"Romm demonstrates that you don't have to be an expert to vastly improve your ability to communicate. He has pulled together the secrets of the greatest communicators in history to show how you can apply these tools to your writing, speaking, blogging — even your Tweeting."*

  What I love about this book: We are all professional communicators. *Language Intelligence* is a relatively short and easy read that gives us the nitty-gritty on the workings of persuasive language. Numerous examples from noteworthy figures of the past and present make the concepts approachable and entertaining.

- *The Culture Code: The Secrets of Highly Successful Groups* by Daniel Coyle

  From the "back-of-book" description: *"In The Culture Code, Daniel Coyle goes inside some of the world's most successful organizations—including the U.S. Navy's SEAL Team Six, IDEO, and the San Antonio Spurs—and reveals what makes them tick. He demystifies the culture-building process by identifying three key skills that generate cohesion and cooperation, and explains how diverse groups learn to function with a single mind. Drawing on examples that range from Internet retailer Zappos to the comedy troupe Upright Citizens Brigade to a daring gang of jewel thieves, Coyle offers specific strategies that trigger learning, spark collaboration, build trust, and drive positive change. Coyle unearths helpful stories of failure that illustrate what not to do, troubleshoots common pitfalls, and shares advice about reforming a toxic culture. Combining leading-edge science, on-the-ground insights from world-class leaders, and practical ideas for action, The Culture Code offers a roadmap for creating an environment where innovation flourishes, problems get solved, and expectations are exceeded.*

Culture is not something you are—it's something you do. The Culture Code puts the power in your hands. No matter the size of your group or your goal, this book can teach you the principles of cultural chemistry that transform individuals into teams that can accomplish amazing things together."

What I love about this book: This is an amazing book about cultural and social dynamics. The concepts are applicable at an organizational level and at a subculture level. *The Culture Code* also discusses social needs that should be considered when creating/delivering messaging. You can use these concepts when thinking about broad organizational change or as you are building groups of culture carriers, working with internal teams, and more.

I'm also a big fan of podcasts, and I listen to a ton of them. Here are the top five that are consistently interesting and insightful. I'll list each of them, provide the description as written in the Apple iTunes podcast directory, and then give you a quick sentence or two about what I love.

- *Hacking Humans* by the CyberWire

  What they say about themselves: *"Each week the CyberWire's Hacking Humans Podcast looks behind the social engineering scams, phishing schemes, and criminal exploits that are making headlines and taking a heavy toll on organizations around the world. We talk to social engineering experts, security pros, cognitive scientists, and those practiced in the arts of deception (perhaps even a magician or two). We also hear from people targeted by social engineering attacks and learn from their experiences."*

  What I love about this podcast: This weekly podcast provides stories about current scams. The podcast is lighthearted but covers the most serious issues facing our people. Hosts Dave Bittner and Joe Carrigan have great chemistry and do a fantastic job delving into the reasons why each scam works and what people can/should do to be more resilient, and their interviews with a wide range of experts are always insightful.

■ *Malicious Life* by Cybereason

What they say about themselves: *"The wildest hacks you can ever imagine, told by people who were actually there. Hosted by cybersecurity expert
and book author, Ran Levi, this is not your average talk-show. These are
fascinating, unknown tales, slowly unraveled, deeply researched. Think
Hardcore History meets Hackable— and come dig into a history you never
knew existed."*

What I love about this podcast: Host Ran Levi is a natural storyteller,
and it shows. His ability to craft a compelling narrative about complex hacks and security events makes the podcast extremely listenable,
maybe even a bit addictive. And, since stories are one of the *Trojan
Horses for the Mind*, it is worth your time to learn from a great security
storyteller not just for the interesting content but to get a sense of how
Ran approaches the task of telling the story itself.

■ *Freakonomics Radio* by Dubner Productions

What they say about themselves: *"Discover the hidden side of everything with Stephen J. Dubner, co-author of the Freakonomics books. Each
week, Freakonomics Radio tells you things you always thought you knew
(but didn't) and things you never thought you wanted to know (but do) —
from the economics of sleep to how to become great at just about anything.
Dubner speaks with Nobel laureates and provocateurs, intellectuals and
entrepreneurs, and various other underachievers. Special features include
series like 'The Secret Life of a C.E.O.' as well as a live game show, 'Tell Me
Something I Don't Know.'"*

What I love about this podcast: Freakonomics Radio gets into why and
how we make the decisions that we make and offers up several obscure
insights and fun facts along the way. While not every episode is as
deeply entrenched in economics as the title would imply, host Stephen
J. Dubner does a masterful job making obscure topics interesting, structuring the pace of information delivery/revelation, and using sound to
cue learning and retention.

■ **The Brainfluence Podcast by Roger Dooley**

What they say about themselves: *"Roger Dooley is the author of
Brainfluence: 100 Ways to Persuade and Convince Consumers with
Neuromarketing, and has been studying the effects of psychology, behavior
research, and neuroscience on persuasion and marketing in business,*

leadership and everyday life. In every episode, Roger shares brain-oriented tactics, along with the expertise of his guests, to increase persuasion with concrete, research-based neuromarketing advice. Guests include best-selling authors and thought leaders like Robert Cialdini, Dan Pink, Guy Kawasaki, Jonah Berger, Chris Brogan, Maria Konnikova, and many more. Learn more and join the conversation at RogerDooley.com."

What I love about this podcast: Simply said, these are solid interviews. They are well done all the way around from a host who knows how to contribute to the discussion without getting in the way. The guests are all masters in their respective fields. This is a great podcast for finding new areas of research and people to follow.

- **The Nir and Far Podcast by Nir Eyal**

  What they say about themselves: *"Nir And Far, a podcast about business, behaviour and the brain by Nir Eyal."*

  What I love about this podcast: Nir Eyal is the author of *Hooked: How to Build Habit-Forming Products*. He bases his work on behavior science principles, and the podcast is primarily made up of short "best of" readings from his book and published articles. Every now and then he does a Q&A episode or has a guest interview. All in all it's a great podcast if you are interested in behavior science.

Be a Realistic Optimist

Every journey starts with a first step. Some of the ideas and goals expressed in the previous chapters may seem difficult to achieve; many are things that you can't achieve on your own. And most require time and consistency to reach their full potential. But, rest assured, there are some short-term wins to be had (phishing training is one such example). But, with some aspects of your program, the journey may, at times, feel difficult.

Always remember your purpose. As a security awareness professional, you are ultimately serving the very people you are seeking to influence. The only way to change them is to have empathy, appreciating who they are and why they struggle. Only then will you be able to find the best method(s) to drive change.

Here's what I know: A transformational security awareness program *will* pay off. In the same way that a steady stream of water over time will create a canyon or that small amounts of money invested will, through the magic of compound interest, turn into large sums of money, your efforts *do* make a lasting impact!

NOTE The best security awareness leaders work from a sense of passion that comes from knowing that they are serving a grand cause: to help build a safer and more secure world, one person, one organization, one family, and one community at a time.

Conclusion

Writing this book was not an easy or short task. But I've thoroughly enjoyed the process. That's something that I can say now but might not have been able to say with a straight face a few months ago. Isn't that like most worthwhile journeys? It's when you take time to reflect upon the distance that you've traveled that you see how far you've come. And when you take time to look back, you know that the journey was worth it. Your program efforts will be like that, too. When you notice the cumulative results of your efforts, you'll begin to appreciate the significance of what you've accomplished. Don't lose perspective. Imagine yourself, your program, your people, and your organization a year from now: *transformed*.

Keep in touch. I'd love to hear your stories or be able to help in any way that I can. And, if you've enjoyed this book and think it's helpful, recommend it to others; or, better yet, buy a copy or two for other security leaders in your network, as stocking stuffers for your kids, or as a meaningful anniversary present for that hard-to-buy-for spouse (he says only somewhat jokingly).

You can connect with me on LinkedIn (`/in/perrycarpenter`), Twitter (@ `perrycarpenter`), or on the Web (`https://TheSecurityAwarenessGuy.com`).

All the best!
Perry

11

Voices of Transformation: Interviews with Security Awareness Program Leaders

Never look back unless you are planning on going that way.

Henry David Thoreau

When I first mentioned this book project on LinkedIn, I had several people send in quotes about the importance of security awareness. Let's read what a few have to say.

> *Security awareness is about putting threat and risk information into terms that everyone can understand. Most people want to be a part of the solution but get frustrated when they don't know or understand what to do.*

Chris Wright, Owner, Citadel Systems

> *As threats against companies and their employees continue to grow year over year, so do the needs for awareness, communications, and education as a deterrent and extra level of security. Investing in people, and not thinking of them as the weakest link but the first line of defense, can be a better preventative measure than some of the most innovative technology that is available. And as advancements in technology and threat vectors occur, there will be a progression of opportunities to educate employees about these risks. A well-designed security awareness program will help to lessen these risks, while creating overall culture change, and in return will have boundless rewards.*

Lauren Zink, Security Awareness Manager, AmTrust

Nothing is 100 percent when it comes to humans, but if we can raise users' consciousness about practicing secure behaviors, we are halfway there. Continuous training helps us do that.

Gail Ricketts, Information Security & Risk Staff,
On Semiconductor

It's only fitting that I yield the last chapter of this book to the voices and words of the people who are fighting the good fight every day: security awareness program leaders. It's fitting that you hear how they phrase their successes, the challenges that they've overcome, and the tips and tricks they've learned. You'll read the stories of people who weren't satisfied with "check-the-box" training. These leaders know that their users and organizations deserve better: they deserve *transformation*.

You'll notice that I'm also including interviews with some consultants as well. I chose to place those interviews in this chapter rather than the "vendor" chapter because these people are out on the front lines creating and implementing full-fledged programs. They are living the life of a security awareness program manager but doing so with and in multiple organizations.

My hope is that by the end of this chapter, you'll have been struck by an insight or two. These may be things that you already know, but for whatever reason, that knowledge may transform into newfound meaning; sometimes profound insights are packaged as familiar truths uttered in ways that are unfamiliar. And, in other cases, you may be blindsided with the *why didn't I ever think of that?* feeling. In both cases, enjoy reading the words of your peers.

Bruce Hallas, Marmalade Box

- **Name:** Bruce Hallas
- **Title:** Owner and principal consultant, Marmalade Box; founder, author, Re-thinking the Human Factor; founder, The Analogies Project
- **Company:** Re-thinking the Human Factor, Marmalade Box, and The Analogies Project

What drew you to security awareness? In short, what's your story?

I am drawn to challenges and environments where there is scope for improvement or where inertia could undermine society or organizations. The human factor, within the context of security, is one of those areas.

I'm genuinely concerned that in the understandable drive to manage the human factor we'll rely more and more on monitoring employees, through the use of increasingly intrusive technology, further eroding trust between organizations and the people who actually make them great.

I see a middle ground where we can improve the chances of employees making choices resulting in what I call positive security outcomes. But this requires the industry to re-think how it currently approaches the challenge of awareness, behavior and culture. That's why I'm here.

I studied law, finance, and marketing. My early career was more focused on business development and marketing. I stumbled into information security 20 years ago where I found my lack of technical skills meant that I could not talk with any confidence about the intricacies of IT. I did however find that I could engage with stakeholders, especially finance, legal, and marketing, in a context and language they understood. This proved helpful to the IT leadership when looking to build a compelling business case for investment in security. We now call what I used to do governance, risk and compliance, but it invariably involved bringing about change within organizations' levels of awareness, behavior, and culture.

Six years ago, I started a program of research called Re-thinking the Human Factor. The research focused on the challenge of raising awareness, influencing behavior, and fostering an appropriate culture to reduce the likelihood and impact of security incidents. The research led to the development of our SABC Framework, which we launched in 2016; the launch of the *Re-thinking the Human Factor Podcast*, and the publication of my first book, also called *Re-thinking the Human Factor*.

Along with a growing team, I help CISOs, education and awareness managers and consultants to develop and deliver demonstrable education and awareness strategies. We also have an ongoing annual commitment to research, which is there to ensure we're always talking about the latest advances in our understanding of awareness, behavior, and culture.

What makes your take on security awareness unique?

The challenges of awareness, behavior, and culture are not unique to the security industry. What makes our approach unique is how we've combined lessons and data from outside of the security industry with lessons from within the industry and then applied this, within a demonstrable framework, to the human factor challenge.

What aspect of security awareness programs are you most passionate about?

Getting the scope right and approved by all stakeholders. If you do this, then you significantly increase your chances of demonstrable success.

What was your biggest "aha" moment when it comes to engaging with people, the "business," etc.?

I remember sitting back and thinking to myself, "What part of information security is not about awareness, behavior, or culture?"

How do you gauge your program's success?

What demonstrable difference has it made?

What's your elevator pitch on how/why security awareness can actually make a difference?

How comfortable would your CEO or legal counsel be in demonstrating that they've taken reasonable and appropriate steps to raise awareness, influence behavior, and build an appropriate organizational culture around security?

What do you love most about your role or mission?

There's a growing momentum for change, which has been building over the past three to four years, and it has been a privilege to have made my own small contribution to this.

Name a book, resource (e.g., TED Talk), or something else that really influenced the way that you think about awareness. Or it could be a book or resource that you always find yourself recommending to others.

My *Re-thinking the Human Factor* podcast. Alternatively, anything by Dan Ariely.

Last thoughts? This is your chance to answer a question that you wish I'd asked but didn't think of. Or perhaps you can offer a piece of advice for readers or a word of encouragement.

Maybe the next big break-through is actually marginal gains across everything we currently do?

Carlos Miró, MUFG Union Bank

- **Name:** Carlos Miró
- **Title:** Director, Enterprise-Wide Cyber Awareness and Training
- **Company:** MUFG Union Bank

What drew you to security awareness? In short, what's your story?

Throughout my career, I've worked to communicate technical and sometimes complicated information in ways that are easily understood by nontechnical internal and external audiences. I have a passion for using my skills and abilities in communication to help my company mitigate the risks introduced into our environment by the human factor. It's an interesting and rewarding challenge. Raising cybersecurity awareness among our staff helps our company and our customers, as well as our employees—both in the office and when at home.

What makes your take on security awareness unique?

We follow a broad, multichannel approach (both for internal and external audiences) that uses traditional communications (including posters), with digital media (including social media), video, and more. In addition, we have a 360-degree, whole-person approach. We teach our staff best practices at the office so that they can carry those home at the end of their day to help their families stay cyber safe.

What aspect of your security awareness program are you most passionate about?

Helping out staff people become more cyber aware and use cyber safe practices both in the office and at home.

What was your biggest "aha" moment when it comes to engaging with people, the "business," etc.?

Helping people understand best practices at home benefits the company when they're in the office.

How do you gauge your program's success?

Internal and external social media clicks, phishing simulation click rates compared to financial industry averages.

What's your elevator pitch on how/why security awareness can actually make a difference?

The human factor is the weakest link in cybersecurity—a great many attacks, for example, begin with a phishing email. And no matter how well configured, no technology is perfect. It often comes down to a user understanding the risks and following best practices.

What do you love most about your role or mission?

Helping people to learn how to be cyber safe both in the office and at home.

Name a book, resource (e.g., TED Talk), or something else that really influenced the way that you think about awareness. Or it could be a book or resource that you always find yourself recommending to others.

Probably my favorite books are those written by Kevin Mitnick—especially *The Art of Deception* and the more recent *Ghost in the Wires*. Both cover social engineering from a former practitioner of the art, who served his time in the penitentiary for his misdeeds and now works to educate others on recognizing and avoiding the "con." His stories are fascinating and entertaining, as well as useful.

Dr. Cheryl O. Cooper, Sprint Corporation

- **Name:** Dr. Cheryl O. Cooper
- **Title:** Security risk manager, speaker, and adjunct professor
- **Company:** Sprint Corporation and Webster University

What drew you to security awareness? In short, what's your story?

I enlisted in the United States Navy when the Internet was primarily only available to the military as what was called back then a "radioman technical controller." Attacks were on government. When I went to work for a private company, it was a natural progression to work in telecom. Working in telecom at that time there was little focus on how the employee contributes to the overall defense-in-depth security strategy. The years passed into the early 2000s, and as technology became embedded into the lives of employees and consumers, security awareness became a greater concern for organizations. Since I worked in network, I knew where the security holes were, and I knew many of them were caused by employees. That drew me to wanting to educate users on the importance of security and safeguarding company assets. With the rise of modern-day hacking, I am even more drawn into helping others protect their work and personal information.

As an educator and security professional, security awareness is just one area of creating a comprehensive security program and a layered defense. Security awareness is important to me because we as security professionals have to address the sociological and psychological elements that drive an individual's behavior to want to support an organization's security program. Security awareness is important to everyone that is connected to the Internet, including children. How can one improve a security program if they don't know why? Security starts at home, and, having children myself, it starts with educating children how to protect themselves. Once an individual understands the importance of security relevant to protecting their own security and privacy, they can translate this to protecting their organization.

What makes your take on security awareness unique?

I am a security risk specialist with the objective of managing risk and compliance with industry regulation and standards. I'm also an adjunct professor teaching cyber security courses for a local university. I bring awareness not just from an enterprise perspective, but I teach my students how to protect their security and privacy on the last frontier, too, e.g., the home front.

My take on security awareness is not unique but holistic and vast because of my many roles that creates many perspectives and an in-depth knowledge of security, threats, and countermeasures. As an adjunct professor, I'm often tasked with discussing threats to an individual's privacy, threats to critical infrastructure, and the types of attacks used to compromise an individual's privacy. From phishing attacks, smishing attacks, vishing attacks to ransomware attacks, I always highlight the importance of security awareness and education. We have to help individuals to understand why it's important— what is the "so what" to me? Why is security important to me? What do I have to lose? What's the skin in the game? If we can achieve that, then we as security awareness educators are one step closer to creating an effective security awareness program.

What aspect of your security awareness program are you most passionate about?

I love telling stories to drive home concepts and why security is important to the individual. People may not remember the term or concept, but they will remember the emotions and the story. I'm passionate about the people. It used to be firewalls were the first line of defense when protecting networks; now it's the people.

This year I've been engaged with bringing security awareness by supporting the growth of the next generation of professionals through formal and informal mentoring working with local universities and security associations.

What was your biggest "aha" moment when it comes to engaging with people, the "business," etc.?

Over the course of my security career, I have found it essential that security awareness training be an ongoing continuous process. It's an absolute for any successful security program due to the ever-changing technology landscape and the sophistication of present-day hackers. My "aha" moment when it comes to engaging people is when I make it relatable through telling stories we can all relate to; I see in their eyes and body language that they get it. Another "aha" moment when it comes to engaging people in discussions about security is sometimes seeing someone's "ho-hum," "I don't care" attitude firsthand;

they feel that adhering to security standards will impact productivity. Unfortunately, all too often organizations have to rely on their security policies to enforce employee adherence to industry best practices.

How do you gauge your program's success?

Gauging our organization's security awareness program success is based on benchmarks. Has the needle moved? For example, my organization performs phishing campaigns. If the results indicate that a high percentage failed the phishing test, this would indicate a need for training. Follow-up phishing campaigns would then be necessary to gauge if the training worked.

What's your elevator pitch on how/why security awareness can actually make a difference?

Security awareness is a critical strategy in any organization's security program because it educates the individuals on how to protect themselves from the bad guys and teaches them how to protect company assets. Human behavior can be our greatest challenge, meaning an organization's weakest link. Education is key in the fight against criminals wanting to rob individuals and organizations regardless of the size of the organization. Education and awareness training reduce the probability of an organization being victimized. Security professionals and educators must teach individuals how to protect themselves against cyber criminals. And employees must take the lessons learned and turn them into everyday habits that are second nature.

A company that implements only technical solutions to protect the organizations' assets will surely become victimized. In today's aggressive technological advances in which everyone is somehow connected to the Internet through cell phones, smart homes, smart cars, medical devices, and much more, we have to educate everyone. From employees working in customer care to executives of multibillion-dollar companies, they all have to stop and look both ways before proceeding—the same lessons we learned in kindergarten when crossing the street. As we as a nation move into the future, we have to build resiliency into our security programs that will allow organizations to quickly identify, respond, and recover from cyber-attacks. With the disappearing of the network perimeter that had been traditionally protect by firewalls, networks are closer to the front door of consumer's homes. Other than common-sense reasons for implementing security awareness training, regulations will drive companies to implement security awareness programs as they too understand that humans are the weakest link.

What do you love most about your role or mission?

My passion currently is mentoring, educating, and creating the growth of the next generation of security professionals. Over the last couple of years, I have mentored many women through formal mentoring programs, as well as informally. I work with local universities and high schools to educate students, as well as educators about security and how to integrate security into the classroom. Looking forward, I am creating an online mentor program for women looking at a career in cybersecurity.

Name a book, resource (e.g., TED Talk), or something else that really influenced the way that you think about awareness. Or it could be a book or resource that you always find yourself recommending to others.

As a security professional in the private industry, and as an educator I have many books I use as references. Certifications are an excellent way to show that you're serious about a security career. If you're looking for a career in security, there are recommended books that support the CISSP. If you're looking at an auditing career, I recommend books that are recommended by ISACA. Of course, there is a vast amount of information and resources that can be found on the Internet. Being in education, I use a host of different books depending on the topic. I would recommend anyone considering learning more about security awareness to use the Internet to search on security awareness resources. Anything you want to learn about, you can generally find on YouTube; it's a great resource. I have used YouTube for a host of topics from security awareness to Cyber Security Pre-Emptive Deterrence. Lastly, the National Institute of Standards and Technology (NIST) has a great framework to provide guidance in creating a security awareness program.

Last thoughts? This is your chance to answer a question that you wish I'd asked but didn't think of. Or perhaps you can offer a piece of advice for readers or a word of encouragement.

When I think about what we can do better as privacy and security professionals, it is to create a security-aware culture. This would bring all employees into the fight against cybercrime. We have to be creative in making security fun! Don't assign security and privacy functions to siloed departments and individuals. Instead, make it a "family" affair and enmesh the entire community. The battle cannot be won with just a few soldiers. We have to enlist all the troops.

Security is only as strong as the weakest link. This is often the human element, the employee.

Krina Snider, Sprint

- **Name:** Krina Snider
- **Title:** Manager, security awareness
- **Company:** Sprint Corporation

What drew you to security awareness? In short, what's your story?

In 2002, I was manager of marketing and communications for the consulting firm, Accenture. A downturn in business forced the firm to make some necessary cuts and being the "low man on the totem pole," I was now in job search mode. Little did I know the most exciting role of my career was about to fall in my lap. After weeks of diligently searching for a new position in marketing and communications, I was contacted by an executive recruiter for the vice president of corporate security at Sprint's World Headquarters in Kansas City.

"But, wait (I thought to myself) … did you say security?!

I'm a marketing chick—are you sure you have the right person?"

The recruiter went on to say that I had been highly recommended by a few of the partners at Accenture for this newly created position to "market" security. Long story shortened, after extensive interviews with that vice president and the seven directors who managed the various functions of security from physical to technical to national, I got the job! They had more than 100 highly technical and talented security professionals in the department, and what they needed was one highly creative person. The company needed someone to market security and help employees not only understand risks but also learn how they can reduce potential vulnerabilities. My job was to develop this new position to

- Create messaging, develop concepts, and deliver an over-arching security awareness program designed to educate Sprint users on technical, traditional, and national security issues.
- Reduce risk to the company and its associates by increasing overall awareness of various security topics using various delivery channels.

What makes your take on security awareness unique?

Three things: make the message easy to understand, make it relevant to the audience, make it memorable (and yes, adding a little "fun" in the mix always helps!).

What aspect of your security awareness program are you most passionate about?

I love the big events when I can deliver more "bang for my buck." There's something special when you can lure your employees away from their desks to provide a targeted event. The annual Safety and Security Information Expo that I coordinate hosts information tables covering all aspects of safety and security from Sprint and the community to help protect employees at home, at work, and online.

What was your biggest "aha" moment when it comes to engaging with people, the "business," etc.?

Know. Your. Audience. It doesn't matter how knowledgeable you are; if you missed the mark on your delivery, you've lost them. I tailor my awareness messaging to meet the needs of my audience. If I'm presenting to executives, the recipe for success is short and sweet … with an added cup of scary statistics, a sprinkle of relevant headlines, and a dash of action items.

Getting to the executives always presents a challenge because they're busy running the company. So, what's the next best thing? Their executive administrators. These are the people who the executives rely on to keep them organized and abreast of important issues. So, I contacted the editor of their quarterly newsletter to include a security message in each issue plus I regularly deliver EA presentations and webinars throughout the year so they can plant those security seeds.

How do you gauge your program's success?

Marketing 101 says you have to deliver a message seven times for it to "stick." I use various communication channels to deliver awareness messaging, which broadens my reach and increases the odds that it's going to "stick." People learn/retain information in different ways, so it only makes sense to reach them through different communication mediums like articles on the Sprint intranet, posters around Sprint facilities, table tents in Sprint cafeterias, visuals on Sprint TV, videos in Sprint training, and in-person presentations to Sprint business groups and departments.

What's your elevator pitch on how/why security awareness can actually make a difference?

It's not a matter of "if" a security incident is going to affect your company; it's a matter of "when." Equipping employees with the tools to help prevent a security incident is the key to creating a culture that padlocks your company and keeps the "bad guys" from getting in. Security awareness protects your *asset*s.

What do you love most about your role or mission?

Seeing the light go on when employees truly understand the issue. I make it clear when I present to audiences that this is big business for the bad guys and they're getting smarter and more sophisticated in their attacks, so we need to be smart(er) and ready. When I receive an email or note that says, "Wow, I had no idea. Thanks for bringing the issues to light—I know what to look for now," that's when I know the message "stuck."

A favorite story (if you want). . .

I try to think of creative ways to deliver security awareness. Each year at our world headquarters, the departments environmental, health and safety, and human resources host a health fair. This is a very well-attended event that provides free flu shots, giveaways, speakers, etc. One October, I wasn't able to have my annual Safety and Security Expo and was looking for other ways to get my message out there, so I contacted the coordinator of the health fair. She was a bit confused as to why I was wanting to participate in the event saying, "Um, this is a health fair and really doesn't have anything to do with security." I told her that I absolutely understood, but that I was going to talk about *viruses of a different kind.* She laughed and admired my creative spin on the theme and then graciously accepted my request to have an information booth with the other vendors. I knew I'd have to ramp it up a bit to get noticed at this health event, so I used monsters and scary props to align with the Halloween timing and to also reiterate how scary security incidents/attacks can be. The event was a huge success, and attendees definitely remembered our booth.

Name a book, resource (e.g., TED Talk), or something else that really influenced the way that you think about awareness. Or it could be a book or resource that you always find yourself recommending to others.

My first day in my position, my director put a book on my desk to read. It was *The Art of Deception* by Kevin Mitnick. This book detailed his many accounts of successful social engineering attacks, which ultimately led to his arrest. Mitnick told his story from the outside looking in and helped me understand how easy it could be to manipulate average, trusting people into disclosing highly sensitive information.

Social engineering was also the reason Sprint realized they needed an awareness program and someone to manage it. A third-party business partner conducted their own social engineering exercise on Sprint, and well, let's just say the employees didn't do so well. This got the attention of the CEO who immediately created the position of manager of security awareness.

That same director also approved for me to attend a workshop, "How to Create and Sustain an Effective Security Awareness Program." This interactive workshop of other security awareness managers not only paved the way for the program I was about to develop, it was also the foundation for the development of the Computer Security Institute's Security Awareness Peer Group, now the International Association of Security Awareness Professionals (IASAP).

Last thoughts? This is your chance to answer a question that you wish I'd asked but didn't think of. Or perhaps you can offer a piece of advice for readers or a word of encouragement.

As a founding member of IASAP, one of the biggest hurdles many awareness managers face is getting their message in front of employees. Creating the message isn't the difficult part; it's the delivery. Who has to approve the message before you can print or distribute? Who is the gatekeeper ... or the road block? To be successful, you have to align with and form working relationships with your corporate communications, real estate, legal, and human resources teams and any other departments who can add fuel/visibility to your message.

Mark Majewski, Quicken Loans

- **Name:** Mark Majewski
- **Title:** Information security evangelist
- **Company:** Quicken Loans

What drew you to security awareness? In short, what's your story?

After many years leading IT software development and architecture teams, I had the opportunity to lead the InfoSec organization at a Fortune 500 company. In security, I enjoyed the technical cat-and-mouse game of trying to outwit the "bad guys." However, I was particularly drawn to the challenging task of securing the "human firewall." Awareness is also a very creative profession. Since we are competing for the mindshare of our team members, content must be creative, engaging, and noteworthy.

What makes your take on security awareness unique?

I believe we are actually charged with building a security culture program, rather than a security awareness program. Employees must know what to do to be secure but also act securely (exhibit secure behaviors). As a result, I have a strong bias toward simulations/tests over training/communications. I believe that the impact of a user being caught by a simulation or test (e.g., email phishing or having their password guessed) can be an effective wake-up call and has a longer memory than a communications/training (CBT/poster/blog etc.). My simulation bias also influences my user surveys. For example, some companies ask their users, "Do you know how to report a phishing email?" in their surveys. I'd rather test their actual behavior than ask about their knowledge in a survey.

What aspect of your security awareness program are you most passionate about?

Delivering content using modern multimedia (especially video) and gamification excite me.

What was your biggest "aha" moment when it comes to engaging with people, the "business," etc.?

Influencing behaviors takes more than awareness. Looking for ways to eliminate the possibility of insecure behavior (e.g., blacklisting common guessable passwords) or assisting employees in real time (e.g., flagging external email messages) are perhaps more important.

How do you gauge your program's success?

Our program measures audience (readers, audience size, game players, etc.) and behaviors (from simulations).

What's your elevator pitch on how/why security awareness can actually make a difference?

The "human firewall" is a critical component of security. A mistake by an employee can bypass some of the best security controls. Yet, one good catch by an employee can prevent a catastrophe. We will be successful when employees *feel* responsible for protecting, *know* how to protect, and *act* to protect company and personal information assets.

What do you love most about your role or mission?

Security threats change constantly. As a result, we are always learning and adapting.

Name a book, resource (e.g., TED Talk), or something else that really influenced the way that you think about awareness. Or it could be a book or resource that you always find yourself recommending to others.

I recommend *Making Things Stick* by Chip and Dan Heath.

Michael Lattimore, Independent Consultant

- **Name:** Michael Lattimore
- **Title:** Cybersecurity awareness evangelist
- **Company:** Presently with Southern California Edison (will be an independent consultant after April 2019)

What drew you to security awareness? In short, what's your story?

I have been a community volunteer since age 7 growing up on Chicago's Southside. I relocated to California in the late 1970s, and with two daughters growing up in the "MySpace era," I quickly became aware of the dangers that kids (and digital immigrants—sometimes seniors) faced on the Internet. I started conducting Internet Safety workshops for families in my neighborhood, and a senior leader at Southern California Edison heard about it and asked me to do a Home Computer Security workshop for the company, promising to sponsor it. We received almost 300 RSVPs for the event, and afterward he offered me a position in information security doing this full-time for the company. Helping people stay safe is a personal mission of mine, so I stepped into my dream job as a security awareness evangelist in 2006.

This chain of events is also what drew me to becoming a founding member of the International Association of Security Awareness Professionals (IASAP).

What makes your take on security awareness unique?

I teach awareness strategies from a personal perspective. I believe that when people are safer at home, they will also be safer in the workplace. I also feel that security awareness has a cultural component and is about addressing the misperception of risk for everyone who participates in online activities. I am a storyteller who adapts the points of wisdom to be relevant to each audience, from elementary school kids to the corporate boardroom leader.

What aspect of your security awareness program are you most passionate about?

The aspect of my security awareness program that brings me the most excitement is seeing the results. I love hearing the stories and seeing the engagement of people who have been in my audiences and have "caught the fire" to become ambassadors and advocates of safe online practices. I am also personally excited about the prospect of raising a generation of security awareness practitioners to step into this as of yet undiscovered profession. In my opinion, the security awareness practitioner is the least known career opportunity in the IT industry.

What was your biggest "aha" moment when it comes to engaging with people, the "business," etc.?

When I witnessed, over and over again, the missteps of those I call the *distinguished users*, I began to become aware of something that I had previously missed. These were individuals who continued to demonstrate that they misperceived the risk involved with using weak passwords, clicking links, sharing their login credentials, and other unsafe cyber behaviors. Some of these behaviors were truly cringe-worthy causing me to ask sometimes, "Um, what were you thinking?"

The big "aha" moment for me was to become aware that these individuals truly did not correctly perceive the risk of their behaviors. They truly did not know, and they did not "know" that they didn't know.

This meant that I needed to learn additional strategies to help them. I realized then that you don't train your puppy with a baseball bat and neither should you punish users for their ignorance.

It was then that I realized the depth and breadth of my mission: to raise awareness and understanding of the risk to them personally. Also, I knew that I had to inspire in them a desire to be safer (sometimes by recruiting them to be ambassadors) and then give them the ability and knowledge to make better decisions. Finally, realizing that we learn best by repetition and emotional involvement, my job was to reinforce the learning so that they could become acculturated to making the right choices in the future.

How do you gauge your program's success?

By measuring the program effectiveness through metrics. Counting what we do—like the number of posters, number of contacts at a security booth, presentations, surveys, etc. Then counting the results—or the impact, like the number of incidents, number of people reporting incidents, and suspicious calls and emails, etc. The more mature your program becomes, the better you get at measuring results (and vice versa).

What's your elevator pitch on how/why security awareness can actually make a difference?

For years corporate leadership believed they could throw a few million dollars at the problem, purchase the best-of-breed firewalls, intrusion prevention, and technology and become a virtual citadel, safe and protected against the hackers.

After billions of records were breached, they discovered that even though they were hard and crunchy on the outside, they were still soft and chewy on the inside because the human firewall was the bastion of last resort. The human firewall is our most valuable asset because machine systems cannot apply nonlinear thinking to an incomplete picture to develop a reasonable hypothesis. Only a human being can do that (although it may not be long before AI is mature enough to astound us in this capacity).

What do you love most about your role or mission?

What I love most is making a difference in the lives of others. I'm excited about promoting the practice and profession for security awareness and the possibility of helping others to create a fulfilling career path in this field. As the sophistication of artificial intelligence increases, it won't be long before we will all need to be proactive masters of the virtual assistants in our lives, protecting the details of our personal lives and even conversations from misuse.

I'm especially excited about what we will create together to counterbalance the unethical use of technology. I am always amazed at human resilience and our power to create solutions that help others, and I am committed to being part of that evolution.

A favorite story (if you want). . .

I have so many … a recent one involves the story of the Iceland police website hack in which the attackers impersonated the Icelandic Police website and pulled off the largest phishing attack in Iceland ever using sophisticated malware and a fake domain name that used the letter i instead of an l. This story really speaks to the power of awareness and how letting down our guard for just a moment can end in disaster.

But one of my most impactful stories comes from the world of "catfishing," in which perpetrators prey on those vulnerable to romantic manipulation. This story involves a recently widowed woman and a newfound romantic interest that went on for quite a while. What made it unusual is that the romantic interest on the other end did not make up stories that begged for money from the potential benefactor.

Instead, the "catfisher" sent her money, lots of it, over a long period of time, purportedly so she could store it for "safekeeping," he said. So they could "live a long prosperous life together," he said. Periodically he would ask her to forward him some of the money, via bank transfer, for various purposes.

But she was allowed to keep the vast majority in her own account. Well, over a period of time, these transfers caught the attention of the Secret Service and Treasury departments, and it was determined that they constituted money laundering. When they investigated further, they discovered that the "cat-fisher" was not one but several actors and that they were leading her on by manipulating her with romantic pretexting.

They were all arrested and prosecuted for money laundering, including the victim (ignorance is no excuse in the eyes of the law), and upon sentencing the judge gave her 10 years—suspended. The judge said that if she tried to continue the "romance," she would be subjected to the 10-year prison sentence.

Even after the preponderance of court evidence showing that these individuals had duped her, she still persisted in the belief that the romantic connection between her and the perpetrator was authentic.

This story speaks to the powerful impact of belief and how easily we can be manipulated if we are not aware.

Name a book, resource (e.g., TED Talk), or something else that really influenced the way that you think about awareness. Or it could be a book or resource that you always find yourself recommending to others.

A really heavy and somewhat sobering look at the cybersecurity state of the nations is detailed in Alexander Klimburg's book, *The Darkening Web: The War for Cyberspace*. It's a thick book (400+ pages) filled with the history of how the Web has been used for nefarious purposes. It also offers some perspective on how we can proactively influence the evolution of the Internet.

Another one is *Glitch: The Hidden Impact of Faulty Software* by Jeff Papows, and it details some eye-opening stories about the software that runs our world and the bugs that you rarely hear about.

Last thoughts? This is your chance to answer a question that you wish I'd asked but didn't think of. Or perhaps you can offer a piece of advice for readers or a word of encouragement.

I'd invite anyone reading this book to consider what they can personally do to participate in creating a safer online environment and experience for themselves and their families. Everyone's personal safe computing practices help to keep us all safe. There are lots of online courses and videos that can help you become more aware and less vulnerable to the increasing attacks. So, don't be a victim or "low-hanging fruit." Instead, be an advocate and maybe even consider a career shift into becoming a security awareness practitioner or a security awareness ambassador in your workplace. There are many opportunities in the industry and in your neighborhood just waiting for you to say, "Yes!"

Mo Amin, Independent Consultant

- **Name:** Mo Amin
- **Title:** Independent consultant
- **Company:** MoAmin.com

What drew you to security awareness? In short, What's your story?

I started out in IT building PCs for clients, and the one thing that I noticed back then was that I enjoyed helping and educating people, especially when it came to demystifying the complex and sometimes arcane jargon that we in the industry use. As I moved into security, it became clear to me that the fundamental issues were the same, only now we live in a world where everything is connected. While this is fascinating, the drawbacks are that the general populace isn't aware of the impact that losing their personal and sensitive information can have on them. Helping people to understand and make sense of things is what keeps me interested.

What makes your take on security awareness unique?

Many moons ago, I spent time in Spain teaching English as a foreign language (TEFL). I taught across all age ranges, and one of the main experiences I took away from there was how to get different people engaged toward a common goal, in that context, getting the class through a curriculum. Over the years, I've combined my TEFL, IT, and security experience with my (allegedly) naturally engaging personality to help clients.

What aspect of your security awareness program are you most passionate about?

As an independent consultant, I'm most passionate in making sure that the security function first raises the level of engagement across the business such that it builds trust. Without the right engagement and trust, everything is effectively built on tenuous foundations.

What was your biggest "aha" moment when it comes to engaging with people, the "business," etc.?

Early on in my IT career, before I actually ventured into security, I discovered that people just want to get their job done; and if you don't create structures and systems to make that as easy as possible, they'll find a way around it to deliver what they need to. One of those moments came when someone said to me "So what! How does this make it easier for me to deliver my project!?!" It was a totally rational and genuine question that we had to think about and change the way we were doing things.

How do you gauge your program's success?

The number-one success factor for me has always been that initial level of engagement. Traditionally, security has always been seen as the blocker, the *Department of No*. Once you start breaking down those barriers and begin to get positive engagement, then your efforts become a little more frictionless. When the business starts approaching *you*, that's when you know you're moving in the right direction.

What's your elevator pitch on how/why security awareness can actually make a difference?

When you demonstrate the why of security to people, the response is a lot more positive than simply dictating the what. Security professionals have to change *their* behavior first in order to help change a layperson's behavior.

What do you love most about your role or mission?

There are so many facets to security and people that this whole field is genuinely interesting. As long as that interest holds for me, I'm here.

A favorite story (if you want). . .

Once upon a time a senior exec said to me, "Mo, the best advice I can give to you is to learn what *not* to do. Take time to look around and see what doesn't work and where the issues and difficulties are. Then you'll be able to see what *to do* to build bridges and fix things." I did. The end. True story!

Name a book, resource (e.g., TED Talk), or something else that really influenced the way that you think about awareness. Or it could be a book or resource that you always find yourself recommending to others.

If you can, spend time living and working in a different culture, ideally one that speaks a different language from yours. You'll pick up things that, at the time, you won't realize or appreciate but later down the line you'll recognize their value. I can guarantee that you'll approach your work differently.

Last thoughts? This is your chance to answer a question that you wish I'd asked but didn't think of. Or perhaps you can offer a piece of advice for readers or a word of encouragement.

Remain interested in your work; the day your interest wanes is the day that you need to look elsewhere. After that point you're only cheating yourself, and you should never cheat yourself in life.

Prudence Smith, Senior Cyber and Information Security Consultant and Industry Speaker

- **Name:** Prudence Smith
- **Title:** Senior cyber and information security consultant and industry speaker
- **Company:** Tier 1 Global Financial Services; small, medium and non-profit enterprises

What drew you to security awareness? In short, What's your story?

I started my security career in 1991 working in a scientific not-for-profit organization that involved opening up public debate, driving government policy change, following the issues in its many guises, and interacting with the media. As the firm moved to a networked and Internet-connected infrastructure, I was put in charge of the project, and as the organization moved online, systems were attacked, and my interest in security grew further. This led me into financial services where I introduced the first global information security help desk that enabled me to introduce basic responses to common reported issues and distribute that to all consultants. On the success of the delivery, I became a technical security consultant working with the business on the security analysis of new and existing services. It was in this role that security awareness was given as a side-of-the-desk job. This was at a time of annual regulatory compliance-driven online training, reporting on uptake of a mandatory training delivered to colleagues, and also around the same time as the global financial crash of the late 2000s. Any research on user behavior was light and, when available, based upon student studies.

There was a distinct awareness that the human was being ignored, and the overall consensus was technology with robust controls was the answer.

- Add a review process
- Add another firewall
- Enable end user protection
- Remove and record privileged access, etc.

Yet breaches were growing, and often controls had broken down due to manual tasking.

This approach made the human the easiest and most lucrative method for adversaries to use to commit fraud, extract data, and install malware. This is because the technology approach follows the rule that if something is authorized, it's approved.

The problem with the technology approach is adversaries know your technology, business processes, suppliers, or at least you should act like they do. The other problem is that some technologies out there are prone to create new security issues, so please research fully and look at the negatives as well as the positive reviews. Security awareness can be seen as a minefield if you are not prepared.

While we get to the stage of human analytics where we can drive configuration changes to prevent loss and protect the user, we must simplify each issue, restrict access to reduce the impact of an attack, raise awareness with the users so they understand why the controls have been put in place, and explain the risk issues they will face with the potential consequences of actions (using real examples). People in general want to do the right thing, so enable them to do so. It is after all not the end user's fault the situation is as it is. People do not know what they do not know.

Organized crime is not called organized crime for nothing. They have the time to investigate and plan and only need to be successful once. Adversaries don't even need to be technical anymore. Why go to all the trouble of learning complicated technology when you can simply buy a criminal service or ask someone to do something?

Not all companies and individuals will face the same adversary, so it is important to identify who is most likely to attack, while keeping an eye on nation-states to see what is coming in the future. This will help you identify how to protect against these adversaries and establish tried and tested mitigation paths to move from fire-fighting every incident to a planned, repeatable response.

Types of adversaries can be drawn into the following categories:

- Nation-states
- Organized crime
- Terrorism
- Fraud
- Insiders

In general adversaries attempt to obtain/conduct:

- Intellectual property
- Money
- Launder
- Malicious, nonmalicious, and accidental privileged access

To combat this level of sophistication and to move away from firefighting every incident, security must be seen holistically and include the security of the physical person, data, technology/cyber, roles, business processes, and the buildings and areas they access at work, at travel, and at home. It sounds like a big job. It is and it isn't.

Humans are vulnerable because:

- Some do not understand security.
- Some don't want to understand security.
- Some consider it someone else's issue.
- Some think security is too complicated; consultants often given differing methods to address the same issue of differing complexities and results. This confuses the end user.
- Some users will act insecurely—the reward is enough.
- There is no magic bullet.
- Some know small bits and think they know what they are talking about; this impacts not only their security but can also make the firm liable should they offer advice that then causes an issue.
- Your systems are likely to be broadcasting its system, version, and probably a lot more. To an adversary, you are just another system but with more fundamental vulnerabilities that are exponentially more difficult to apply to a human than any system.

It wasn't until 2105 that we now knew how much this was costing the global economy, when the FBI reported an estimated annual loss to cybercrime of around $665 million per year. A 2018 study by the University of Surry projects losses by 2021 of $19 trillion, and we are on track to reach that number. When I speak to students, I receive laughter at this figure. It is too ridiculous to contemplate, but we are on projection. This issue is at a critical level globally.

What makes your take on security awareness unique?

The approach requires commitment, budget, and buy-in from the very top. If your awareness program does not have budget and senior executive buy-in, you will struggle to deliver. When I say struggle, I mean fail. You are unable to make a cultural change to any business by yourself, and if this is the case, you are best approaching other high-risk issues that are more easily solved and easier to relate to senior management. However, if you are driven to make a change, there are other ways you can help us all raise our game by raising awareness. These can include getting onto boards, talking at local schools, old people's homes, clubs, universities, and charities.

A training and awareness program must be all-inclusive, innovative, and educational. People learn differently. What works for one will not work for another. A program that works together across industries, utilizing key central messages, that refines technology to prevent cyber crime while also, in the interim, educating end users to the types and techniques each type of user faces.

What aspect of your security awareness program are you most passionate about?

As a security professional, I am passionate about learning and being an expert in my field. Awareness is another string to my security experience, and it is a method that studies show, if applied correctly and thoroughly, can mitigate 80 percent of cyber attacks, just by applying the same basic controls that security consultants have been recommending for years.

In my view, the Internet came too quickly. Everyone wanted local admin rights, then an email address, then the Internet. Security was not considered a risk, and this is where the problem lies. We have all been dormant for too long when it comes to humans, and adversaries appear to have the upper hand. But they do not. If we all take ownership of our data and online life, we will be safer and secure.

What was your biggest "aha" moment when it comes to engaging with people, the "business," etc.?

Humans are too fickle for any awareness program to work 100 percent.

How do you gauge your program's success?

Statistics and metrics. Those can be hard to get at because of the holistic nature of a cybersecurity awareness and training program. While reporting on a technical system appears easy, gauging user behavior change is far more difficult, and often metrics and stats result in how many messages were sent out or read, how many were printed, or a poster posted. None of this gauges human behavior change. We must look at specific issues to relate that change in behavior.

A great place to start is phishing. Phishing whether by email or voice is the number-one method to commit fraud, extract data, and install malware and one of the main metrics used to show the resiliency of a firm. I have come across free phishing products, but I am always wary of free products. If you are a small company, set up your own phishing campaign using the techniques used by adversaries such as spoofing and measure the success rate of who responds. Conducting your own phishing campaigns does have its drawbacks, but if you have a limited budget, you will be able to enable a landing page, or attachment, that contains the training and awareness required and analyze the log files for who accessed those sites.

For those who act correctly and do not open or respond, this is your firm's resiliency rate. Remember, phishing exercises must not be considered training. Phishing simulations are awareness exercises and should not be threatening. Any metrics reported can be used to show where the gaps are in email security. If you can, enable DMARC so people cannot spoof your domain name, and make sure that you are consistent with your customers and clients about the messages and how you relate these.

Never send an email link without it being the full address and underlying address and do not deviate from your normal website addresses. Better still, have all communication available through your secured website so visitors can access the material centrally. Do not forget to educate your customers on how you will talk to them and when remembering and advising colleagues and customers that adversaries are always waiting to take advantage and probably know of your communication plans. I have heard of a company who experienced business email compromise (BEC) with a new vendor before the first payment.

What's your elevator pitch on how/why security awareness can actually make a difference?

I frame elevator pitch interactions like this:

Hello, my name is <insert name>, and my role is to change culture when it comes to cyber and data risk. I raise awareness of the cyber risks you face in your day to day work, home, and traveling activities. Do you know how to report an incident? <<Yes/No>>. <if Yes, move to the next paragraph>, <if No, please continue>. You don't, just type <easy url for people to find it/ i.e. cyber\ or \security> into a browser; it's all there.

Did you know that cyber crime is currently costing the global economy $XXXX, and that's a conservative estimate. It's estimated to rise to $XX trillion by 2021. The number-one method of attack is phishing. Did you receive my recent email <mention the latest phishing simulation>? Well, the firm's click rate was X% <stress amazing or bad depending on the results>.

If you're interested, I can come along and speak at your next team meeting and go through your department's resiliency. Or why not become a champion yourself? It's volunteer and great on your annual review. You'll have specialized training with certification and learn of all the latest attacks and you can be the cyber go to person for your row, team, department, or country. Put on events or drives. Visit the website for everything you need and join the chat channel.

A favorite story (if you want). . .

I delivered a technical defense and attack-driven technical attack simulation in order to identify new cyber and information security talent. Working with a startup firm I had been working with for a few years, an eight-hour cyber attack was delivered using cloud technology. As part of the delivery, a leader board was created that went into detail about how well each team was on each step. It was clear that every person taking part was 100 percent on attack and no one was fully on defense. It was then that I realized that the industry was failing our future and our future was attacking our present.

Name a book, resource (e.g., TED Talk), or something else that really influenced the way that you think about awareness. Or it could be a book or resource that you always find yourself recommending to others.

Get involved in cyber and information security in all avenues in your life. Look at all of the topics and become an expert in a few. Learn statistical analysis and Microsoft Excel (everyone needs an Excel expert). Become proficient in putting your analysis into strong charts and graphs.

Last thoughts? This is your chance to answer a question that you wish I'd asked but didn't think of. Or perhaps you can offer a piece of advice for readers or a word of encouragement.

Know your scope and remit and get that signed off by your stakeholders. These are a few traps to avoid:

- Don't become the team to identify the high-risk users. This is not the role of the training and awareness team. High-risk users are a business risk and therefore identified and owned by the business. After all, they know their applications and services and who has access to them.

Be also aware that often training and awareness include the training of security professionals too. Be careful of this scope crawl as this is a large issue within itself.

■ Training on skills required to perform a role is in general an issue between immediate management, senior management, and HR. You will also find that due to the high cost of cyber training that it will eat all of your available budget.

These are some hints and tips:

1. Be consistent in your messages and make life easy for the end user.
2. Use online resources to reduce turnaround time as long as the message is correct for your firm/project/piece of work.
3. You cannot change attitudes to cyber and data use without top-level approval and direction that cyber is a top risk to the firm. There will be times when an incident may involve a senior executive or an activity requires their support, and if you cannot gain their swift approval, you will be unlikely to succeed.
4. You should behave as though your systems and data have already been compromised.
5. Be aware of "zero-day attacks," which basically is malcode that is so new that it has not yet been picked up by systems and will not be identified and/or contained. This includes attacks that process so occasionally (for example, once every 25 years) that they will most likely not be picked up by any IPS/IDS system.
6. Any security technology put in place is only as good as the information that it knows, such as how it's configured and managed ongoing.
7. Once any systems are online, you need to own them, manage them, and keep them updated—if your supporting systems allow it and it has been thoroughly tested away from live/production systems. This is true no matter how small the organization.
8. If you can, enable mobile device encryption as well as the ability to remotely wipe devices if they are lost, stolen, or when an employee is no longer with the organization.
9. To get your board of directors on your side, show them the facts. Board members really are no different from anyone else.
10. Remember it is not the end users' fault if they make a mistake.

If you do not have these things, you may find that your awareness messaging will be prevented or altered until you fail.

Thom Langford, (TL)2 Security

- **Name:** Thom Langford
- **Title:** Founder
- **Company:** (TL)2 Security, an InfoSec consultancy

What drew you to security awareness? In short, What's your story?

For me, awareness gives us the single most cost-effective, "bang-for-the-buck" investment any organization can make into security. Given the statistics on the level of "insider threat" and the number of incidents caused by negligent or ignorant employees, I find it amazing that more effort isn't put into it.

Additionally, I also enjoy interacting with people in a way that speaks to them, engages them, and impacts their day-to-day lives. It is one thing to help them make a difference at work; it is something else to help them change bad habits and practices across their lives, at home with their family, or even with their friends.

What makes your take on security awareness unique?

I don't think I have a unique take on it, but the emphasis I like to place on it is not always replicated across our industry. There is still a lot of placing people in a room and shouting PowerPoint at them for an hour and then expecting a fundamental shift in their behavior. One-off exercises don't work.

The more we think of awareness as an infinite game (one without rules, with no end, and with no defined winner), our mind-set will change. The purpose of the game is to increase awareness across everyone we encounter and leave them wanting to continue to play the "game" with you. That is very different to annual, one-off security training.

What aspect of your security awareness program are you most passionate about?

That it isn't prescriptive. Setting out do's and don'ts doesn't help anyone in an evolving and changing environment. The threats, the antagonists, and the technology changes all the time. Giving one-dimensional advice results in one-dimensional thinking, and so when new threats emerge, they aren't perceived as threats until it is too late.

The other element I feel very strongly about is ensuring we make a visceral connection with people. Maya Angelou was quoted as saying that people will forget what you show them, or do for them, but they never forget how you made them feel. If we can connect at that basic level of human emotion with people concerning security awareness, then we will have reached the tipping point and really made a difference.

What was your biggest "aha" moment when it comes to engaging with people, the "business," etc.?

Regarding people in the context of security, I have always maintained that every interaction we have with anyone should leave them as fanatical advocates of security and of us. That means making them truly understand why we are doing things a certain way and how we are truly helping the organization rather than hindering it. Again, that visceral response is key, and personally I use humor. By that I don't mean I do 30 minutes of standup at every meeting but rather take a slightly lighter view of circumstances to raise the mood and put everyone at ease. The awareness campaigns I have rolled out include humor as a core part of the approach for this very reason.

And regarding the business as a whole, it was about doing my level best to never say "no" to anything. It is not my job as a CISO to act as the last bastion of security, ensuring the organization avoids risk at all costs. That way leads to the stifling of innovation and the sidelining of us as a security team. We should be informing them of the risks and helping them address or ignore the risks as appropriate. Our main purpose is to help the business sell more stuff, whatever that stuff is, and that means taking calculated risks, being cognizant of what might be coming.

How do you gauge your program's success?

There are so many ways, formal and informal, and many of them unique to your organization. For instance, perceived wisdom is that security incidents will go up after training as people will be more willing and informed to report incidents. But what if the training worked well and people stopped doing certain risky activities? Fewer phishing links clicked, for instance? One study found that people who had been trained to spot phishing attacks subsequently clicked through on more attacks than those that haven't because they felt over confident about their abilities. Success factors and KPIs will always depend on the environment and culture. Reporting incidents may be culturally frowned upon, perhaps seen as whistleblowing, so that will confuse traditional stats.

Of course, you should always start measuring from months before the training to see the baseline, and that way any significant deviation can be interpreted as a result of the training. Once the change is seen, it can be interpreted through surveys, watercooler discussions, or any kind of forum (as long as the culture supports that kind of information gathering. . .).

What's your elevator pitch on how/why security awareness can actually make a difference?

Simple, security awareness/education is the crowd sourcing model for promoting the behavioral equivalent of virtually any security technology you roll out. It may not take you all the way, but it is significantly cheaper than trying to implement technology to fix everything.

What do you love most about your role or mission?

That when it is done properly, watching people's reactions and changing attitudes as the revelation hits them that security will not only help secure the business but propel it onto new heights. It is that fanatical advocate moment that I live for, because we have fundamentally shifted somebody's worldview on how we can and should be working as a modern, digital company.

A favorite story (if you want). . .

Complexity is always the enemy of success. Many years ago I was charged with ascertaining the organization's potential for loss of personally identifiable information. I formed a small team, and an amazing spreadsheet was created; it would alter what questions were asked based on previous responses, consolidate responses, feed into a master spreadsheet—the works. A month after having sent out this 200-question masterpiece, and with multiple reminders, about 10 percent of the target audience had filled it out. I had failed to meet my deadline, by a significant margin, and was rightfully reprimanded.

The advice I was given was "don't let perfect be the enemy of good." We rallied, created a 15-question spreadsheet, and got over 85 percent of the target audience to respond. Good enough.

We were never going to get a 100 percent response (as much down to the culture as anything else), but we had a damn good idea of what the scale of our risk was, and that was good enough. Detail is good, but always know when that level of attention is required and especially when it isn't.

Name a book, resource (e.g., TED Talk), or something else that really influenced the way that you think about awareness. Or it could be a book or resource that you always find yourself recommending to others.

Storyscaping by Gaston Legaboru and Daz McColl. It is actually a marketing book, but I learned some very valuable lessons from it around creating "experiences" for people; it goes back to the visceral response I mentioned. The algorithm they gave that has always stuck with me is Value + Story = Experience. We security people can all provide the value, it is our skillset after all, but by driving a story behind the content, by helping people make emotional connections to the content, you get experience, and if they experience it, they feel it. And that is what they will remember the most.

Last thoughts? This is your chance to answer a question that you wish I'd asked but didn't think of. Or perhaps you can offer a piece of advice for readers or a word of encouragement.

Security is not a funny topic, but that doesn't mean you can't have fun.

Tory Dombrowski, Takeform

- **Name:** Tory Dombrowski
- **Title:** IT Director
- **Company:** Takeform

What drew you to security awareness? In short, What's your story?

Being in small business for most of my professional career, security has always been an afterthought. This is unfortunate because these businesses are now becoming the target of attackers, due to their lax security. We had an event where a lookalike domain was used to target our accounts payable team in an attempt to solicit funds immediately for a fictional invoice. The attacker pretended to be our CEO and used a very similar-looking domain. Our team wasn't having it; they weren't about to pay without a matching PO. I was dragged into the ordeal when they were trying to figure out why we didn't have a PO. My keen eye spotted the fake domain, and the attempt was foiled.

After everything was cleared up, I wanted to develop a strategy should this ever happen again. I did the forensics work to find the lookalike domain and contacted their registrar and had them banned. But how was I going to stop an attack like this in the future? No amount of email filtering could catch something like this, and I had to answer to management as to a strategy moving forward. That's when I decided that I am not the only person smart enough to catch this stuff; people just needed to be trained to identify this sort of attack. Security awareness became my strategy. That was just the beginning.

What makes your take on security awareness unique?

Security can be a scary topic for end users. I think of the line in *Men in Black* when Will Smith's character finds out there are real live outer-space aliens living on Earth (in the movie). He states to his soon-to-be partner that people can handle this information. Tommy Lee Jones replies simply, "A person is smart. People are dumb, panicky, dangerous animals, and you know it!" I agree with that statement. If you attack security head-on, you will see a lot of people become panicky about everything that happens in their digital world. While that can be beneficial, it can also be cumbersome.

My unique spin on security awareness is to encourage users to be part of a team effort in defeating these rogue elements. If even I get concerned when watching some security blogs and webinars, end users are certain to get worried. It can be overwhelming to see all the ways an attacker can (and will) infiltrate networks and trick users. Instead of scaring users, I treat them as intelligent individuals who can be a part of the solution. I make light of current events, use funny memes, and create reward programs. One of my favorite lines is, "I am more carrot than stick," meaning I'd rather reward than punish. I don't favor shaming users who make mistakes but instead offer praise for users who caught particularly tricky phishing emails.

What aspect of your security awareness program are you most passionate about?

I love making training/awareness fun and attainable. It is easy to launch a training campaign, it is hard to make that training effective long term. I have heard some sales managers talk about maintaining "mind share" with our reps. They are talking about keeping our product lines on the top of the sales rep's minds. Our reps tend to sell several different product lines, so how do we keep our products on the forefront of their minds when they are talking to potential customers? This has inspired me to come up with creative ways to keep security on the top of a user's mind while still being relatively fun and engaging.

I have created annual themed campaigns where users can earn badges, mentions in newsletters, and awards. I choose a fun theme that works along with the idea of users being fish and the attackers being fisherman. My first year was a "Shark Week" theme (like on Discovery Channel). I like the idea of empowering my users, with an image of them being a fierce creature and the attacker being a weak one. Weekly I would review the reported phishing emails and award badges to users who reported them. The badges were simply an image of a shark with their name (like a digital trophy). There were two main levels initially. One was a smaller basic shark; the other was a Great

White. I also created a few special badges when I noticed people going above and beyond. At the end of the year, the top people earned physical awards with their name on them. I still see a few of them on their desks.

What was your biggest "aha" moment when it comes to engaging with people, the "business," etc.?

We have a C-level executive who has been infected and hit with ransomware more than once. Unfortunately, many other higher-level executives don't think they have the time (or see the need) for training. He did not participate in the training. He recently got hit with ransomware again, and this time it partially affected our network. Luckily, some protections we had in place stopped the spread, and backups were available to get us back in action. We had identified this user as the source of the infection and tackled him as he walked in the door. I wrestled him to the ground and ripped his precious laptop from his grip before he could further the infection. OK, maybe I'm exaggerating, but there was at least an emotional struggle.

This user had to go without a computer for almost an entire day while we tried our best to clean up. He was incessantly pestering me for when he would have his laptop back. I repeatedly reminded him that had he done the training, this would not have happened. I saw the email that caused the infection, and it was ripe with red flags. In fact, a few others in the company had received the same phishing email and easily identified it as phishing. After a day without his system, he finally agreed he would do the training. To my surprise, it was not just lip service. He did do the training, and the next time I saw him he told me how surprised he was that he could identify phishing emails. I will not say he has been a perfect user ever since, but his eyes were opened to the possibility that he could identify dangerous emails without my help.

How do you gauge your program's success?

Weekly I review our Phish Alert messages along with every phishing test and training campaign. Based on the types of feedback I get through the phish alerts, I can see which users are actively aware of potential threats. When I see the level of Phish Alert messages taper off, I tend to send out more colorful newsletters. There is a correlation to the amount and quality of my security newsletters and the level of Phish Alerts we receive. Obviously after a particularly effective phishing or training campaign, I like to run a phishing test to see how we are doing.

What's your elevator pitch on how/why security awareness can actually make a difference?

Any worthy IT person will have at least some form of basic firewall, AV, and backup solution in place. The next best place to invest is on the biggest and easiest target, the users. Making end users aware of the security threats and landscape will almost naturally enforce some basic security protocols. Users don't want to be the source of a breach, so if you offer them knowledge of how they can be part of the solution, they will take it. I have personally witnessed some of the most vulnerable people turn around and become one of the least vulnerable/most secure users after some basic security training.

I have had users who would fall for phishing emails simply because the phishing email had the email signature for a known sender. When I showed one particular user how easy it is to mimic an email complete with signature, he still didn't believe me. However, after the security training, he became one of our security evangelists and the picture of a secure user. That user and his story inspired others to give training a chance. Often after training, users would comment on how surprised they were about what they learned. Some users even asked for more training.

What do you love most about your role or mission?

I enjoy teaching people. One of my personal joys in life is taking a subject and sharing it in a way that people can associate with the topic. Our security training program has many different available methods of communicating the materials, which makes for a diverse training program. I also enjoy inventing creative campaigns to keep my users aware and on point. While a training program is easy enough to launch, the real trick is to keep the subject top of mind for users. I enjoy creating engaging content in regular newsletter-style emails. I incorporate an annual theme to develop imagery/memes and awards to capture users' attention and imagination.

A favorite story (if you want). . .

One of my favorite campaigns was a "Phishing Derby"—in a single month I sent out nine phishing tests. The "Phishing Derby" was advertised for a period before it began. The concept was that during the month-long event, any users who didn't click simulated phishing links (and reported the most phishing tests) would be our winners. I didn't pull any punches and started the campaign with a phishing email that promised to include a link to the derby rules. Users were on guard after that, but I still caught quite a few of our better users when I took advantage of inside information to send very targeted phishing tests. When users complained about how I used inside information against them,

I was able to demonstrate (and drive home) how such a targeted campaign could really happen. When the campaign ended, I had 13 users with perfect scores. In the following months we had some phishing tests with 0 percent click-through.

Name a book, resource (e.g., TED Talk), or something else that really influenced the way that you think about awareness. Or it could be a book or resource that you always find yourself recommending to others.

I prefer live events, like webinars. I have picked up a lot of good information from webinars and online communities. I don't know if I could point to one specific book, article, or video. I do recommend webinars whenever I see a good topic.

Last thoughts? This is your chance to answer a question that you wish I'd asked but didn't think of. Or perhaps you can offer a piece of advice for readers or a word of encouragement.

People can learn how to be a part of the solution. Often in IT, we treat users like simpletons. How often is the phrase "I don't know how they tie their shoes in the morning" been uttered in IT offices? I am passionate about bridging the gap between IT departments and end users. There is some truth to the stereotype that many people in the IT fields can struggle when communicating with nontechnical people. However, we as a community need to remember that while we may excel in the technical fields, there are others who excel at their fields as well. It is our job to not only set up hardware and software and fix problems but to also help end users engage the technology we provide for them. This includes using those tools safely.

Appendix: Seven Key Reminder Nudges to Help Your Recall

1. The three realities of security awareness
   - Just because I'm *aware* doesn't mean that I *care*.
   - If you try to work *against* human nature, you will *fail*.
   - What your people *do* is way more important than what they *know*.
2. Trojan Horses for the Mind
   - Emotion
   - Visuals
   - Sound
   - Words and story
3. Behavior shaping
   - System 1 versus System 2 thinking
   - Fogg Behavior Model (B=MAP)
   - Framing and context
   - Nudge theory
   - Variability of reward
   - Cialdini's principles of persuasion
4. The power of culture lay in the fact that humans are social creatures.
5. Think about your awareness program outreach in three areas: *content*, *experiences*, and *relationships*.
6. Understand the lives, actions, and interactions of your users. Think through each point of your user's routines where you might be able to intersect.
7. A transformational program has more in common with a *conversation* than it does a *monologue*.

Index